BLOODY TYRANTS
& LITTLE PICKLES

STUDIES IN
THEATRE HISTORY
AND CULTURE

HEATHER S. NATHANS

series editor

BLOODY TYRANTS & LITTLE PICKLES

STAGE ROLES *of* ANGLO-AMERICAN GIRLS *in the* Nineteenth Century

MARLIS SCHWEITZER

UNIVERSITY OF IOWA PRESS, IOWA CITY

University of Iowa Press, Iowa City 52242
Copyright © 2020 by the University of Iowa Press
www.uipress.uiowa.edu
Printed in the United States of America

Design by Richard Hendel

Printed on acid-free paper

Library of Congress Cataloging-in-Publication Data
Names: Schweitzer, Marlis, author.
Title: Bloody Tyrants and Little Pickles: Stage Roles of Anglo-American Girls
in the Nineteenth Century / Marlis Erica Schweitzer.
Description: Iowa City: University of Iowa Press, 2020. | Series: Studies in
Theatre History and Culture | Includes bibliographical references and index.
Identifiers: LCCN 2020006526 (print) | LCCN 2020006527 (ebook) |
ISBN 9781609387365 (paperback) | ISBN 9781609387372 (ebook)
Subjects: LCSH: Theater—United States—History—nineteenth century. |
Theater—England—History—nineteenth century. | Theater—Commonwealth
countries—History—nineteenth century. | Fisher, Clara, 1811–1898—Criticism
and interpretation. | Lander, J. M. (Jean Margaret), 1829–1903—Criticism and
interpretation. | American drama—nineteenth century—History and criticism. |
English drama—nineteenth century—History and criticism.
Classification: LCC PN2248.S39 2020 (print) | LCC PN2248 (ebook) |
DDC 792.0973/09034—dc23
LC record available at https://lccn.loc.gov/2020006526
LC ebook record available at https://lccn.loc.gov/2020006527

For Isaac,
my own "Little Pickle"
&
for my mom, who ignited
my interest in naughty girls
with her tales of
Messy Bessie

CONTENTS

ACKNOWLEDGMENTS

The cover of this book is imprinted with my name but it would not exist without the support, collegiality, dedication, and encouragement of an entire community of research assistants, project participants, research collaborators, editors, curators, librarians, journals, funding institutions, academic associations, and loved ones.

I have been fortunate to have worked with an incredibly talented group of students over the duration of this project, several of whom have gone on to pursue their own graduate-level studies of theatrical girlhood. For their help exploring many archival nooks and crannies and bringing to life the words spoken by girl actresses over a century ago, I offer heartfelt thanks to Ryan Boulet, Tenihkie Brant, Adam Brewer, Adam Corrigan-Holowitz, Denise Rogers, Samantha Everts, Thea Fitz-James, Heather Fitzsimmons Frey, Anna Griffith, Signy Lynch, Tegan Macfarlane, Jenna MacNeil, Anne Marsh, Julie Matheson, Mark Matusoff, Jayna Mees, Marlene Mendonca, Marjan Moosavi, Rhys Naylor, Colette Radou, Anthony Sansonetti, Ashley Stevens, Molly Thomas, and Rebecca Tran.

Research colleagues and collaborators have offered indispensable advice and feedback over the years, inspiring me with their scholarship and critical insights. My thanks to Natalie Alvarez, Christopher Balme, Roberta Barker, Sarah Bay-Cheng, Susan Bennett, Robin Bernstein, Gilli Bush-Bailey, Leo Cabranes Grant, Barbara Crow, Tracy C. Davis, Heather Davis-Fisch, Barry Freeman, Lisa A. Freeman, Heather Fitzsimmons Frey, Benjamin Gillespie, Darren Gobert, Julia Henderson, Erin Hurley, Monique Johnson, Stephen Johnson, Kirsty Johnston, Magdalena Kazubowski-Houston, Sasha Kovacs, Laura Levin, Derek Miller, Sarah Parsons, VK Preston, Rebecca Schneider, Kim Solga, Jenn Stephenson, Matthew Wittmann, Harvey Young, Belarie Zatzman, and Joanne Zerdy.

Editors deserve their own mention for helping to mold earlier pieces of this project. My deep gratitude to Tobias Becker, Jen Boyle, Leo Cabranes Grant, Jim Davis, Heather Davis-Fisch, Stephen Johnson, Wan-Chuan Kao, Kedar A. Kulkarni, Laura Levin, and Joanne Tompkins. Thanks as well to the following presses and publications for granting permission for me to reprint revised versions of articles and chapters that first appeared in their pages: *Nineteenth-Century Theatre and Film*, Playwrights Canada Press, Punctum Books, *Theatre Journal*, and *Theatre Research in Canada*.

Heather S. Nathans is everything an author could wish for in a book series editor: insightful, responsive, dedicated, and a source of engagement. I am grateful to her and to the other members of the editorial team at the University of Iowa Press, including Meredith T. Stabel, Daniel Siba, Jacob Roosa, Susan Hill Newton, and Noreen O'Connor-Abel. And of course, my deep gratitude to the two anonymous reviewers who read the manuscript in an earlier form and offered thoughtful, challenging food for thought. This book would be nothing but for your incisive critiques and generosity.

This project has also benefited from the generous support of funding bodies, including a SSHRC Insight Grant from the Social Sciences and Humanities Research Council of Canada, an Andrew W. Mellon Research Fellowship Endowment from the Harry Ransom Center, a Short-term Fellowship from the Folger Shakespeare Library, and Minor Research Creation grants from the School of the Arts, Media, Performance and Design at York University. This funding supported travel to the Folger Shakespeare Library, the Library of Congress, the British Library, the New York Public Library for the Performing Arts, the Houghton Library at Harvard University, the Harry Ransom Center at the University of Texas, Austin, and the New-York Historical Society. Many thanks to the librarians, curators, and archivists who answered questions, offered advice, and helped nudge this project along. I am likewise grateful to the following academic associations and research gatherings for providing opportunities for me to share my research with their members: American Society for Theatre Research; Canadian Association for Theatre Research; Canadian Historical Association; "Emotional Journeys: Itinerant Theatres, Audiences, and Adaptation in the Long 19th Century" at the German Historical Institute–London;

"Translating Theatre Histories" at LMU (Munich); MacKay Lecture Series, Dalhousie University; Victorian Studies at York; and York Circle.

Finally, thank you to my family for sustaining me on a daily basis with their joy, creativity, friendship, and love: my parents Edmond and Karen, my husband Daniel, and my sons Marcus and Isaac.

PROLOGUE

This book opens with a cute and seemingly benign object—a Stafford-shire figurine of a child of indeterminate gender dressed in a kilt and broad feather hat. The figurine is one of several hundred Staffordshire figurines in the Harvard Theatre Collection and spends much of its time swaddled in layers of bubble wrap in a temperature-controlled facility. In fall 2014 I had a chance to remove these layers (carefully) and to examine the figurine in all of its nineteenth-century glory. Placing it upright onto the library desk, I noticed the figurine's rosy cheeks and stocky legs, the green and orange patterning of its kilt, the royal blue of its bodice, and the jaunty blue and gold plumage on its hat. The light in the reading room made the figurine's glaze coating shimmer. With its left arm upraised it looked as if it was about to speak.

The Harvard Theatre Collection contains dozens of Stafford-shire figurines representing the celebrated actors and actresses of the nineteenth-century stage: Sarah Siddons, Edmund Kean, Charles Macready, John Philip Kemble, Charlotte Cushman, and many others. In some cases, as with Siddons, the library has multiple versions of the same figurine, distinguishable by color and painting but presum-ably made from the same mold. This multiplicity points to the rapid growth of the English pottery industry in the early nineteenth century and to the intensification of the market for commodities bearing the likeness of the famous *and* infamous, not just actors and actresses but also criminals, politicians, singers, dancers, actors, royalty—a veritable who's who of Victorian celebrity culture.

The Harvard archival records say nothing about when the figurine I viewed was made or who owned it. This is not unusual. As theatre his-torian Ellen MacKay observes, since most figurines lack the potter's sig-nature or mark, it is almost impossible to situate them "across a given artisan's oeuvre or a given factory's output," which poses additional challenges for tracing the "social life" of a specific figurine.[1] I can never-

FIGURE 1. *A Staffordshire figurine of Jean Margaret Davenport.*
Uncat. Figurines, Box 14, Houghton Library, Harvard University.

theless speculate that the figurine emerged from its mold in the pottery district in the 1830s and was later sold at a market stall, fairground, or holiday resort in or around Staffordshire.[2] Most likely, it then journeyed to a home, where it found pride of place on a bookshelf or parlor mantelpiece. Additional clues arise from the figurine itself. Staffordshire potters typically referred to engravings, sheet music covers, photographs, paintings, illustrated newspapers, and the like when creating the mold for a new figurine; indeed, the explosion of print culture in the nineteenth century was critical to the creation and proliferation of Staffordshire figurines and celebrity culture more broadly.[3] Knowing about this symbiotic relationship is a major boon to the performance historian.

Thanks to the diligent sleuthing of literary scholar Robert Simpson Maclean,[4] whose visit to Harvard preceded mine by several decades, I know that the figurine represents the girl actress Jean Margaret Davenport in the role of Young Norval from John Homes's Romantic tragedy *Douglas*. Maclean first identified the figurine as Davenport in a 1995 article entitled "The Case of the Silent Figure: A Phenomenal Art Mystery Revealed." In it he describes his process of discovery, which involved close consultation with Harvard curators and specialists in nineteenth-century pottery as well as cross-media analyses of Davenport's image. Comparing the figurine with a colored engraving of the actress in the same role, Maclean highlights similarities in costuming, posture, and gesture. He asserts that the potter who first created the figurine mold most likely used the engraving—or an earlier, reversed version—as the basis for his design. "Although the Staffordshire figure of the Scottish lass will always retain an inscrutable silence," Maclean wistfully concludes, "young Jean will be poised to dance her Highland fling as Young Norval for innumerable centuries, thanks to the enduring art of the Staffordshire potters."[5] To him, she is forever young— caught in time—a fixed representation of a bygone moment.

Maclean's romantic musing on the Davenport figurine, silenced yet poised on the edge of dance, anticipates Robin Bernstein's influential writing on the power of "scriptive things," objects that assert a strong emotional pull on the humans who encounter them. Such things guide human performances in much the same way that a play script encourages particular gestures or embodied actions.[6] Rather than inviting identical acts, however, the Jean Davenport figurine contains multiple scripts that move across bodies and over time, impelling a host of new, different performances, including those that occur inside the archive. What makes an object like the figurine such a valuable source for a study of theatrical girlhood is the way it offers access to the repertoires that surrounded its creation and circulation. As Bernstein writes, "Within a brick-and-mortar archive, scriptive things archive the repertoire—partially and richly, with a sense of openness and flux."[7] In other words, attending to the materiality of the Davenport figurine—paying attention to its size, color, design, weight, and so on—can reveal previously hidden repertoires of human interaction that confirm or complicate historical narratives. Thus while Maclean imagined the figurine as silent and silenced, Bernstein's scriptive thing offers a way to hear the figurine speak again.

What does the Davenport figurine say, then? Some helpful clues arise in considering the figurine's function as a collectible item purchased for display in the home. Despite its diminutive size (no more than six inches high), its fragility scripts careful touch (remember the bubble wrap): this is no toy but an object to be handled gently and placed on view, out of reach of tiny fingers and awkward elbows. According to Victorian scholar Rohan McWilliam, Staffordshire figurines and other collectibles enlivened the "mental and emotional world of the mantelpiece," making it "a space for memory and pleasure."[8] Compared with clothing, accessories, or other objects associated with public performance of class, Staffordshire figurines mediated a kind of "public intimacy" from their place on the parlor shelf, scripting micro-performances of domesticity, commemoration, and celebration.[9] For Joseph Roach, "public intimacy" arises when celebrated figures produce a feeling of closeness within their admirers, directing the desire for greater intimacy toward practices of consumption, theatrical or otherwise.[10] As miniaturized effigies, Staffordshire figurines brought the public world of the stage into the privacy of the home, inviting those who had missed seeing a much-lauded performance or a favorite actor in person to feel connected to a broader theatrical sphere.[11] Of course, the intimacy afforded by a figurine was informed by its size and form, not to mention its fragility, and yet I can imagine that the placement of the figurine in the home made the real-life Davenport appear simultaneously familiar ("she is in our house and part of our family") and strange ("we have access to her through her role / the figurine but only in a very limited way"). This constant toggling between familiarity and strangeness is one of the defining characteristics of celebrity culture and the It effect. "'It,'" Roach writes, "is the power of apparently effortless embodiment of contradictory qualities simultaneously: strength *and* vulnerability, innocence *and* experience, and singularity *and* typicality among them. The possessor of *It* keeps a precarious balance between such mutually exclusive alternatives." [12]

The Staffordshire figurine expresses Davenport's apparent "It" qualities through sculpted pottery. Curiously, a very similar figurine now held by the Victoria & Albert Museum in London has been identified "as a companion piece to a figurine of the young actor Master Betty" in the role of Young Norval. [13] This confusion over the figurine's (gender) identity calls attention to the plasticity of a girl actress like Jean Davenport—to her ability to slip in and out of character, to occupy multiple roles of varying ages and genders, to pass as a boy onstage and be mistaken as a boy offstage as well. For all of its material solidity, the figurine as an effigy of the long-gone girl offers evidence of her malleability, of her ability to fit (quite literally) into a mold, as well as her ability to break out of it.

The figurine's perpetual performance of Jean Davenport *as* Young Norval also raises questions about repertoire—why did the Staffordshire potter represent the girl as a male character, and why this one specifically? What does this decision—a decision undoubtedly informed by other images in circulation—reveal about audience tastes for cross-dressed girls? To what extent did the production and circulation of figurines like this one naturalize the relationship between performers and their repertoires? And if, as I've suggested, the Jean Davenport figurine enjoyed pride of place in the home of a middle-class family, how did this object influence the development of other gendered repertoires, not just on the stage but in parlors and kitchens as well? Did young girls shape their own appearance and behavior in Jean Davenport's image? Did they seek the same kind of plasticity that she modeled onstage? This book hopes to answer these and other questions by analyzing the formation of a distinct repertoire for girls in the first half of the nineteenth century; this repertoire delighted in precocity, plasticity, and playfulness and offered up a model of girlhood that was similarly joyful and fluid.

BLOODY TYRANTS
& LITTLE PICKLES

INTRODUCTION

Bloody Tyrants and Little Pickles: Stage Roles of Anglo-American Girls in the Nineteenth Century traces the repertoire of a small group of white Anglo-American actresses as they reshaped theatrical girlhood in Britain, North America, and the British West Indies during the first half of the nineteenth century. It is a study of the possibilities and the problems girls presented as they adopted the manners and clothing of boys, entered spaces intended for adults, and assumed characters written for men. It asks why roles like Young Norval, Richard III, Little Pickle, and Shylock came to seem "normal" and "natural" for young white girls to play, and it considers how playwrights, managers, critics, and audiences sought to contain or fix the at times dangerous plasticity they exhibited. Starting with but looking beyond the metropole of London where they first performed, this book follows young white girls as they traipsed across the stage in tragedies, comedies, and farces; as they transformed the pages of scientific manuals and serialized novels; as they crossed the Atlantic onboard ships in service to imperial ambitions; as they modeled new forms of idealized whiteness; as their images and names were repeated in objects bearing their likenesses; and as they found their way into the semiprivacy of the scrapbook and the domestic scenography of the mantelpiece.

Historians have documented the kind and range of roles girl actresses played over the course of the nineteenth century,[1] yet few have considered why, how, or when these roles entered their repertoire.[2] In fact, most studies of eighteenth- and nineteenth-century acting, including those within the dynamic field of "actress studies," overlook girls altogether, directing their attention to the adult women who were most obviously responsible for innovations in acting style.[3] But reading the development of adult repertoire apart from the development of children's repertoire has led to an incomplete understanding of girls' contributions to Anglo-American performance culture in this period. As

1

Jeanne Klein observes, "the forcible separation of child actors from adult actors" in the late nineteenth and early twentieth centuries via later labor laws "has led theatre academics not only to dismiss 'children's theatre' ... but also to neglect the significant impact of children on the very history of ... theatre."[4] This book expands Klein's geographic focus on US theatre to argue that child performers, especially young white girls, joined adult playwrights, managers, critics, and audiences in the development and expansion of an increasingly *transatlantic* theatre repertoire in the early nineteenth century. This evolving repertoire reflected shifting perspectives on girls' place within Anglo-American society, including where and how they should behave, and which girls had the right to appear at all.[5]

In its focus on repertoire, *Bloody Tyrants and Little Pickles* moves beyond full-length dramas to analyze a broad range of performances, following Tracy C. Davis in understanding repertoire "as a theorised descriptor of nineteenth-century performance practice."[6] Davis stresses the circulatory and relational aspects of repertoire, the way it develops over time and across the bodies of performers and audiences who recognize existing performance vocabularies, absorb new tropes, and remake old ones, thereby ensuring a kind of durability where meaning is concerned.[7] When certain gestures, songs, or tropes disappear from the repertoire due to cultural rupture or the passage of time, they can seem confusing or ridiculous when revived.[8] Taking a cue from Davis, this book attends to the wider cultural shifts, audience obsessions, individual preferences, and critical conversations that shaped the repertoire of the girl actress in the first half of the nineteenth century with the goal of decoding "the archive of meanings that no longer circulate" around particular plays and performance genres.[9] Repetition is critical to the establishment of repertoire, as it is to all performance, following Richard Schechner's famous definition of performance as "twice-behaved behavior."[10] Yet for a performance to enter the repertoire it must be repeated multiple times and across multiple bodies. It is worth asking why and how some performances—tropes, songs, dances, roles, comic bits, and so forth—invite repetition while others do not. How and when does repertoire change and what do these changes reveal about the cultural preoccupations of a particular historical moment? With these questions in mind, each chapter not only investigates the arrival and subsequent uptake of a specific role into the repertoire of nineteenth-century girlhood, but also considers how that role engaged larger concerns about girlhood, girls' education, father-daughter relations, and familial formations.

Although shifts in repertoire affected the lives and performances of many young girls over the course of the nineteenth century, *Bloody Tyrants and Little Pickles* maintains a tight focus on two star actresses: Clara Fisher [Maeder] (1811–1898) and Jean Margaret Davenport [Lander] (1829–1903). This duo was not alone in thriving on early nineteenth-century stages, yet their unique relationships with audiences, managers, playwrights, critics, and others gave rise to new roles and acting opportunities that had longstanding effects on the profession. Despite their differences in age—Fisher was older than Davenport by nearly two decades—their careers followed an eerily similar trajectory (thanks in no small part to some deliberate mirroring by Davenport's manager-father). Both enjoyed professional success as pre-adolescent girls in Britain and North America, specializing in Shakespearean male roles, Romantic heroes, and hoydenish boy characters; both had plays specially written to showcase their individual talents; and both delighted audiences with their rapid character transformations and skillful singing and dancing.[11] Playing everything from scheming merchants and heroic revolutionaries to naughty boys and dutiful daughters, Fisher and Davenport stretched the confines of nineteenth-century theatrical repertoires and pulled at existing definitions of girlhood. Close analysis of their repertoire thus reveals the extent to which deep cultural anxieties, personal rivalries, national interests, racial hierarchies, imperial politics, and shifting social dynamics played out, in, and through the bodies of young girls as they moved across oceans and stages in the first half of the nineteenth century.

These girls were far from average—phrenologists measured Clara Fisher's head for evidence of her brilliance; Jean Davenport was viciously immortalized by Charles Dickens in *Nicholas Nickleby*—and for this reason, their repertoire influenced the lives of hundreds, if not thousands, of other girls (and boys) who were their theatrical contemporaries. Indeed one of my goals in this book is to draw out the unseen connections between the exceptional and the average, to identify the originating impetus and material conditions whereby exceptional girls set performance templates that inscribed or challenged very particular cultural norms.[12] For example, the otherwise silly farce *Old and Young;*

or the Four Mowbrays becomes discernible as a sharply satirical commentary on the performativity of gender and age when read against the critical discourse surrounding Clara Fisher as she matured. So too, recognizing that the character of Little Pickle was originally written for the comic actress Dorothy Jordan illuminates how shifts in the repertoire of adult actresses rippled through the repertoire of girl actresses. Focusing on the careers of exceptional performers makes such discoveries possible.

This book nevertheless reaches beyond the exceptional to consider long-forgotten plays and performance pieces. Where previous historians have often privileged "overtly child-oriented literary dramas" in arguing for the validity of children's theatre,[13] I investigate a broader range of performance forms, including relatively unknown afterpieces and farces. In this, I acknowledge the mobility of performers and audiences and the mixing of genres that often constituted a single night's entertainment.[14] The eighteenth- and nineteenth-century Anglo-American stage was highly regulated, rigidly hierarchical, and extremely competitive. Although most bills at London's "legitimate" theatres varied from one night to the next, they typically included: a prologue introducing the themes of the main piece delivered by one of the leading actors; a full-length play lasting two to three hours; several short interludes of singing, dancing, or both; a brief epilogue presented by another leading actor; and a short, usually comic, afterpiece.[15] Spectators present for the full evening's entertainment learned to expect frequent variation in setting, genre, and mood. Should they return the following evening, they would find an entirely different bill presented by many but not all of the same actors and actresses. Since it was extremely rare for London's patent companies, Theatre Royal Drury Lane and Theatre Royal Covent Garden, to present the same plays from week to week, performers had to master a diverse repertoire in order to meet managerial needs and audience expectations. The practice of casting plays according to strictly observed "lines of business" meant that emerging performers had to bide their time in supporting roles until an opening presented itself. Such openings could be rare, however, as leading actresses like Sarah Siddons and Dorothy Jordan continued to occupy their most successful roles well into their later years. Actresses hoping to rise to leading lady status had to contend with shifting managerial allegiances and scheming rivals; some went so far as to take advantage of their rivals' time away from the stage during periods of ill health or childbirth; others sought favor with the theatre manager, a popular playwright, or an influential patron.[16]

These access issues make the arrival of girl actresses onto the nineteenth-century stage fascinating to consider. Of course, girls were hardly new to the theatre. Those born into theatre families often made their first stage appearances as infants and small children in nonspeaking parts before graduating to pages, servants, royal children, and other supporting roles.[17] In the mid-eighteenth century, playwrights began writing more actively for children and children's companies, creating farces, masques, and afterpieces that emphasized the charm and vitality of young performers, while occasionally positioning them as erotic subjects. One telling example is George Colman's *A Fairy Tale* (1763), an adaptation of *Midsummer Night's Dream*, which concluded with a sexually charged epilogue delivered by a five-year-old Miss Hopkins who flirted with male audience members.[18] Such performances delighted in testing the boundaries of childhood by turning girls into sexualized commodities.[19] However, as Kristina Straub observes, not "all child performances in the Georgian theatre carried this sexual charge or the threat entailed in marketing children's bodies."[20] Playwrights deployed girls (and boys) to promote unified visions of empire in masques like Colman's *The Fairy Prince* (1771).[21] Managers also called upon girls to evoke audience pathos in Shakespearean tragedies, most often as Prince Arthur in *King John* or as the young princes in *Richard III*, who in Colley Cibber's 1699 adaptation enjoyed additional stage time, new lines, and a graphic onstage murder.[22] Girls therefore assumed increasingly important positions on the eighteenth-century stage as sexualized beings and objects of pathos—but what elevated them from supporting players to transatlantic stars?

This book argues that a series of interconnected developments supported the spectacular ascent of girl actresses like Clara Fisher and Jean Margaret Davenport. These included innovations in transatlantic transportation, the proliferation of print media, the rapid growth of consumer culture, and the corresponding rise of celebrity culture. Nineteenth-century girls in the theatre were publicly *visible* in ways that earlier child actresses were not; they appeared in illustrated newspapers, as figurines, in scientific lectures, on city streets, and they traveled extensively, playing for audiences throughout Britain, North

America, and the West Indies, where they inspired fans to emulate their appearance and behavior and purchase goods marked with their names and images. But more than this, girl actresses appealed to audiences in and through their performances of girlhood during a time of evolving gender roles, shifting class formations and corresponding adjustments in family life, competing approaches to childhood education, advancing imperial interests, and new research on human development. In sum, the stage offered a critical site for experimenting with competing identities in and through the performances of girls.

Performing Girlhood

Bloody Tyrants and Little Pickles places girls at the center rather than at the margins of theatre and performance history. In so doing, it rejects the way "girls have been doubly marginalized as both females and youth" in keeping with the larger aims of girlhood studies.[23] A wideranging field,[24] girlhood studies challenges women's studies for overlooking, dismissing, or undervaluing the contributions of girls in its desire to celebrate the political advances of women; at the same time, it critiques tendencies within childhood studies to lump boys and girls together under the category of the "child," a move that fails to account for the very different material conditions that distinguish girls' experiences from those of boys.[25] Girlhood studies foregrounds the construction, formation, and performance of "girlhood" as a historical category, while heeding girls' lived experiences. As such, it offers a much richer account of the gendering, racialization, classing, and nationalization of girlhood and brings to light the many ways that girls assert political and social agency.[26]

But what is a girl and at what point does she transition from girlhood to womanhood? "While it seems every woman has been a girl and every female child is one," girlhood studies scholar Catherine Driscoll writes, "it is not clear what this means."[27] When does a girl become a woman? At the point of menstruation, sexual activity, marriage, childbirth, or some other major life moment? Is chronological age a measure of girlhood or does girlhood exceed age? And what about gender?[28] Catherine Robson found that many nineteenth-century men lamented their "lost girlhood," a preadolescent period during which they indulged in the pleasures of domestic life before assuming the mantle of Victorian manhood. Robson's study foregrounds the distinctly performative nature of girlhood, demonstrating how it achieves a certain kind of naturalization over time through what Judith Butler famously described as a "stylized repetition of acts."[29] The performative acts that collectively gender and age a body vary according to time, culture, and geography. If girlhood has a constant, then, that constant is change. Driscoll characterizes girlhood as "an idea of mobility preceding the fixity of womanhood and implying an unfinished process of personal development."[30] Girlhood is about plasticity, experimentation, and the capacity to change.

The concept of plasticity offers an evocative framework for approaching the repertoire of nineteenth-century girls. Plasticity involves processes of molding and behind molded, of (im)pressing into and leaving a mark upon the surface of matter and being vulnerable to marking by an outside force. A plastic girl is open to transformation and capable of transforming others through her charm, cuteness, wit, or intelligence.[31] It is this ability to give as well as take form that distinguishes plasticity from cognate terms such as flexibility and elasticity. Turning to dictionary definitions, philosopher Catherine Malabou observes that flexibility refers to "that which is easily bent" and to "the ability to change with ease in order to adapt oneself to the circumstances." Yet flexibility also connotes docility, passivity, a willingness to yield to external forces without resistance: "To be flexible is to receive a form or impression, to be able to fold oneself, to take the fold, not to give it."[32] Elasticity likewise refers to the ability to adjust to varying degrees of force or pressure. Yet elastic movements tend to occur along a linear plane—expand, contract, expand, contract—and an elastic object can only be stretched so far before it snaps. By contrast, plasticity is about "the power to create, to invent or even to erase an impression, the power to style."[33] To be plastic, then, is to remake the world, to challenge accepted norms, and to forge new ways of being. But not all forms of plasticity are benign. For Malabou, "plasticity is also the capacity to annihilate the very form it is able to receive or create. We should not forget that *plastique* ... is an explosive substance made of nitroglycerine and nitrocellulose, capable of causing violent explosions."[34] Whereas flexibility supports the reproduction of the status quo,[35] plasticity leaves open the possibility for irruption and disruption, for tension and resistance, for fluidity and change.[36]

The girls at the center of this study were undeniably plastic, not just in their ability to give and take form, but also in the way they pushed against, and in some cases exploded, notions of what it meant to be a girl. Playing old men and old women, precocious boys and rowdy sailors, bloody tyrants and Little Pickles, they assumed multiple forms, confounded binaries of gender and age, and resisted the easy equation of femininity with girlhood. Indeed, one of this book's unexpected discoveries is that girl actresses not only performed new models of precocious girlhood but also offered appealing representations of *boyhood*—to the horror of some and the delight of many. Simply put, girl actresses like Clara Fisher and Jean Davenport queered evolving conceptions of gender, urging audiences to resist binary thinking if only for the duration of their onstage performances.[37]

Though many theatregoers found pleasure in watching girls skate seamlessly across the borders of gender, age, class, and nation, others fretted about their fluid performances and sought to dissect or otherwise contain them within discrete categories. These anxious observers perceived girls as slippery, unfixed, unknowable, untrustworthy, and therefore dangerous, not simply because they were susceptible to change but because their circulation as actresses gave them unique opportunities to influence others.

It would be a mistake, however, to assert that those who perform plasticity always enjoy the freedom their actions seek. Karen Sánchez-Eppler soberly observes that the perceived mutability of children and childhood itself might "be one of the reasons it has proven so easy to dismiss childhood as a place of cultural meaning, to view childhood teleologically in terms of the goal of adulthood than as significant in itself."[38] In other words, when girls (and boys) are understood as subjects in process—as incomplete beings who have yet to reach a state of maturity—their opinions and actions matter less to those in positions of authority. There is nothing inherently liberating about being plastic, and plasticity in itself cannot protect individuals from harm—for if plasticity is about taking and giving form, then it can also result in bruises and broken bones, violence and annihilation.[39]

Plasticity can also connote fakeness and cultural theft. As film scholar Kristen J. Warner details, twentieth-century black musicians coined the term "plastic soul" as a commentary on the appropriation of black music by white artists. Warner introduces the broader con-

cept of "plastic representation" to critique the hollowness and superficiality of cultural producers' efforts to enhance "visual diversity" on-
screen, which "uses the wonder that comes from seeing characters on
screen who serve as visual identifiers for specific demographics in order
to flatten the expectation to desire anything more."[40] The history of
nineteenth-century performance is brimming with creators' use of cultural appropriation to stabilize racial hierarchies. The white girls who
danced across transatlantic stages were hardly immune to such forms
of plasticity; indeed, many were active (if also unwitting) participants
in the advancement of white supremacist interests.

Historical Developments

The history of girlhood nestles within, alongside, and in tension with
the history of boyhood and the history of childhood more broadly. Definitions of childhood, girlhood, and boyhood blur and overlap in many
studies, even as scholars attend to differences of gender, race, sexuality,
class, ability, and nationality or region. Such blurring makes it difficult to extrapolate whether certain observed historical developments
applied to *all* children, or to one particular group, especially when the
term "childhood" is most often associated with the experiences of white
boys.[41] Yet the gendered categories now recognized as boyhood and
girlhood almost always developed in tandem with one another.[42]

Like their twenty-first-century counterparts, nineteenth-century
parents, writers, scientists, and educators often disagreed on the nature of childhood. Some clung to the older Calvinist belief that all children were born tainted by original sin and thus required strict discipline to help them find the path to spiritual redemption and eventual
glory lest they face damnation.[43] Others followed the philosopher John
Locke, who in his 1693 treatise *Some Thoughts Concerning Education* described children as *tabula rasa* or blank pages of paper waiting to be written upon. Given the child's impressionability, Locke ad-
vised, parents and caregivers should avoid pressing too firmly into the
child's character and forever deforming it[44] and instead use a "steady
hand" to guide their children's wills to states of "compliance and suppleness" such that obedience "seem[s] natural to them."[45] By contrast,
Jean-Jacques Rousseau argued in *Émile* that parents and other educators should avoid subjugating the will of the impressionable child

and should instead allow the child to develop a free will, albeit under the tutelage of an adult observer.[46] Locke's and Rousseau's views found expression in late eighteenth- and early nineteenth-century parenting tracts and children's stories, which urged children to make good, moral decisions within family and social groups. These pragmatic texts emphasized collaboration, cooperation, negotiation, and self-legislation, positioning children alongside adults on the path to maturity.[47]

Enlightenment perspectives on childhood also informed the writings of Romantic poets like William Wordsworth, who celebrated the innocence and purity of the mythical young child born "trailing clouds of glory."[48] Whereas Locke and Rousseau encouraged children's development through education and parental guidance, the Romantic poets sought to preserve the metaphorical, decontextualized "Child" in a state of permanent innocence, free from the influence of outside forces and adult ways. Children who appeared too educated or too self-possessed were to be pitied for their early exposure to the pitfalls of the adult world. This idealistic perspective set the stage for what some historians identify as a full-fledged "cult of the child" in the mid- to late nineteenth century, when children were reified in art and literature as pure, innocent beings capable of softening even the hardest adult heart.[49]

Yet attitudes toward childhood did not evolve in a smooth or linear fashion.[50] Even the era's most passionate writers sometimes reversed their previously stated positions and failed to practice what they preached.[51] Such competing views reflect the tremendous social and political changes that were remaking the Anglo-American world in the first half of the nineteenth century. Throughout the eighteenth century, most working- and middle-class children contributed to their family's economic well-being through piecework and other menial labor. But the rise of factories and the corresponding increase in middle-class wealth in the first decades of the nineteenth century meant that children no longer had to labor in the same way. Rather than prizing children for their economic value, middle-class families began valuing children for their emotional value (i.e., what Viviana Zelizer describes as their "pricelessness"), devoting considerable resources to supporting their physical, intellectual, and spiritual growth.[52]

This perspective on children shifted in tandem with the rise of consumer culture in Britain and North America and the growing recognition of children's influence as consumers.[53] Contemporaries noted that children's perceived susceptibility to influence made them highly vulnerable to advertising, and parents eager to provide material evidence of their love (or class status) often yielded to their children's demands.[54] Consumption, of course, is its own form of labor, one that requires the careful assessment, acquisition, and display of goods.[55] From the late eighteenth century onward, women and children, especially girls, marked their family's wealth and class status through the quantity and range of goods they consumed. And what better place to display this wealth than at the theatre? The privileging of the child within the family unit affected Anglo-American theatre as well, leading to an increase in shows created specifically for the amusement of children and young families.[56]

White, middle-class children frequented Anglo-American theatre culture well before the mid-nineteenth century, when managers like P. T. Barnum actively pursued women and children with the introduction of special matinee performances. Challenging received histories of children's theatregoing in the United States, Jeanne Klein has shown that managers in New York and Philadelphia offered half-price tickets to "children under 10 [or] 12" during holiday seasons or for specific performances in the first two decades of the century. Managers intensified their efforts in the 1820s, hoping to lure family audiences away from cheaper amusements with comparable pricing.[57] By April 1838, a playbill advertising a Juvenile Gala Night for Caroline Fox and Miss F. Jones at Boston's National Theatre made an explicit appeal to children: "The Misses Fox and Jones hope to see many of their *little friends*, with their *great friends* on this occasion."[58] Not surprisingly, boys enjoyed greater freedom to attend the theatre alone or with friends, while girls were almost always accompanied by family members. Nevertheless, both enjoyed a diverse range of plays performed by many of the leading artists of the day: Charles Mathews, William Charles Macready, Master Burke, and others.[59] Similar developments unfolded in Britain. A playbill for Jean Davenport's 1836 debut as Richard III included the following notice: "That the Younger Branches of Families may have an opportunity of witnessing Miss Davenport's Performance, all under Twelve Years of Age will be admitted at Half Price. Also Schools at Half Price. For this Night only."[60] While there is limited evidence that children's presence at the theatre directly influenced play selection, managerial marketing efforts suggest that they were certainly aware of this audience constituency.

Not all families could afford to attend the theatre, however, and not all children enjoyed a privileged position within the family unit. Indeed, the emergence of an idealized vision of childhood in the early to mid-nineteenth century hinged on the careful exclusion of nonwhite and working-class children from the category of the "child." Although social reformers in England, the United States, and elsewhere began agitating for labor laws that would protect very young children from horrible working conditions early in the nineteenth century, it would take most of a century for governments to implement any longstanding policy changes. These reforms did little to disrupt the equation of childhood with whiteness, however, and African American, Asian, Indigenous, and other racialized children suffered the indignities of nineteenth-century racial hierarchies and white supremacist ambitions.[61]

For their part, white Anglo-American children occupied key roles in broader nationalist and imperialist projects. Novels, periodicals, and other published matter encouraged British children to treat "imperialism and empire as a normal part of the world," "to accept the values of imperialism" without question, and to imagine themselves as the literal "king [and queens] of the castle."[62] Outside the home and school, the theatre also functioned as an important site of transfer for nationalist and imperialist ideologies.[63] Often, as I document throughout this book, girls like Clara Fisher and Jean Margaret Davenport served as ambassadors of empire, representing imperial values, aesthetics, and political aims as they traveled throughout North America and the British West Indies.[64]

Fisher and Davenport experienced the empire in a way that few of their contemporaries could. Most white middle-class children learned to adopt an expanded view of the world and their place within it even as the home became a site of protection, oversight, and insularity. New models of middle-class family life urged parents, especially mothers, to take careful note of their children's physical, emotional, and moral development in order to "understand better the workings of human reason and intelligence" and identify the first signs of sickness or poor health.[65] Doctors like Andrew Combe, brother of the phrenologist

George Combe, maintained that parents who closely observed their young children's gestures could discover unarticulated needs and desires. Such attention to the life of the child further demonstrated that there was "a shape, moving in the body ... something *inside*: an interiority."[66] This emphasis on parental surveillance and the relationship of age to ability offers one explanation for the growing popularity of child performers. Playbills celebrating the achievements of girls and boys who were "only five" or "only six" years of age encouraged parents to attend the theatre to compare the skills of the onstage performers with the talents of their own progeny.[67]

Many late eighteenth- and early nineteenth-century writers, artists, and commentators enjoined parents to pay special attention to girls who, like all women, possessed a "natural" tendency toward lying and deception.[68] Kept in check, girls could serve as a vital stabilizing force within the domestic sphere. Others wrote specifically *for* girls, offering them scripts for life. In her widely circulated conduct book, *Daughters of England* (1843), Sarah Stickney Ellis charges her girl readers "to prolong rather than curtail the season of their simplicity and buoyancy of heart" and to be "contented to be a girl, and nothing more."[69] Rejecting models of girlhood plasticity, Ellis calls for girls to embrace stability and stasis, to restrict their movements and their emotional maturation in order to preserve the well-being of fathers and brothers.[70] It was acceptable for boys to venture out into the world to learn and discover through lived experience, but girls had to endure greater degrees of surveillance within the home so that they might reproduce its values when they became wives and mothers.[71] American authors likewise celebrated girls' redemptive potential, especially in temperance literature wherein young daughters are often shown sacrificing themselves to save their wayward fathers.[72] Throughout the Anglo-American world, then, daughters were called upon to serve the interests of fathers and brothers and to provide a stable, healthy foundation for male activity outside the home.[73]

The question arises: if parents and educators were so eager to promote a model of respectable white girlhood that would secure and stabilize dominant social norms, why did audiences take such delight in watching girls misbehave onstage?

For years historians have bandied about numerous theories to explain the popularity of nineteenth-century child performers on Anglo-American stages.[74] Carolyn Steedman insists that audiences watched children perform for clues to human interiority and for "the artful display of childhood's artless little ways on the stage."[75] James R. Kincaid agrees that what made child performers so alluring to their adult admirers in the late Victorian period was the belief in a firm divide between childhood and adulthood.[76] This perceived separation made children "available to desire [by] making it different, a strange and alien species."[77] Marah Gubar and others have since complicated Kincaid's thesis, arguing that the Victorians understood the line between childhood and adulthood as porous and that adults were drawn to child performers for reasons that extended beyond the erotic.[78] She maintains that British audiences found child actors appealing because they were talented and capable and seemed to blur the line between innocence and experience, challenging attempts to separate the worlds of adults and children. Gubar's critical intervention offers a valuable starting point for considering why girls so frequently attracted (and repelled) audiences in the first half of the nineteenth century. The girls who fill the pages of this book refused to fall into simple categories. Their precocious range and ability to slip easily in and out of character threatened to destabilize the status quo, and this made them both delightful and terrifying.

My argument here departs from earlier claims about girl actresses, including those made by Elizabeth Reitz Mullenix in *Wearing the Breeches: Gender on the American Stage*, one of the few studies to acknowledge the political significance of girl actresses as *girls*. Mullenix attributes the popularity of girl actresses in the antebellum United States to a combination of charm, innocence, and contained transgression of gender norms. These performers were ultimately nonthreatening, she argues, because their excursions across the borders of gender and class were perceived as playacting: "The 'pretty little girl' who played Shylock or Richard III was less threatening than the adult woman, for children's actions were seen as unconditionally innocent: as men, they were perceived to be at play rather than at work."[79] The "pretty little girl" might succeed at playing with masculinity, but she would never succeed in destabilizing categories of gender and sexuality because her destiny was womanhood.[80] Mullenix's assertion that audiences viewed girl actresses as precocious innocents is persuasive, but it underestimates the complex responses that such performers elicited and the explosive plasticity they brought with them to the theatre.

Like most professional performers, girls were always learning new material—new songs, dances, and afterpieces—to enhance their repertoire, test their range, and showcase their virtuosity. Girls' mobility and plasticity—their frequent crossing and recrossing of geographic borders *for* performance, not to mention their crossing of borders of race, gender, and class *through* performance—marked them as different from many of their girl contemporaries in the locations they visited. It is this aspect of the girl actresses under consideration here that makes them such ideal subjects for investigating the circulation and transmission of multiple, at times competing, even polarizing notions of girlhood. They were anything but static, and attempts to render them knowable and unthreatening did not always succeed, much to the chagrin and consternation of those who wished otherwise.

Finding Girls Onstage

One of the ongoing challenges of children's history in general, and the history of girlhood in particular, is the relative silence of children as historical subjects. Since much of the evidence of girls' lives comes from adults, historians must consult these sources with caution, even when reading memoirs or autobiographies written by adult women about their own girlhoods.[81] Ample documentation of nineteenth-century girl actresses exists in journalistic accounts, scientific reports, plays, memoirs, autobiographies, sketches, paintings, photographs, and souvenirs—to name some of the most readily available sources—but this evidence does not (necessarily) offer access to the thoughts and impressions of the girls themselves. With these limitations in mind, I do not presume to speak for the girls that are this book's central focus but instead look to identify how and why their repertoire developed. I nevertheless remain attentive to moments when girls voices' or perspectives arise from the text—or from the pages of a scrapbook. In this regard, I am inspired by recent methodological innovations in actress studies, which model "multi-faceted modes of thinking about how to critically assess the evidence we do have and how to creatively consider how to theorize meaning from the absence of tangible documentation."[82] Such approaches include detailed microhistories, practice-based experimentation, and speculative fiction.[83]

I also pay heed to texts that work against the association of plasticity with girlhood by purporting to explain, fix, or otherwise stabilize the figure of the girl actress. These performative documents include reviews written by experienced theatre critics; playbills with notes about the limitations of a girl actress's engagement; fictional accounts of backstage life; sketches, illustrations, and commissioned portraits; angry letters to the editor; scientific treatises; recollections of theatre managers; and (ironically) memoirs written by the actresses themselves. In addition to offering valuable details about individual girls' performances, these texts suggest that girl actresses were a source of excitement, confusion, and anxiety for adult audiences, especially men. I also realize that in reflecting back on their careers at the end of the nineteenth century, some actresses may have downplayed the more controversial or liberating aspects of their girlhood performances or wished to advance a particular narrative about themselves or their families, and so I pay attention to texts that show evidence of strategic rewriting or careful erasure.[84]

Beyond these sources, I look to objects and related ephemera for evidence of how audiences consumed girl actresses and their repertoires. As I observed in the Prologue, the widespread production of Staffordshire figurines in the early nineteenth century made it possible for fans to collect little effigies of cherished performers like Jean Davenport and display them in the comfort and privacy of their homes. So too, audiences hoping to relive something of a favorite performance could purchase scripts and sheet music to play for family and friends. Thus the onstage repertoire of the girl actress and details about her offstage life became accessible throughout the Anglo-American world to an increasingly diverse group of men, women, and children, many of whom sought to signal their admiration through consumption and imitation. Finally, in an effort to acknowledge the contingency and uncertainty of all historical research, I use interludes to make my presence as a researcher known. I discuss the challenges I faced interpreting sources and use critical self-reflection to think through my own assumptions, mistakes, and biases.

The Repertoire of This Book

Bloody Tyrants and Little Pickles borrows the structure of a typical evening of nineteenth-century theatre to explore the breadth of the girl actress's repertoire. A prologue and epilogue bookend five main chapters, while a series of interludes runs throughout. The chapters themselves follow a similar progression from "serious" Shakespearean drama to comedy and farce, although this structure is by no means intended to support the still-lingering cultural hierarchies that privilege "legitimate" theatre over all other forms.[85] To the contrary, by paying attention to interstitial matters, I join other historians of popular performance in promoting an expanded view of the nineteenth-century stage, one that acknowledges the complex networks and relationships—personal, professional, emotional, intellectual, sexual, and so forth—that made Anglo-American theatres and their repertoires.[86]

The first two chapters focus on roles that migrated from the repertoire of adult actors and actresses into the repertoire of the girl actress (Richard III and Little Pickle in *The Spoiled Child*), with a specific focus on Clara Fisher and her older sister Jane. The third chapter considers how critical anxiety about Clara's occupation of roles originally intended for men spurred the development of new plays (*Old and Young*) that offered a subversive take on the performativity of age and gender. The final two chapters turn to Jean Margaret Davenport, whose career in the 1830s and 1840s was ghosted by the presence of Clara Fisher and guided by her manager-father Thomas. In leaping forward by two decades from Fisher to Davenport I do not wish to suggest that they were the *only* girl actresses in this period (there were many others!) but rather to identify transitional moments in the development and circulation of repertoire. Like Fisher, Davenport influenced the theatrical representation of girlhood as she traveled throughout the empire, embodying the emerging ideal of the dutiful daughter even as she trod the boards as Richard III.

The chapters are separated by brief interludes, which describes an object or performance that extended the reach of the girl actress.[87] Running as a counterpoint to the book's chapters, these interludes track the transatlantic circulation of theatrical girlhood via scripts, toys, memoirs, objects, song, and dance. They investigate how the transmission of repertoire across bodies, geographies, and temporalities serviced imperial aims, propped up class and racial hierarchies, and facilitated bold new expressions of girlhood. Across the interludes, I acknowledge the methodological challenges that arise for historians when trying to grasp the experiences of girls who lived two centuries ago, and I mark my own place as a white cis-gender scholar grappling with the beautiful fragments of past lives.

INTERLUDE 1
BETTYMANIA

One of my favorite archival finds from the Folger Shakespeare Library is a book of paper dolls published in 1811. Titled "Young Albert, The Roscius, Exhibited in a Series of Characters from Shakespeare and other Authors," this second edition booklet includes seven pages of colored illustrations depicting such characters as Falstaff, Hamlet, Othello, Young Norval, and Richard III, each with an opening for one of "Young Albert's" (white or black) heads. On the facing pages, short excerpts offer clues to the dramatic moments the dolls are meant to inhabit. As a uniquely scriptive thing, the booklet invites those who encounter it to quite literally play with Albert's repertoire, to familiarize themselves with the gestures, costumes, settings, and narratives that defined each role, to imagine crossing borders of gender, age, race, class, and genre, and to delight in the fluidity of performance and the vantage points of the characters' heroic lives.[1]

"Young Albert" is almost certainly modeled on the real-life Master William Henry West Betty (Master Betty for short), the twelve-year-old "Infant Roscius" who captivated London audiences in the 1804–1805 season. Betty's repertoire included Young Norval in *Douglas*, Romeo in *Romeo and Juliet*, Achmet in *Barbarossa*, and the title role in *Hamlet*. As one of the first child celebrities of the modern era, he circulated within an evolving economy of cuteness wherein he was valued for his size, charm, and vulnerability, especially when he was ill or indisposed. Audiences admired Betty's physical appearance and collected biographical pamphlets, caricatures, and souvenirs bearing his likeness. Such objects, including the booklet of paper dolls, contributed to the production of a nascent celebrity culture, mediating the relationship between Betty and his audience. The development of Betty's distinctly masculine repertoire and the mania that surrounded him offstage is the focus of this short interlude.

Born in Shrewsbury in 1791, Betty made his stunning debut in Belfast in August 1803, several weeks shy of his twelfth birthday, playing the role of Osman in Aaron Hill's *Zara*, one of the era's most iconic Romantic heroes. But it was a very different Romantic model that had first drawn Betty to the stage. According to his biographers, Betty fell in love with acting after attending a production of *Pizarro* (1799), Richard Brinsley Sheridan's tragedy about the Spanish conquest of Peru starring the celebrated actress Sarah Siddons in the role of Elvira, the title character's Spanish mistress. Siddons's performance, which enhanced the character's "mixed dignity and tenderness" and the "virtuous struggles of repentance and remorse,"[2] so entranced young Betty that when he returned home "his conversation ran upon the character of Elvira and the fascinations of the drama."[3] He set about learning all of Elvira's emotional speeches "in imitation of Mrs. Siddons," which he then recited to his parents and their friends.[4] I linger on the events of Betty's first theatre outing to emphasize how his passion for acting arose through cross-gender identification, his fascination with both Siddons and the character of Elvira. Ultimately, Betty's parents gave in to their son's pleas and hired Mr. Hough, the Belfast Theatre's "ingenious and experienced prompter,"[5] to train Betty for the stage. In a critical, if unsurprising, development, Hough steered his young charge away from Siddons and Elvira, thereby forestalling any risk of the boy overidentifying with the actress and her repertoire. Instead, Hough prepared Betty to embody a range of tragic warrior heroes, including Osman, Young Norval in *Douglas*, Rolla in *Pizarro*, and Achmet (Selim) in *Barbarossa*, John Brown's tragedy about the Algerian ruler. Such roles indulged theatregoers' orientalist and imperialist fantasies,[6] while inviting them to compare the boy with the leading male actors of the day. In this way, Hough aligned Betty with the ideals of Romantic masculinity and the demands of empire, creating a template that later child actors would follow.

Following his Belfast debut,[7] Betty embarked upon a series of provincial tours, performing in Dublin, Cork, Edinburgh, Glasgow, Birmingham, Sheffield, and Liverpool, where large audiences greeted him with excitement bordering on hysteria.[8] It was during this period that Betty (presumably under Hough's guidance) first introduced Rich-

FIGURE 2. *Master William Henry West Betty.*
By permission of the Folger Shakespeare Library.

ard III into his repertoire. A review from an August 1804 appearance in Birmingham noted that "the variety of conflicting passions which the crook-backed tyrant at all times was a prey to, were depicted by the young Roscius in the most able manner."[9] Here, the critic compares Betty to the first-century Roman actor Quintus Roscius Gallus, who was so widely lauded in his time that his name became an "honorary epithet" for subsequent generations of actors.[10] Another newspaper described how audiences responded in astonishment to his death scene, wherein Betty as Richard *"gnash[ed]* his *teeth* in such a manner, as to give the highest promise of *future excellence!*"[11] Tellingly, the critic acknowledges Betty's potential, while hinting that the boy is not yet ready for such a challenging role.[12]

After a year spent touring the provinces, Betty made his London debut at Covent Garden in December 1804. London audiences swarmed the theatre, primed by the glowing tributes and word-of-mouth accounts that had preceded his arrival. They were not disappointed. Critics praised Betty's technical skill, his "bold, correct and grace[ful]" attitudes, his "striking and elegant" posture, and his convincing portrayal of strong emotion. His admirers included the Prince of Wales, the Duchess of York, and other members of the royal household, as well as the Prime Minister and members of Parliament.[13] Thanks to a loophole in his contract with Covent Garden, Betty also played at Drury Lane during his London engagement, doubling the public's opportunities to see him.[14]

Theatre historians have long wondered at the underlying factors that fueled Bettymania. Some scholars echo Kristina Straub in attributing the boy's popularity to his physical attractiveness and charisma, noting the hype that surrounded each performance, the number of male and female theatregoers who purchased goods bearing his image, and the crush of fans that gathered outside his home and followed him on his travels.[15] Commenting on claims that Betty's Richard III "gratified the female part of the audience," Jim Davis opines that women (and men) may have been aroused watching "the implicit sexual 'otherness' of Richard embodied and mediated through the 'innocent' child performer."[16] Childhood in this context is read through the body of a (pre)pubescent boy whose attractiveness arises from the startling juxtaposition of his onstage character with his real-world self, a self that is seemingly innocent, both morally and sexually. However, an emphasis on

Betty's appearance alone does not account for the range of responses he elicited. While some audiences expressed combinations of maternal and sexual desire for the boy, others viewed him as a refreshing escape from the anxieties of war and the threat of a Napoleonic invasion.[17] George Taylor reads Bettymania "as a sign that people do indeed turn to the theatre in times of crisis, not necessarily to see their concerns enacted, debated or rehearsed, but to escape from anxiety."[18] Jeffrey Kahan concurs, observing that London newspapers devoted more column inches to covering Betty's December 1804 debut than to Napoleon's coronation as emperor of France the same week.[19] This was no accident. Betty's widespread popularity with Londoners and the surging crowds that greeted his performances at Drury Lane and Covent Garden gestured toward the public's brewing dissatisfaction with contemporary politics and a surge in pro-revolutionary critiques of royalty and the aging aristocracy. As a "symbol of juvenescence," Betty offered an appealing alternative to the decadence, disease, and corruption that characterized the nation's rulers.[20] Through his portrayal of Romantic heroes, men willing to sacrifice themselves for family and nation, he invited theatregoers to imagine their own "man of destiny."

Public hunger for youth and vitality, fueled by the production and circulation of goods bearing his name and his own frequent theatrical appearances, transformed Betty from a charming boy into a celebrity.[21] Betty's audience avidly consumed his image[22] and indulged in gossipy tidbits about his private life. "The attraction of the young Roscius is not limited to the stage," claimed one report, "for he cannot walk along the streets without drawing crowds, who naturally press after him."[23] Here the desire to see the boy stretched beyond love and admiration to include stalking and other threatening behavior. Those unable to get tickets to see Betty perform would wait in the street outside his Southampton row house, hoping to catch "a peep before his *drawing-room curtain!*"[24] Pushing beyond public into private space, the crowds pursued Betty with a hunger tinged with violence. The harder it became to access Betty's physical person, the more desirable he became.

The hysteria surrounding Betty suggests that the boy possessed the requisite balance of "contradictory qualities" that Joseph Roach identifies as critical to the full flowering of the "It-Effect": onstage he appeared as a strong, valiant warrior; offstage he was a cute child in need of support.[25] This aspect of Betty's celebrity became dramatically apparent when the boy fell ill and had to cancel several scheduled performances. Audiences were so overcome with worry that the Drury Lane management published a notice with letters from Betty's father and doctor verifying the young boy's illness, complete with vivid details of "bilious vomiting" and "cold and hoarseness" that rendered his voice barely "audible in his room."[26] London papers followed suit, publishing regular updates on Betty's progress, with graphic accounts of the specific treatments administered (e.g., enemas, bloodletting), while Betty's family posted notices outside their door to address the "numerous and incessant enquiries of the Nobility and Gentry."[27] This intense interest in Betty—the public's demand to know *everything* that was happening to his body behind closed doors—hints at the ugly underbelly of celebrity culture. Such extreme reactions to Betty's ill health also highlight the role of vulnerability, weakness, and distance in the accentuation of cuteness, an "aesthetic category" associated with smallness, delicacy, pliancy, and defenselessness.[28] Although, as cultural historian Lori Merish asserts, "what the cute stages is, in part, a need for adult care,"[29] the cute can also arouse feelings of possession and domination. When Betty became sick, his already attractive boy body became the focus of public scrutiny and heightened desire, a desire further stoked by his sudden inaccessibility. Hidden in the inner sanctum of his bedroom, Betty was literally untouchable, even by members of the nobility and gentry, which only made him seem more fascinating, more defenseless, and more desirable.[30]

But Betty was not without detractors. Some critics remained skeptical of his abilities, observing that he was much less convincing as a romantic lover like Romeo[31] and that his performances of other Shakespearean characters prompted giggles and laughter.[32] Other writers expressed concern about Betty's status as a prized commodity and accused his father of demanding ever-higher rates for his son's services.[33] In the mock poem *The Young Rosciad*, the pseudonymous Peter Pangloss refers to Betty as "thy father's prop" and "the public's toy."[34] In Pangloss's narrative, Betty is a pathetic object created to serve his father's ambitions. Corresponding imagery of forced public consumption framed Betty as an agentless being, the antithesis of the brave heroes he played onstage. Professional artists likewise rejected Betty or damned him with faint praise. Some actors simply refused to perform alongside the boy actor, while others withdrew from the stage entirely during Betty's "reign," either because there were no roles for them or because they did not wish to be associated with him.[35] The playwright Elizabeth Inchbald sarcastically commented that "had I never seen boys act before, I might have thought him exquisite," while Sarah Siddons concluded that he was "a very clever, pretty boy, but nothing more."[36] Tellingly, both Inchbald and Siddons acknowledge Betty's boyish charm but refuse to see him as anything more than a "clever, pretty boy" in a long string of clever, pretty boys. Their exhaustion with Betty, and with an industry that privileges youth and boyhood, is palpable.

Such criticism did little to deter fame-hungry parents and managers from lobbing their own little wonders at the stage. In 1805, the caricaturist William Holland captured this phenomenon in a drawing entitled "A Cart Load of Young Players on their Journey to London," in which a dozen or more miniaturized boys and girls stand in the back of a farmer's cart, dressed in costumes representative of Betty's most famous roles.[37] The image flattens the children's miniaturized cuteness into the single category of "young players," although the discernible presence of girls within the group suggests that parents did not consider their daughters' gender an impediment to questing for stage glory. The craze for child performers was not limited to London, either. "Infantine acting is growing into a rage of the day," declared a writer for the *Morning Herald* as early as December 1804, citing the recent example of a nine-year-old boy "brought forward" at the Chester Theatre.[38] Several months later, Theatre Royal, Weymouth announced the engagement of six-year-old Master Dawson, the "Conte Roscius," who would appear in *The Beaux' Stratagem*; in June 1805, the four-and-a-half-year-old Master Wigley played the bugle at Drury Lane.[39] Girls with such monikers as "the Infant Billington" also made their way onto the stage. By late 1805, over twenty infant Roscii (boys and girls) had "sprung up" in theatres across Britain,[40] shadowing Betty's repertoire in the hope of acquiring a piece of his celebrity.[41] This surge in mini-Roscii led to a corresponding boom in acting schools, private tutors, and related training institutions for aspiring child performers; by November 1804, one source reported that as many as four hundred children were actively training to "become *Roscii*."[42] Bettymania even crossed the Atlantic to New York, where a fourteen-year-old John Howard

Payne made his own bid for theatrical stardom in 1809, playing Young Norval in *Douglas* and many of the other roles that had elevated Betty to stardom.[43]

To date, most analyses of Bettymania have focused squarely on the celebrated boy, casting only cursory glances at the other child performers who pursued a similar path to stardom. One exception is Miss Mudie, a cute yet seemingly untalented girl of eight who infuriated critics like Leigh Hunt, who found the practice of casting children "in characters irreconcilable to their age and size ... systematically absurd."[44] When, during an 1812 performance of *The Country Girl*, the audience loudly disapproved the sight of the tiny Miss Mudie dressed in breeches, the girl stood her ground and insisted that she had "done nothing to offend you." She then resumed the scene, to a more raucous response, but "did not appear to be in the slightest degree chagrined or embarrassed, but went on with the scene as if she had been completely successful."[45] As the hissing and murmuring continued, Covent Garden manager John Philip Kemble pleaded with the audience to allow Miss Mudie to finish her performance, promising that she would never return to the stage. But it was only after another (adult) actress assumed Miss Mudie's role in the last act that the audience ceased their jeers, marking the end of what critic David Erskine Baker described as "the most imperfect performance ever witnessed on a London stage."[46]

Miss Mudie's failure is frequently cited as one of the most unfortunate products of Bettymania.[47] This, in turn, has left the impression that girls were poorly equipped to compete with someone of Betty's stature. But this view is too limited. Certainly Betty's repertoire emphasized a particular kind of heroic masculinity that was not (immediately) accessible to girls. Yet in the midst of all the hype some of the loudest praise was directed at Jane Fisher, the "Young Roscia," whose diverse repertoire included both male and female roles: Jane Shore, Rosalind, Young Norval, and Richard III. As the following chapter explores, the secret to Fisher's success was her emotional range, facility with language, and, perhaps most important, her ability to portray a *kind* of masculinity that, while charming and legible, afforded opportunities for disguise.

CHAPTER 1
The Tyrant King

ON GIRLS PLAYING RICHARD III

With Christmas 1817 fast approaching, holiday audiences gathered at the Theatre Royal Drury Lane to watch a company of girls between the ages of six and thirteen perform an adaptation of David Garrick's *Lilliput* (1756). Critics applauded the juvenile company but they reserved their highest praise for six-year-old Clara Fisher in the role of the Prime Minister, Lord Flimnap.[1] "The affected gravity, and jealous whims of the diminutive Lord, are hit off by this surprising child with astonishing cleverness," one writer commented.[2] A second enthused that she "manifested an almost miraculous power of conception of character."[3] What impressed the critics even more was Fisher's uncanny portrayal of Richard III in the last act, when the company performed a masque for the Lilliputian Majesty. "It was really *Richard* in movement, gesture, language, and we had almost said, in looks, seen in miniature as through an inverted telescope," the *Morning Herald* proclaimed.[4] Another writer declared that Fisher's "miniature *Richard* [was] the finest specimen the Stage ever produced."[5] Watching the tiny girl play the tyrant king was akin to viewing a scientific spectacle, at once strange and wonderful.

Fisher's stunning debut marks a curious moment in the history of girls on stage. As the *British Press* wryly noted, the decision on the part of Drury Lane management to present a children's company composed almost entirely of girls "was a very hazardous one—for, since the period when the good fortune of [M]aster Betty called forth a host of *Roscii* and *Rosciae*, the tide of public feeling has run violently against the exhibition of children on the boards of our great theatres."[6] Here the paper refers to the meteoric rise of Master Betty, whose overwhelming popularity throughout England, Ireland, and Scotland had spawned a host

MISS CLARA FISHER,

as Richard 3.ᵈ

A weak invention of the Enemy

FIGURE 3. *Clara Fisher as Richard III.*
By permission of the Folger Shakespeare Library.

of other child performers of varying ages and talents, all hoping to ride the Roscian wave. But the tide turned quickly; critics and caricaturists soon pounced on Betty and the Betty wannabes, accusing them of usurping the rightful place (and roles) of adult performers.[7] Those cast aside by the public desire for "infant phenomena" likewise voiced disgust and concern.[8] Gradually audiences tired of watching boys and girls pretend to be grown men and women, and "Bettymania" waned. Yet while some critics in 1817 questioned whether London was ready to be entertained by yet another child prodigy, the public's embrace of Clara Fisher indicated that it was. "The time seemed to be ripe for my appearance," Fisher remarked in her autobiography years later, "and I had the whole field to myself."[9]

It would be wrong, however, to assume that the "ripeness" of Clara Fisher's arrival was distinct from Bettymania or that her rise to stardom owed nothing to the experiences of the Roscii who had constellated around the boy a decade before. Nor is it accurate to say that she had the whole field to herself. To the contrary, this chapter argues that Fisher's ascendancy was a peculiar by-product of Bettymania, one that can be traced through the Fisher family and the early career of Clara's eldest sister, Jane.

Jane Fisher was one of more than twenty boys and girls who followed Betty onto the stage in the first decade of the nineteenth century. In 1805 a writer for *Universal Magazine* declared that she was "a clever sprightly little girl, and probably one of the best of the Roscia swarm."[10] Yet this aspect of her life is entirely obscured from biographical accounts of Clara Fisher or other members of the Fisher family. The reason for this apparent erasure is unclear: perhaps their father, Frederick George Fisher, wished to represent his youngest daughter as a unique phenomenon, untainted by the negative associations that in 1817 still clung to Betty's name. Or perhaps Jane Fisher had no desire to relive the earliest years of her career.

This chapter restores Jane Fisher's name to the history of nineteenth-century girl actresses and acknowledges her contribution to the development of a distinct repertoire for girls. It also initiates this book's lengthy engagement with Clara Fisher, who effectively reshaped the contours of theatrical girlhood in Britain and North America. The Fisher girls negotiated a wider range of roles than boys like Betty, playing male and female characters across the genres of tragedy, comedy, and farce. Such repertorial diversity attests to the sisters' dynamic plasticity and the demands placed on subsequent generations of girls, who had to develop the vocal, gestural, and physical skills to transition from women to men, old ladies to little boys, and so on. Whereas boys like Betty specialized in a particular brand of heroic masculinity (as the previous Interlude detailed), girls learned to delight audiences with the breadth of their repertoire, playing high and low, masculine and feminine, old and young, all in the name of entertainment.

This chapter also explores an intriguing development in the history of cross-dressed Shakespeare: the introduction of Richard III as a role for girls. Adult actresses had long specialized in breeches roles, such as Rosalind and Margery Pinchwife, wherein a female character assumes the guise and dress of a man out of necessity or in pursuit of love. In plays with breeches roles, Celestine Woo explains, cross-dressing "occurs as a feature of the narrative, and as a decision by the character."[11] Most breeches roles delight in the sexualized display of the female body, especially the legs, and conclude with the character's return to dress "befitting" her gender, an action that reaffirms gender binaries and patriarchal norms. On occasion, actresses also donned breeches to play a male character for the duration of the play, wherein the act of crossing gender was "exterior to the narrative and plot."[12] These travestied[13] interpretations gave actresses greater opportunities to test their range, challenge audience expectations, and perhaps most important, assume the clothing, gestures, and actions of men without interruption. Between 1775 and 1805, Sarah Siddons asserted her right to play Hamlet, offering a startlingly sympathetic vision of the prince that invited provincial critics and audiences to take her seriously in the role.[14] Her contemporaries Peg Woffington and Ann Barry similarly tested their mettle with comic roles like Sir Harry Wildair in *The Constant Couple* and Lothario in *The Fair Penitent*.[15] But none of these actresses ever approached Richard III—or left no record if they did—which makes the role's subsequent incorporation into the repertoire of the Fisher girls rather peculiar.

By 1822 Clara Fisher had performed Richard III an estimated two hundred times in theatres across Great Britain.[16] Other girls followed suit. In the early 1840s, Jean Margaret Davenport introduced her Richard to audiences as far reaching as Kingston, Jamaica, and Montreal, Quebec, while a decade later Ellen Bateman delighted British and US audiences with her star turn as the tyrant king.[17] Boys like Master Betty and Master Joseph Burke also played the role,[18] but Richard's privileged place in the repertoire of the era's most celebrated girls, and their less-celebrated counterparts, suggests that it served as something of a litmus test for emerging female talent.

Historians have offered various theories to explain why audiences took such delight in this seemingly incongruous form of "age transvestism"—Marah Gubar's term for the practice of "children impersonating adults and vice versa"[19]—yet they have stopped short of asking why girls (and their managers) gravitated toward Richard III specifically.[20] This chapter does just that, tracing Richard III's migration from the repertoire of adult male actors into the repertoire of girl actresses at the beginning of the nineteenth century. If, as Jim Davis observes, "The history of Shakespearean performance by children has much to reveal about the shifting and sometimes contradictory perceptions of childhood in the nineteenth century," what does an analysis of girls performing Richard III reveal about shifting attitudes toward girls as prodigious subjects?[21] Is it simply that audiences enjoyed seeing girls play such a complicated, divisive character, or was their response indicative of a larger cultural fascination with Richard's fierce intelligence, ambition, and desire? The answer, this chapter argues, has much to do with the way the role allowed the Fishers to showcase their knowledge of Shakespeare, to charm audiences with their cuteness and youth, to assert their right to stand center stage, and, perhaps most important, to take delight in Richard's monstrous plasticity. In asking why and how Richard III found such a privileged place in the repertoire of girl actresses this chapter also traces contemporary debates about girls' education and intellectual development. It highlights the tension between Frederick George Fisher's desire to promote his actress daughters, while protecting them from public scrutiny. And it concludes with a discussion of the phrenologist who promised to explain the mystery of Clara Fisher's talent, including what (in his view) made her such a superior Richard III.

The Young Roscia Plays Richard III

Jane Merchant Vernon sits on the fringes of theatre history; her name appears in passing references and occasional footnotes. In later life, she enjoyed success as a comic actress in the United States following her 1827 marriage to George (Verrall) Vernon, after which she was known as Mrs. Vernon. Born in Brighton around 1792,[22] her first years were spent in relative comfort and in the company of books, within a growing family of artistically inclined children.[23] Her father, Frederick George Fisher, was an educated man and a one-time amateur actor. From the 1790s to the early 1800s, he was proprietor of two circulating libraries, one in Eastbourne (est. 1790) and the other in Brighton, which catered to visiting members of the social elite by providing books and "also reading lounges with all the London newspapers, music and billiard tables."[24]

Fisher was an avid Shakespeare scholar and collector and author of such volumes as *The New Brighton Guide* (1800), a travel guide for visitors to the seaside resort town, and *A Catalogue of the Various Articles Contained in Clara Fisher's Shaksperean [sic] Cabinet* (1830), a fascinating collection featuring sketches and descriptions of the Globe Theatre, Anne Hathaway's cottage, and other Shakespearean structures. Fisher's abiding interest in Shakespeare was the metaphorical glue that held the Fisher family together. Hours spent reading his plays tightened the bonds between father and children and left a deep imprint on his daughters' lives. "He read Shakespeare incessantly," Clara Fisher later wrote of her father, "and took great pride in teaching me."[25] Jane Fisher likewise inherited her father's love of the Bard. In his *Players of a Century*, Henry Pitt Phelps remarks that Mrs. Vernon's "education was liberal" and her word "was considered final" in any dispute over the interpretation of a Shakespearean passage.[26]

Fisher's "incessant" reading to his daughters is consistent with the rise of a distinctly sentimental model of family life in the late eighteenth and early nineteenth centuries wherein fathers were tasked with overseeing their children's education and guiding them onto a moral path that, in the case of daughters, would ensure that they became good wives and mothers.[27] Fisher's dedication to teaching his daughters Shakespeare is notable, however, given contemporary debates about whether to introduce girls to the vulgarities of Shakespeare's plays. Some critics claimed that exposure to "unadulterated Shakespeare," meaning plays featuring grotesque violence or passionate expressions of sexual desire, threatened the mind and soul of young girls, jeopardizing their potential for future happiness.[28] These writers called for "responsible parents" to closely supervise their daughters' reading and guide them away from the enticements of the Bard.[29] Anxiety about girls reading "raw" Shakespeare led to the publication of two important volumes for children, Charles and Mary Lamb's *Tales from Shakespeare* and the Bowdlers' *The Family Shakespeare*, both of which supported the "development of feminine graces—modesty, patience, and gentleness."[30] Published in 1807, these volumes offered adaptations of Shakespeare's plays cleansed of the goriest or most sexually explicit passages, thereby reassuring nervous parents that they could read to their children without fear of "falling unawares among words and expressions which are of such a nature as to raise a blush on the cheek of modesty."[31] Significantly, neither the Bowdlers nor the Lambs included *Richard III* in their volumes—an absence that marks the play as somehow aberrant and dangerous.

Not everyone agreed with such aggressive protectionism, however. The publisher William Godwin, who worked closely with the Lambs, wrote against the practice of parents locking volumes of books away. "Trust him in a certain degree with himself," Godwin wrote in *Educational Writings*, "Suffer him to wander in the wilds of literature."[32] Curiously, Godwin stops short of advising parents to free their *daughters* into the "wilds of literature," implicitly supporting gendered divisions in reading practices.[33] Although I have found no direct evidence that Frederick George Fisher knew Godwin or was familiar with contemporary writing on children's education, I can nevertheless conjecture that as a librarian and bookseller he would have had ample opportunity to follow debates about children's reading. Indeed, it is safe to assume that his profession would have *required* some degree of familiarity with the arguments about girls and Shakespeare. Fisher's actions, then, speak volumes. Rather than shielding his daughters from the dangers of Shakespeare, Fisher did the opposite, enthusiastically inviting them into the world of *Richard III*.

In 1803, the Fisher family fortunes took a turn for the worse when Fisher declared bankruptcy and had to sell six cottages, a garden, two houses and stables, as well as four thousand volumes, twenty-two pianos, and a harpsichord from his library.[34] Not long after this period of distress, Fisher seems to have drawn on his training as an amateur actor to prepare his eldest daughter for the stage.[35]

Jane Fisher made her London debut at Drury Lane in the winter of

1804–1805, performing *The Spoiled Child* for "seven successive nights" to "great Applause."[36] Although originally written for Dorothy Jordan, the role of Little Pickle was ideally suited to the energy and physical charms of a young child (as I discuss in the following chapter). During this engagement, Fisher also played "the favourite Character of [Shakespeare's] Rosalind," another celebrated Jordan role that invited audiences to compare Fisher, "justly styled the Phenomenon Roscia," with the adult actress.[37] More important, however, were comparisons between the young "Roscia" and the "young Roscius" himself, who had just made his London debut. Although Fisher's appearance at Drury Lane followed closely on Master Betty's, she apparently held her own and secured a contract for the following season.[38]

Riding the wave of Bettymania, Jane Fisher appeared as Richard III at the New Theatre Royal in Cheltenham in July 1805, much to the "astonishment of a brilliant audience" who were impressed by the twelve-year-old girl's "combination of power and judgment."[39] The character of Richard III demands "great judgment and discrimination, and a constant attention to stage effect," one critic wrote, before declaring that the young girl's "remarkably expressive" countenance and strong, flexible voice gave her "a decided superiority over her rival of the opposite sex," that is, Master Betty.[40] As the critic makes plain, Richard III is a challenging role for *any* actor, one that requires considerable stamina, a strong memory, and deep knowledge of the human psyche.[41] In all areas, Jane Fisher exceeded expectations:

> The first soliloquy of *Richard* was delivered with judgment and force, and the scene, in which he murders *King Henry*, was played with peculiar skill and discrimination, and drew down loud and deserved applause. In the celebrated scene with Lady Anne, he was uncommonly happy; though perhaps occasionally rather too loud. —Where Richard presents her with his sword to stab him, we think she mistook the meaning of the author, and was not sufficiently plaintive and pathetic; for, it is under tenderness of manner and external feelings that he best conceals his perfidious hypocrisy. The expression of "To the Tower, to the Tower!" was admirably delivered; and in the soliloquy, after the young princes are sent thither, she was uncommonly happy in describing the vices of men, and the ambition of *Richard*. The quarrel with Buckingham,

a very difficult scene, was excellently played.—The news of his defection, and of the invasion of Richmond, was received in a manner which astonished the audience; and the celebrated exclamation, "Off with his head!—so much for Buckingham!" drew down thunders of applause. The Tent Scene and the battle Scene close the life of the Usurper; and these were played in a very superior style of excellence. Perhaps her action is rather too sudden, and her utterance, at times, too voluble, but the spirit, the energy, and the fury of a disappointed Usurper, were never more admirably delineated. In her dying scene, she was eminently successful.[42]

Here the author assumes audience familiarity with both Shakespeare's play and previous actors' interpretations of the tyrant king. He is awed by Fisher's sophisticated grasp of the character, her ability to handle "very difficult material," her energetic presentation of celebrated lines, and her spot-on interpretation of Richard's energy and fury at his defeat. Such achievements were impressive, the writer notes, since "she had travelled the whole of the preceding night without the refreshment of slumber" and had never seen "the play of *Richard* acting before!"[43] Despite identifying some weaknesses—too loud and too quick in certain moments, possibly misreading Shakespeare's intent in others—the writer celebrates Jane Fisher as a natural prodigy untainted by adult influence.

Comparisons with Betty were inevitable—and perhaps desired. The Cheltenham critic concluded that Fisher's portrayal of the tyrant king greatly "exceed[ed] that of her well-known rival."[44] The following week, the critic commented again on the similarities to Betty, noting that "the same interesting elegance of form and action that has attracted such notice in this wonderful Boy, characterizes the performance of this wonderful Girl." In naming Fisher a "wonderful Girl" (with a capital G), the writer pairs her with Betty's "wonderful Boy," the Roscia to his Roscius. Like Betty, Fisher was "great and astonishing" in "scenes of combat and death" and similarly demonstrated an appropriate "tone of voice and volatility." In fact, Fisher's facial expressiveness "and the brilliant clearness of her voice, when raised to the extreme pitch of enthusiasm or madness," made her superior to the Young Roscius.[45]

Throughout the summer of 1805 critics continued to praise Fisher as a natural talent. In a July 20, 1805, letter to the editor of the *Glo-*

cester [*sic*] *Journal*, a writer going by the initials T.P. explained that Fisher had "no instructor, her father's dissidence preventing his undertaking the task" and "that the book is put into her hand, or, as is generally the case, only the part she is to perform, *and that her own ideas alone* are to direct her, candour will not be at a loss to see the evident disadvantage under which she labours in comparison to her Rival."[46] Though acknowledging that the absence of formal training may have limited Fisher's development as a performer, at least in comparison to her "Rival" (i.e., Betty), T.P. characterizes the young girl as a naturally gifted artist granted the autonomy to make her own acting decisions. Like the idealized child of nature, her performances exhibit spontaneity and a kind of unvarnished freedom. T.P. further notes that when she performed Young Norval alongside her father in *Douglas*, his "extreme agitation and attention to her, throws her off her guard, of which, the difference between her manner when he was on the stage with her, and when not, afforded a palpable proof."[47] For all his love of Shakespeare, Frederick George Fisher does not appear to have been a particularly skilled actor.

From what I can tell, Jane Fisher never realized her full potential during her Roscia years. Later references to performances in Bath, where her repertoire included more standard ingénue fare like Desdemona and Miss Hardcastle in *She Stoops to Conquer*,[48] suggest that she made a career for herself during her teen years. But the abrupt end of Bettymania and the annoyance, if not latent violence, with which many critics greeted the prospect of child actors in the period immediately following helps explain her apparent disappearance from the historical record (for a decade or so). By 1806–1807, the visibly teenaged Master Betty no longer delighted audiences, and the deficiencies in his acting made him a topic of ridicule. As Jeffrey Kahan concludes, "Betty had overexposed himself through performances, pamphlets, newspaper reports, and a seemingly endless variety of cheap knickknacks."[49] Where such objects had once secured Betty's status as a cute child and desirable celebrity, they now exposed Bettymania's superficiality. As the taste for Betty soured, so did the taste for other Roscii.[50]

Yet the "Young Roscia" remains an important figure for this study as one of the first actresses to play Richard III. Jane Fisher came to the bloody tyrant out of necessity—out of the need to impress audiences with her talent and to perform a kind of masculinity that invited

CHAPTER 1

comparisons to Betty's displays of Romantic heroism. But the Roscia/o rivalry does not explain why Fisher opted to play Richard III over Romeo or Hamlet, for example—roles that Betty had also attempted and which later found favor with actresses like Charlotte Cushman and Sarah Bernhardt—nor does it explain why Fisher's sister Clara returned to the role two decades later. A closer look at the role and the dynamics of the Fisher family suggest that what ultimately drew the Fisher girls (and their father) to *Richard III* was the way it allowed them to showcase their intelligence, emotional range, and plasticity, while avoiding the trappings of celebrity culture and the dangers of overexposure.

Playing *Richard*: Strategies of Overexpression

Richard III enjoyed a prized place in the repertoire of most leading actors of the eighteenth- and nineteenth-century stage, thanks in no small part to Colley Cibber's expansion of the role and his emphasis on Richard's psychological complexity.[51] Although Cibber's 1699 adaptation was surprisingly faithful to the plot and structure of Shakespeare's original, he introduced substantial changes to the character of Richard, adding monologues that more closely articulated the tyrant's aims.[52] These changes, theatre scholar London Green asserts, served to "sensationalize the evil ambition of [Shakespeare's] protagonist and bring Richard's unwelcome battle with his conscience to the center."[53] While enhancing Richard, Cibber diminished, or in some cases completely eliminated Edward IV, Margaret, Clarence, and Hastings, while lending greater pathos to the character of Anne.[54] The result was a role ideally suited to the needs of the star actor and a play that delivered a more straightforward vision of villainy and corruption.[55] Small wonder that *Richard III* found favor with later generations of actors looking to elevate themselves to stardom.[56]

With *Richard III*, Cibber also created a role that offered protection from the glare of public life. Theatre historian Julia Fawcett argues that Cibber's decision to make his tragic debut as Richard rather than Hamlet or another "noble prince" was shaped by the actor's desire to keep his private life private.[57] Wary of growing fascination with actors' off-stage lives and nervous about his own "physical eccentricities,"[58] Cibber opted for a role through which he could appeal to audiences without subjecting his personal life and appearance to their scrutiny. To achieve this, he engaged in what Fawcett calls "overexpression," a performance strategy that "allows its practitioners at once to invite and to disrupt the public gaze, paradoxically, by enhancing or exaggerating the features through which they might be recognized and evaluated by their spectators."[59] Critical to Cibber's performance of "overexpression" was his physical embodiment of Richard, a character who relishes descriptions of his deformities and uses his eccentric features "to secure his power" and "frustrate the reinterpretations that might undermine it."[60] By actively inviting a clinical gaze, Richard asserts his subject status, refusing to be seen as an object of pity or derision. "I have no brother, I am like no brother," he boldly declares after stabbing his brother and king, Henry VI. "And this word 'love,' which graybeards call divine, / Be resident in men like one another / And not in me: I am myself alone."[61] For Fawcett, such moments of self-determination defy those who seek to understand Richard's actions or "to read him against earlier narratives or within predetermined rules about anatomy as a key to character."[62] This aspect of the character made him an ideal choice for actors who likewise wished to avoid the piercing gaze of the public eye, or for parents, like Frederick George Fisher, who sought to protect their daughters from easy commodification.

Fisher fiercely guarded his daughters' privacy and studiously avoided the trappings of celebrity culture. As Clara Fisher recalls in her autobiography: "He had a great aversion to my being seen or talked to, and would frequently say, 'My child, now that you are on the stage, and so young, keep yourself from public view, except professionally, and let nobody come near you. The less you are seen and known as Miss Clara Fisher, outside of your immediate duties in your respective characters, the better for you.'"[63] Fisher offers no explanation for her father's "great aversion" to her circulation in public or his insistence on the strict separation of her onstage characters from her offstage self. Perhaps he wished to protect her from the circus that had greeted Master Betty as well as the innuendo and titillation of plays like Colman's *A Fairy Tale*.[64] Whatever the cause, Fisher's cautious parenting meant that Jane and Clara Fisher did not appear in public as cute, sexualized commodities. Instead, they played Richard III.

A question dangles: why did Fisher train his daughters to play the tyrant king instead of the doomed princes, roles frequently played by

young girls?[65] Cibber's adaptation offers some clues. Rather than diminish the roles of the princes, Cibber added new lines and increased
their stage time, providing exciting new opportunities for young performers.[66] In doing so, however, the actor-manager deemphasized the
wit and sophistication that arises from Shakespeare's text, wherein the
princes appear to Richard and his ally Buckingham as "sharp-witted,
precocious, and capable . . . equals and adversaries rather than innocent victims."[67] Tapping into sentimentalist modes of feeling, Cibber
instead represented the princes as "'tender babes' or 'gentle lambs,'"[68]
and set their murder onstage, where their pitiful cries played powerfully on audience emotion, especially when they came from the mouths
of actual children.[69] As sweet, innocent victims, the girls and boys playing the princes regularly moved audiences to tears but enjoyed fewer
opportunities to showcase their virtuosity or intellect.[70] Is it any wonder that Fisher wanted his daughters to play the king instead?

Richard III is more than a flashy role. It is a dynamic, complex role
that invites disguise and dissembling. Through Richard, the Fisher
girls erected a barrier between their onstage performances and their
offstage lives, behind which they explored the privilege and power of
monstrous masculinity without succumbing to its worst abuses. Just as
Cibber negotiated audience desire to breach his privacy by "assuming
a body that is 'too much a body,'"[71] the Fishers used the "too-much-
ness" of Richard to protect themselves from prying eyes. Yet in portraying a king with a "strange" and "abject" body, they also marked themselves *as girls*, distinct from the adult male roles they performed.[72] This
paradoxical effect was achieved (in part) through a strategic play with
scale.[73]

This performative strategy is visible in numerous images of Clara
Fisher, including this book's cover and the cover illustration for the
Lilliput sheet music (Figure 4). Here, Fisher's tiny Richard stands in
the middle of the page surrounded by other girls and the considerably
taller adult actor playing Gulliver. For all of her miniaturized ferocity,
she seems peculiarly out of place. Indeed, critics frequently compared
watching Fisher onstage to looking at an object through the wrong end
of a telescope, a metaphor that evokes Susan Stewart's claim that "We
imagine childhood as if it were at the other end of a tunnel—distanced,
diminutive, and clearly framed."[74] The image of the miniaturized girl
also nods toward the heightened ocular-centrism of early nineteenth-

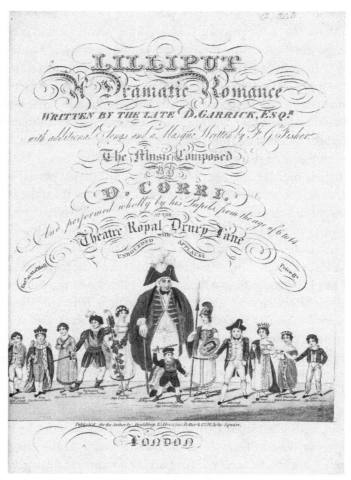

FIGURE 4. *The cast of* Lilliput, *with young Clara Fisher as Richard III.*
Courtesy of the British Library.

century theatre culture. The mediating technologies of the Drury Lane proscenium arch, combined with the auditorium's three-thousand-person capacity and the very recent introduction of gas lighting, further enhanced the miniaturization of the girl performer.[75] Such technological innovations led actors to adapt their performances to the dimensions of the stage, increasing the size and grandeur of their gestures to make them legible to members of the audience seated at the back of the auditorium.[76] While written accounts and pictorial evidence suggest that child actors like Betty and the Fisher sisters used similar techniques, the effect of seeing a child playing an adult role alongside other adults would have been both strange and wonderful. Yet even as the emphasis on miniaturization invited close observation, the character of Richard III allowed the girls to avoid the peering eyes and grasping hands that had reached so desperately for Betty.

Size and scale alone do not explain the Fisher girls' embrace of Richard III or the role's eventual migration into the repertoire of the girl actress. A further factor in their adoption of Richard III seems to have been the play's unique exploration of the human will, an attribute that appealed to the Romantic appetite for "exceptional but ambiguous and contradictory personalities."[77] Alongside "Napoleon, Milton's Satan, and the Byronic hero," Nicoletta Caputo writes, Richard III "acquired almost superhuman connotations" for Romantic authors and admirers. As early as 1801, the writer Charles Lamb defined his vision of a Romantic Duke of Gloucester in a letter to a friend, writing, "I am possessed with an admiration of the genuine Richard, his genius, his mounting spirit, which no consideration of his cruelties can depress."[78] Like Lamb, poet Samuel Coleridge was drawn toward Richard's fierce intelligence, vaulting ambition, and the forcefulness of his will, which he recognized as a reflection of "Shakespeare's own gigantic intellect."[79] The experience of reading the play or watching an actor perform Richard III thus afforded unique access to the Bard himself. Is it any wonder that Frederick George Fisher seized on such a role for his daughters?

The "Astonishing" Clara Fisher

Sometime before 1815, the Fishers and their six children relocated to London where Frederick George Fisher established himself as an auctioneer on Great Russell Street. Jane Fisher appears to have withdrawn from the professional stage at this point, although she continued training under the tutelage of Domenico Corri, an Italian composer, dancing master, and theatre manager who also specialized in preparing girls and young women for the stage.[80] It was around this time that the three-year-old Clara began exhibiting a startling gift for imitation. Following a trip to the theatre, she surprised her family by replicating Eliza O'Neill's performance in Nicholas Rowe's "she-tragedy," *Jane Shore*, "blend[ing] the madness of *Alicia* with the tenderness and distress of *Jane Shore*."[81] On another occasion, Clara reproduced a comic dance she had observed at the Olympic Theatre, complete with facial grimaces and gestures. Her mimetic talents extended to music as well: "soon after she could walk, [she] took a great interest in music, learning any tune with the greatest correctness, after hearing it played over one or twice on the piano."[82] Fisher's 1819 biographer characterizes Clara as a naturally gifted prodigy, a mysterious and otherworldly creature destined for a life on the stage, yet curiously avoids referring to Jane Fisher's own time as a "Young Roscia." While I can only speculate on the author's reason for excluding such details, I assume that Clara benefited considerably from her eldest sister's expertise and years of training.

In the summer of 1817, Corri approached the management of Drury Lane about bringing a juvenile production of Garrick's *Lilliput* to the stage.[83] Whereas previous productions had featured casts of boys, Corri proposed an all-girl version "with the exception of Gulliver."[84] With Drury Lane's encouragement, Corri began preparations and appealed to Frederick George Fisher to allow his three youngest daughters, Caroline, Amelia, and Clara, to perform in the piece. Fisher not only consented, but also agreed to adapt Garrick's script for the juvenile company, "writ[ing] songs and new characters in order to introduce his [Corri's] musical pupils to the public attention."[85] The new material included a masque wherein the character of Lord Flimnap performs the "tent scene" from *Richard III*. Fisher's involvement in *Lilliput* is significant.[86] As noted already, Richard III was not a role associated with female performers—adults or children—nor was it a play considered appropriate for young girls to read. By including a large chunk of the fifth act so prominently in the revised *Lilliput* Fisher made clear his investment in the play and his daughter's career (in her memoirs Clara Fisher confirms that it was her father who taught her to read the role).[87] Of course, he must also have known that his daughter's appearance in the tent scene would invite comparisons with the brilliant new star, Edmund Kean.

Kean embodied the Romantic ideal. When he debuted his Richard III in 1814, he upended decades of sentimental interpretations by indulging in the king's darkness, brooding intellect, and perverse delight in the suffering of others. His passionate performance style, characterized by "intense emotions and marked mood swings," stood in

FIGURE 5. *Edmund Kean as Richard III.*
By permission of the Folger Shakespeare Library.

marked contrast to the restrained, neoclassical style embodied by Sarah Siddons and her brother John Kemble. Where their performances typically featured a series of statuesque poses, chanting vocal passages, and carefully modulated outbursts of emotion, Kean brought speed, volcanic bursts of energy, emotional intensity, and surprising variety to Drury Lane's three-thousand-seat theatre.[88] Audiences were thrilled, seeing in Kean's Richard the qualities that Coleridge, Lamb, and others had identified as ideally suited to the aesthetic and ideological needs of the current moment. They wondered at Kean's fresh interpretation, especially his ability to convey the character's rapid thought processes through facial expression, quick gestures, and innovative line deliveries, all of which captured an emotional and psychological depth that struck audiences as refreshingly realistic.[89] "He fought like one drunk with wounds," William Hazlitt enthused in his description of Kean in the final act, "and the attitude in which he stands with his hands stretched out, after the sword is taken with him, had a preternatural and terrific grandeur, as if his will could not be disarmed, and the phantoms of his despair had a withering power."[90] Kean's Richard exhibited the intense will, superhuman intellect, and dark masculinity that Romantic writers had longed to see.

It is a testament to Clara Fisher's unique abilities that audiences responded to her first Richard as loudly and enthusiastically as they had for Kean's three years prior. Critics marveled at her "astonishing cleverness" and "miraculous power of conception of character," proclaiming her a prodigy.[91] At the same time, they called attention to her "studied precision" in gesture and commented on the "accuracy" and "correctness" of her interpretation, including "her knowledge of the text, and an acquaintance with stage effect" that the *British Press* found "really surprising."[92] Such accounts implied that Fisher's performance was the product of extensive study and careful training, while others asserted that her talent was innate.[93] A writer for the *Morning Herald* argued for the latter in his account of the "extraordinary little creature," echoing Romantic theories of the malleable child: "children, it is well known, are very plastic creatures; but previous discipline, method, and memory, never could produce what this child is without premature endowment of the most extraordinary kind."[94] As "plastic creatures," most children could learn to impersonate others given the appropriate time, instruction, and memory, yet often such imitation resulted in stilted performances that did not originate naturally from the child herself. Here the writer's reference to Fisher's "premature endowment" hints at her exceptional mental qualities. Similarly, the *Birmingham Commercial Press* acknowledged that the "little creature has, no doubt, undergone a thorough course of training," but could not deny her originality and phenomenal talent, calling special attention to her ability to "adapt to her circumstances, which sufficiently proves that she is not the creature of mere imitations."[95] The *British Press* likewise praised the quality of Fisher's mind and the sophistication of her characterization:

> There is a *mind* about it [her performance] which proves that it is not the mere offspring of imitation. We have seen children so tutored as to do many things that amazed us. They have danced—they have played on various instruments—they have recited—they have executed fancy works, in an elegant style. But still they were little more than *automata*. A particular line was marked out for them, and they never strayed beyond it. But the variety which appears in the acting of the little *Richard*—a variety always in unison with the character—evinces a precocity of genius, a quickness of perception, a maturity of judgment, which we cannot contemplate without astonishment.[96]

The *British Press* identifies a critical difference between the imitative abilities of other child *automata*—perhaps an oblique reference to the offshoots of Bettymania—and Fisher's variety, genius, and maturity. Whereas the generic child actor displays a plasticity that lends itself to a particular set of carefully demarcated lines set out by adult tutors, Fisher follows her own lines and defies easy categorization. Again, it is the *"mind"* behind the performance that astonishes, a mind that apparently frees Fisher to imbue Richard with vitality without stepping beyond the bounds of believability.

This emphasis on Fisher's mind, especially her quick wit, adaptability, and confidence, echoes the critical discourse surrounding Kean, and indeed critics were quick to compare the two. One newspaper referred to Fisher as "the Lilliputian Kean" and another described her Duke of Gloucester as "an exact miniature of Kean."[97] As it happens, Fisher and Kean knew one another and often performed on the same bill. For example, the playbill for Fisher's spectacular debut in *Lilliput* includes an announcement that "Mr. Kean . . . will have the honour of resum[ing] his professional Duties on Monday next, when he will perform the Character of King Richard the Third."[98] Fisher had ample opportunity to see and study Kean's acting, a fact she makes plain in her autobiography. "Oh, what an actor Kean was!" she enthuses. "Earnest, impetuous, and full of fire! ... Edmund Kean made you jump!"[99] "I have seen all the great actors, and played on the same evenings with many of them," she continues, "but I never saw any one surpassing Kean."[100] Kean attended Fisher's performances as well. Fisher recalls visiting Kean's box in between the acts of *Lilliput* where "the great actor took the child upon his knee and chatted pleasantly with her for a few minutes."[101] While some critics later implied that Fisher modeled her Richard on Kean's, Fisher claims that she never saw Kean perform his most celebrated roles. "My only instructor was my father," she insists, although she acknowledges that he "probably had seen them all [i.e., other performances], and no doubt taught me what he thought best." Here, Fisher leaves open the possibility that aspects of her performance were inspired by Kean but goes on to assert that she was much more than a capable student and often shared "notions" of her own about a character or specific stage moment. "Children who are in earnest can occasionally originate," she asserts, "and I was very earnest, and very observant too, for my years."[102]

Beyond her talent for observation and originality, what distinguished Clara Fisher most was her excellent memory and her ability to quickly master long passages of text. Although at age six she lacked the strength and endurance to realize a role as large as Richard, she possessed a strong musical ear and could learn one hundred lines of text within one hundred minutes.[103] After concluding her contract at Drury Lane in 1818, Fisher (via her father) accepted a contract at Covent Garden where she performed in *Harlequin Gulliver*, a variation of *Lilliput* complete with the fifth act tent scene from *Richard III*. Gradually, she expanded her grasp of the role until she could perform the play in its entirety.[104] By age seven Fisher regularly performed a full version of the play alongside her older sisters Amelia and Caroline (as Henry the Sixth and the Earl of Richmond),[105] with appearances in Dublin, Edinburgh, Glasgow, Newcastle, Leeds, Manchester, and Liverpool, among other cities.[106] And by the time she was eight she had "played the character through the entire play for more than two hundred times," affirming her billing as "the Lilliputian Wonder."[107]

For four "continuous" years the Fisher family traveled throughout Britain, with Clara Fisher's name and reputation leading the way.[108] When not performing as Richard, she impressed audiences with her Shylock, Falstaff, and Young Norval, roles typically associated with male actors. The work, Fisher recalls, was "rather hard but pleasing," as the exigencies of the road meant that the family had to travel by carriage almost every day. But she insists that she had no trouble getting "sufficient rest" since the Fishers owned their own carriage and ensured that in "the larger cities and longest engagements" she only played "every other night."[109] Wherever Clara Fisher traveled, she was greeted with loud applause and rousing acclaim by critics who recognized her talent. As one writer concluded, "Without entering into the cant of minute criticism, I shall merely say of this fascinating little creature, that her performance does not require the indulgent standard by which juvenile pretension is ordinarily estimated. Miss Clara Fisher may safely submit her pretensions to the scrutinizing test by which such actors as a Kean, a Blanchard, or a Jordan, have attained popularity. No allowance is requisite on the score of age or stature."[110] For this critic, Fisher is more than equipped to handle the "scrutinizing test" of public opinion; she does not require indulgence or public pity for her age or limited training. One man took this idea of a "scrutinizing test" even further: the phrenologist George Combe, who set out to pinpoint the source of her talent.

Reading Clara Fisher's Head

In May 1820, just two months shy of her ninth birthday, Clara Fisher and her parents visited the Edinburgh Phrenological Society.[111] By this point, the girl had delighted audiences in London and the provinces with her expanding repertoire and full-length interpretations of Shakespeare's male villains. Now in Edinburgh for her second season, Fisher caught the eye of the charismatic George Combe.[112] A longtime admirer of the stage, Combe proposed making a plaster cast of Fisher's head to ascertain, first, "whether great mental power is ever found at an early period of life, in concomitance with a small brain," and second, "what particular combination of faculties is essential to success in the histrionic art [that is, acting]?"[113] Creating a cast of the girl's head would allow Combe to answer these questions through phrenological analysis. Frederick George Fisher's willingness to permit Combe to analyze his daughter is somewhat curious given his previous efforts to protect her from public view. Perhaps, like any parent eager to understand their children's inner workings, he was persuaded by phrenology's claim to scientific innovation and Combe's promise to discover what made Clara Fisher so unique.

Phrenology enjoyed immense popularity in the nineteenth century thanks to the proselytizing efforts of men like Combe, whose 1828 book *The Constitution of Man* became one the most widely read publications of the period. Combe's ideas derived from the earlier work of Franz Joseph Gall, a Viennese physician, and his student J. G. Spurzheim.[114] Through close analysis of human remains and living subjects, they discovered what they believed was a direct correlation between the size of the brain and its constitutive organs.[115] Working from this premise, phrenologists grouped each of the brain's faculties into two orders and six genera for a total of thirty-three separate faculties, each tied to a specific organ.[116] These ranged from Order 1 feelings of philoprogenitiveness (love of offspring), self-esteem, and benevolence to Order 2 intellectual faculties, which included the senses, perceptive faculties, and faculties related to external objects (such as time, tune, language). By measuring the brain's faculties and understanding their relation to one another and to specific actions, phrenologists believed that they could develop a fairly accurate reading of an individual's behavioral tendencies. No mind was indecipherable ... or so phrenologists claimed.

Combe founded the Edinburgh Phrenological Society in 1820 with his brother Andrew and several other colleagues who shared the brothers' belief that the mysteries of the human mind could be plumbed through phrenological analysis. Eager to establish itself as a leading center for phrenological research, the society sought donations of skulls and casts. "No adequate idea of the foundation of the science can be formed," wrote Combe, until phrenologists had inspected "*a number* of heads; and especially by contrasting instances of extreme development with others of extreme deficiency."[117] Early acquisitions included the "Skull of Kapitapol, a Canadian Chief, presented by Henry Marshall, Esq. Surgeon to the Forces in Scotland," the "Cast of the Head of an African, Ditto, of a Deaf, Dumb and Blind Individual," as well as casts of "Heads of Three Ladies" and the "Head of a Boy, with a large Cerebellum."[118] In addition to encouraging donations, Combe and his associates began an active program of creating casts of important figures and unique individuals. In this they were aided by sculptor William Scoular, whose mentor John Graham had been "introduced to the academy casts from the most celebrated antique statues" during his own education.[119] Trained in classical sculpting methods, Scoular brought technical skill to the society and was entrusted with making casts of significant human remains, including the skull of the legendary Scottish hero Robert the Bruce, whose skeleton had been unearthed in 1818.[120] Unfortunately for Clara Fisher, Scoular's classical training does not appear to have prepared him for the challenges of casting a living human child.[121]

In her 1897 autobiography, Fisher describes the discomfort and terror of the cast-making process. Together father, mother, and daughter visited the society's headquarters, where Combe and presumably Scoular "prepared [her] face." As Fisher recalls, "the committee of gentlemen first put some wash on my face, then plastered it all over with the preparation of lime, or whatever it was, and finished by placing some straws in my nostrils."[122] But one of the straws was too long and when Scoular removed it to make the adjustment he accidentally knocked the other one out. "I believe I should have smothered to death," Fisher matter-of-factly observes, "if my father, who saw me endeavoring to get back the straw, had not jumped forward and replaced it."[123] After this, Fisher sat immobilized while the committee completed the casting process. Though she acknowledges that Combe was "as nice as he could be," the traumatic experience left a deep imprint in her memory, as her recollection of it seven decades later suggests.[124]

Fisher's account of her experience at the Phrenological Society foregrounds the eerie aspect of the cast-making process for living human subjects, a practice that seeks to fix or immobilize facial plasticity. To achieve this effect, subjects must remain absolutely still while the wet plaster is layered over their faces and must continue to hold their position as the plaster slowly hardens. As such, the casting process temporarily silences the living body, quite literally holding it in time and place as the plaster changes physical states. "Like the photograph," writes Ute Kornmeier, the cast "freezes its image in that instant, which will already have passed before the first viewer sees it. This is what makes the cast image so trustworthy; it shows what somebody looked like at one particular time, nothing less and nothing more."[125] It was the cast's appar-

Miss Clara Fisher

Aged 9 Years

FIGURE 6. *Phrenology sketch of Clara Fisher's head, created during her 1820 visit to the Edinburgh Phrenological Society. Author's collection.*

ent "trustworthiness" through its temporal fixity that made it such a valuable document for phrenologists like Combe. But not all casts are trustworthy, especially when children are involved. Indeed, as Combe outlines in his 1824 publication *Elements of Phrenology*, phrenologists generally refrained from measuring the heads of infants and children because "in infancy the brain and skull are imperfectly developed" and therefore any assessment would be incomplete or inaccurate.[126] In other words, the plasticity of children's brains, their ongoing physiological development, rendered them poor phrenological subjects.

The question arises: if phrenologists generally avoided making casts of children because their brains were unformed, why was Combe so intent on casting Clara Fisher? Although Combe does not address this question outright, several possible answers arise from the report and the phrenologist's subsequent actions. First, as noted earlier, Combe's goal was to ascertain whether "great mental power" could be discerned at an early age despite the brain's smaller size and what "particular combination of faculties" afforded individuals success in the acting field.[127] By analyzing Fisher's cast, Combe promised to end nagging debates that dogged both phrenology and the theatre profession. It is also possible that the phrenologist hoped to fix the unfixable, to hold the nearly nine-year-old girl in time and thereby assert his own interpretive powers and the legitimacy of phrenology as a science.[128]

Combe read his "Report Upon the Cast of Miss Clara Fisher" to the Phrenological Society on December 26, 1820, and published it in 1824 as part of the society's proceedings, along with an illustration of Fisher based on the cast (Figure 6). He begins by responding to the question about the relationship of brain size to "great mental power," noting that Fisher possesses an "uncommonly large" head and a unique combination of mental faculties that equip her for excellence in the theatrical arena. "In all her acting," he observes, "she displays so much comprehensiveness of mind, that, when the full expression of intellectual power and deep feeling is heard from her lips, and her whole manner is perceived to be in unison with that expression, her age and diminutive stature are instantly forgotten and she is listened to with that fixed attention which genius alone can command."[129] Rather than take offense at a young child playing a role intended for an adult, audiences "instantly" forget her age and size because they are so overwhelmed by the seamless combination of "intellectual power" and "deep feeling."

After this initial assessment, Combe details all thirty-three of Fisher's organs, before isolating the four faculties that explain her prodigious abilities: secretiveness, imitation, "concentrativeness," and ideality. The first two faculties are "essential requisites" to skillful acting, as indicated by his previous observations of "several individuals in private life."[130] (Here Combe alludes to his friendship with theatre professionals like the actress-manager Mrs. Henry Siddons.)[131] Secretiveness, Combe continues, helps the individual to hide her "natural character" and therefore embrace fully, through imitation, another character. Ideality "adds splendour to the performance" by inspiring "the glow and colouring of fancy" and "the spirit of poetry." Individuals with above-average ideality possess dynamic imaginations that breathe life into their performances, as distinguished from "mere mimickry."[132] Finally, concentrativeness allows actors "to support a variety of faculties in a state of simultaneous and combined activity." Actors like Fisher, whose concentrativeness measured "rather large," appear effortless onstage, showcase a range of emotions through voice and movement, and express their characters' thoughts through dialogue with "force and expression."[133]

Combe's analysis of Fisher's mental prowess is important when considered alongside Romantic notions of the ideal child. On the one hand, his conclusion that "great mental power" is identifiable at an early age supports Romantic arguments about the capabilities of the "natural" child born free of sin; on the other, his identification of the specific faculties necessary for success in the "histrionic art" complicates assumptions about childhood innocence and the absence of artifice. Rather than attributing Fisher's success to her status as a child and a universal set of values, he argues that what sets her apart from her peers is the distinct combination of her faculties and her application of them.[134] Thus, while she appears to be a "child of nature," a pure, innocent being unadulterated by artifice or the heavy burdens of the world, she is not just an innate talent, but a skilled performer who makes the most of her abilities through study, preparation, and hard work.

The phrenologist is careful to note, however, that mere possession of faculties like concentrativeness or imitation does not a successful actor make, nor does possession of similar faculties equip all actors to play the same roles. An actor devoid of tune, for example, would likely fail to portray a character required to sing or speak a melodious piece of text regardless of imitation and secretiveness. Combe's argument here might be read as a defense of casting practices associated with lines of business, which operated on the assumption that certain actors were better equipped to play certain roles. But he goes on to note that while an actor may share certain faculties with the character he or she is portraying, "it does not follow ... that an actor, in his [or her] personal conduct, must necessarily resemble most closely those characters he [or she] represents to the best advantage."[135] Combe credits Fisher's success as Richard III to the presence of many of the "elementary qualities" that constitute the character. Her "high and full forehead gives her the [tyrant's] intellectual energy," while her "immense *love of approbation, firmness* and *cautiousness*" allow her to embody his "ambition," "determination," and "coolness." At the same time, the girl's strength in the faculty of ideality, which casts "the colouring of poetry" over her performance, prevents her portrayal of the king from becoming "too diabolical" and therefore too distasteful to audiences.[136] Perhaps most important, her strengths in the higher faculties of benevolence, justice, and adhesiveness clearly demarcate "the real character of Miss Fisher" from her representation of the bloody Richard.[137] In other words, she is simultaneously not Richard and not *not* Richard.[138]

In the last section of his report, Combe steps beyond the usual bounds of phrenological analysis into the world of performance criticism, weighing the merits of Fisher's Richard against those of Edmund Kean.[139] While praising the "intense intellectual energy" of Kean's Richard, he argues that the actor's interpretation departs in detrimental ways from Shakespeare's conception of the role, especially where the king's passion and intellect are concerned. "In Kean's acting," writes Combe, "*Richard* storms, rages, and vociferates.... The ever-presiding intellect is dethroned, and rage and cruelty, and ambition, constitute the man."[140] Moreover, Kean's Richard displays frustrating inconsistencies that, in Combe's estimation, prevent audiences from understanding the character's inner life and motivation. By way of example, Combe points to Kean's first scene with Lady Anne in which his Richard appears as an honest, repentant man, leading the audience to imagine that he has truly changed; but later in the play, Kean explodes this interpretation, descending into "outrageous bursts of passion" that "dethrone" the king's "ever-presiding intellect."[141] By contrast, with Fisher, the tyrant's rage "is the storm of a mighty intellect, imbued with hate," in accordance with Shakespeare's depiction of Richard as an "intellectual fiend."[142] Where Kean's portrayal is frustratingly mercurial, Fisher's performance never wavers from exposing the king's hypocrisy and deception; her consistent portrayal of the king's emotions and desires thus renders her Richard more lifelike, more convincing, and ultimately superior to Kean's—in Combe's estimation.[143]

Curiously, Combe's analysis of Fisher's Richard III avoids any reference to the girl's other roles, even though the diversity of her repertoire was on full display during her 1820 visit to Edinburgh.[144] Perhaps these portrayals seemed trifling compared to Shakespeare and Richard III; or perhaps Combe worried that acknowledging Fisher's constantly shifting repertoire challenged notions of an easily diagnosed, decipherable self.[145] The diversity and richness of her repertoire tells a different story, as the following chapters reveal. Ultimately, Combe's lengthy analysis of Fisher's Richard III furthered his report's underlying claim: namely, that there was nothing mysterious or undecipherable about the girl. Her Richard was consistent, balanced, and legible, despite the character's despicable qualities; therefore, so was she. Ironically, Combe's assertions were at odds with the complexity of the role itself, most notably Richard's rejection of spectators' assumptions about his monstrous body and its perceived legibility. As noted earlier, Richard III defies those who seek to read anatomy as an index of character[146] and thus also rejects the promise of the scientific gaze. This aspect of the role made it ideal for actors looking to protect themselves from the public eye. But Combe insisted otherwise, denying the threat of Clara Fisher's plasticity or her (father's) desire for privacy by quite literally transmuting the potentially explosive substance of her being into a cast that he could carry about with him on his lecture tours of Britain and North America.

Coda: The Transatlantic Journey of Clara Fisher's Cast

George Combe's traveling performances with Clara Fisher's plaster cast powerfully demonstrate how girls became caught up in larger pedagogical (not to mention racist) projects during a period of colonial expansion and imperial domination. As a star prop appearing in print and onstage alongside the heads of criminals, the physically disabled, and representative samplings of African, Asian, and South American "nations," the cast of Clara Fisher's head embodied white, Anglo-American ideals—the promise of civilization in the form of a young girl's brain. In this respect, Fisher's cast became a potent thing, an animate object that exceeded its object status in order to secure Anglo-American racial hierarchies. That Clara Fisher herself had little control over her cast's production or its circulation—the cast-making process quite literally silenced her—points to the troubling way that the girl, and indeed all phrenological subjects, became nonconsensual participants in phrenology's imperialist project.

Fisher and her cast continued to perform precocious white girlhood across the pages of Combe's publications. In 1824 Combe and his associates published the *Transactions of the Phrenological Society*, a collection of the best lectures and presentations given by members of the society in the first four years of its existence. Included is Combe's "Report Upon the Cast of Miss Clara Fisher," along with a full-page illustration of Fisher in profile, one of only five engraved plates published in the book. Illustrator A. N. Henderson Dell captures much of the young girl's focus and determination in her facial expression, while her short curly hair and rounded cheeks testify to her age. Fisher's image appears in the opening pages of the volume—not quite a frontispiece but immediately following the title page—bestowing a kind of blessing on the contents that follow. The engraving's prominent placement suggests that Combe and his colleagues were eager to emphasize their connection to Fisher and her tacit endorsement of their ideas. Even a casual browser must flip past the attractive illustration of Clara Fisher's head.

The *Transactions'* table of contents offers a testament to the phrenologists' interest in extreme cases, especially individuals exhibiting medical conditions or atypical behavior. Topics covered include a lengthy discussion of color perception, an essay by Andrew Combe (George Combe's brother) on "the Effects of Injuries of the Brain upon the Manifestations of the Mind" as well as a study by A. Hood on a "Patient who forgot the use of Spoken and Written Language." Combe's study of Clara Fisher, the seventh essay in the volume, directly follows an essay on the "Cerebral Developments of King Robert Bruce" and precedes a lengthy case study of a ten-year-old boy, identified only by the initials J.G. As with the illustration plate, the placement of the "Report" between a study of the celebrated Scottish king and a lengthy diagnosis of a child who had been discovered "miserable and starving on the highway" seems deliberate. Combe's complimentary observations about Fisher and her embodiment of royal traits provide a strong foil to the detailed discussion of the boy J.G., who possessed a peculiar "combination of great deficiencies and great endowments" and who required serious intervention on the part of doctors, teachers, and charitable societies to "rescue [him] from the dominion of his lower facul-

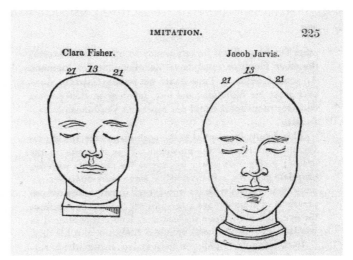

FIGURE 7. *Illustration from* Lectures on Phrenology *by George Combe, 1839; BF870 .C65 1839. Photography © New-York Historical Society.*

ties, and elevate him into a moral and intellectual being."[147] Juxtaposed with J.G.'s challenges, Clara Fisher's unique abilities are amplified; she is marked as an ideal specimen, an astonishing girl possessed of wit, intelligence, and cunning.

Combe used juxtaposition to similar effect in his 1830 *System of Phrenology*, a volume that includes numerous illustrations of ethnic and racial "types" from around the world, along with a sampling of criminals (predominantly murderers) and celebrated individuals from the past and present.[148] One need only look at *System*'s "List of Figures" to observe the white supremacist logic that underpins much of Combe's phrenological project.[149] Clara Fisher appears three times in *System*, first as an example of an individual possessed of considerable secretiveness, a faculty Combe indicates that he has "uniformly found ... large in the heads of actors and artists";[150] then as someone possessed of a large "Love of Approbation," a characteristic that aligns her with King Robert Bruce; and finally as someone with moderate benevolence. Significantly, Fisher is not associated with any of the "national" types featured elsewhere in the volume. When she is compared with other individuals, they are invariably white.[151]

The phrenologist crafted a similar narrative when he embarked on his lecture tours of Great Britain, Europe, and North America, traveling with a large collection of casts, busts, and skulls, which he arranged in such a way as to give his audience conclusive "proof" of phrenology's merits, often through the use of strategic juxtaposition. For example, when he lectured on imitation, he used five busts, including that of Clara Fisher, to show how and where the faculty manifested itself: "This organ is situated on the sides of Benevolence. It gives a squareness to the frontal part of the coronal region, constituting a sort of table-land. . . . In this of Voltaire it is still more strikingly developed, rising, indeed, higher than Benevolence. This is the head of Clara Fisher, taken when she was eight or nine years old, and much distinguished. In it you see the same conformation. In this head of Jacob Jarvis it is small."[152] In *Lectures*, two sketches illustrate the profound differences between Fisher and Jarvis, offering "conclusive" evidence of the former's superior imitative abilities: Fisher's head is gently rounded whereas Jarvis's is surprisingly pointy. Elsewhere in Combe's lectures, we learn that Jacob Jarvis was a man from Cork whose benevolence organ was "extremely developed," so much so that he could "never resist any solicitation" from friends or associates. For decades, Clara Fisher's head played a significant role in Combe's phrenological repertoire, onstage and in publications, long after Fisher herself had retired from the stage. Transported in his luggage from town to town and across the Atlantic, her head offered a powerful object lesson in support of white racial superiority and the larger aims of phrenology as a science.[153]

Yet the object could only contain so much. George Combe's efforts to cast the girl actress as a singularly knowable subject were at odds with the performance practice that was a hallmark of her success. Despite offering a detailed assessment of her Richard III, Combe said nothing about her ability to portray multiple characters of varying ages, genders, and ethnicities in protean farces like *The Actress of All Work* and *Old and Young*, which I discuss in Chapter 3, as well as more conventional breeches roles like Little Pickle in *The Spoiled Child*, the subject of the next chapter. Such pieces gave nineteenth-century women and girls unique access to roles and behavioral repertoires that traditional casting practices prevented them from inhabiting. Perhaps Combe worried that referencing these roles would diminish or undermine his argument by highlighting Fisher's plasticity. Although he claimed to have solved the mystery of her astonishing mind, the actress's ever-expanding repertoire gave proof that she was not so easily fixed.

A BRIEF HISTORY OF THE TOMBOY

Was Clara Fisher a tomboy? Her short hair and androgynous appearance hint at an answer, but what is a tomboy anyway? The *Oxford English Dictionary* dates the first recorded use of the word to 1553, when it was used to describe "A rude, boisterous or forward boy." Over time, the word's gendered associations changed. By the 1570s, the word "tomboy" referred to girls as well as boys, and by the 1590s it was used almost exclusively to describe "a girl who behaves like a spirited or boisterous boy; a wild romping girl; a hoyden."[1] The term "hoyden" followed a similar etymological path, from defining "a rude, ignorant, or awkward fellow" in the sixteenth century to "a rude, or ill-bred girl (or woman): a boisterous noisy girl, a romp" in the seventeenth century.[2] However, as literary scholar Michelle Ann Abate explains, a "hoyden was more closely associated with breaching bourgeois mores than female gender roles," and was later subsumed into the category of the tomboy.[3]

Most histories of tomboyhood focus on the tomboy as a distinctly American figure who emerged in the 1840s and 1850s when new economic realities placed greater pressure on young white working- and middle-class girls to leave home and contribute to their family income.[4] Where once the ideal girl had been mild and retiring, now she embraced life with vigor.[5] Tomboys were strong, physically active, brash, and daring, fully capable of handling themselves and helping others. As such, they were critical to the formalization of racial hierarchies in the United States. Abate sees a close correlation between the rise of anti-immigration sentiment in the mid-nineteenth century—much of it in response to the arrival of families fleeing famine in Ireland—and the celebration of active, healthy, resourceful WASP girls who exuded confidence and the resilience to handle life's many challenges.[6] Such girls would make fit mothers for the next generation, the racist logic of the era promised, and thereby secure familial and racial legacies. Extending Abate's arguments, Renée Sentilles observes that "the celebration of white middle-class tomboys strengthened the whiteness of girlhood, because such behavior was perceived as 'tomboy' only in girls with white bodies."[7] Black girls could not afford to exhibit tomboy behavior for fear of confirming stereotypical associations of blackness with wildness and savagery.[8]

Yet this equation of whiteness and tomboyhood was hardly new, nor was it unique to the United States. Though individual performances of tomboyhood varied from one cultural context to another—as with all performances of gender—many of the tomboy's defining characteristics can be found in eighteenth-century plays like Isaac Bickerstaff's *The Romp*, which audiences in North America consumed as avidly as their British counterparts. In turning briefly to *The Romp*, I wish to emphasize how the figure of the tomboy circulated as an attractive and transmutable transatlantic construct.[9]

Priscilla Tomboy made her first appearance in Isaac Bickerstaff's opera/musical drama *Love in the City*, which premiered at Theatre Royal Covent Garden on February 21, 1767.[10] Although now regarded as Bickerstaff's "best full-length comic opera," *Love in the City* was a critical and popular failure at the time due to its unflinching critique of the middle class.[11] Undaunted, Bickerstaff decided to rewrite the play as a straightforward comedy, now retitled *The Romp*.[12] After several successful performances outside London, the revamped play premiered at Covent Garden in March 1778, and its central female character became a cultural touchstone.[13]

Priscilla Tomboy is a fascinating albeit troubling girl—strong-willed, feisty, self-determining, quick-tempered, the epitome of tomboyhood. Historian Peter A. Tasch describes her as "an unloveable spoiled child,"[14] yet she is not so much unlovable as willful. The daughter of a wealthy Jamaican planter, she is also a desirable marriage prospect, but Priscilla has her own ideas where marriage is concerned. She rejects social norms, manipulates the men around her, and bridles when others correct her posture and manners.[15] "E'cod, last Sunday, if we had not been in church, I would have hit her a slap in the face," Priscilla warns her friend Penelope when discussing Penelope's overbearing cousin Molly Cockney.[16] Her threats are far from hollow: Priscilla responds violently when provoked—throwing stools, beating governesses, pushing over dancing masters—in a manner consistent with masculine behavior. But it is ultimately her intelligence, self-confidence, and refusal to be treated as a commodity that defines her as a dangerous woman. When her guardian and Penelope's uncle Barnacle Cockney threatens to send her back to Jamaica for refusing to marry his nephew (and Penelope's brother), Young Cockney, she hatches her own plot. "They are as frightened as the vengeance now about my going to Jamaica, because they think they shall lose my money," she matter-of-factly informs the milliner Madame La Blond, and so sets about convincing Young Cockney that she will run away with him to Scotland when in fact she is conspiring to marry the man of her choice.[17]

Priscilla Tomboy is gutsy, brash, and independent. She is also an outsider. Indeed, her hoydenish behavior is bound up with her status as a West Indian creole—a connection Bickerstaff highlights in the play's first few pages. *The Romp* opens with Priscilla and Penelope sitting in a grocer's shop embroidering a large canvas, much to the frustration of Young Cockney, who worries that the women's activity is impeding his customers' access to the shop. With business foremost in his mind, he begs the girls to retire to a parlor or inner room where they will be out of the way. But Priscilla refuses to move, asserting her right to occupy public space. At his wit's end, Young Cockney threatens to report her to his uncle, at which point Priscilla throws her stool at him, crying, "There, take your stool, you nasty, ugly, conceited, ill-natured ——."[18] Young Cockney is shocked at Priscilla's "unmannerly" behavior and wonders aloud that she is "not ashamed" of herself. He concludes that her behavior is the product of "the breeding you got in the plantation—You know you was turned out of Hackney boarding-school for beating the governess, and knocking down the dancing-master—I believe you think you have got among your blackamoors—But you are not among your blackamoors now, Miss."[19] Bickerstaff makes effective use of Young Cockney's rant to disclose critical details about Priscilla's personal history and family heritage. He reveals that she was raised on a plantation, presumably in the West Indies,[20] and that she has been sent to London to refine her education. He further reveals that she has been kicked out of Hackney boarding school for violent acts directed at the headmistress and dancing master, the instructors most directly responsible for (re)shaping her gendered movements. Young Cockney concludes

FIGURE 8. *Hand-colored scene from* The Romp *with Mr. Dodd as Young Cockney, Mrs. Jordan as Priscilla Tomboy, Mr. Barrymore as Captain Sightly, and Miss Barnes as Miss a la Blond. Published in London by S. W. Fores on January 3, 1786, Harry Beard Collection. © Victoria & Albert Museum, London.*

that Priscilla's behavior is attributable to plantation life and overfamiliarity with African slaves—her "blackamoors."

In his rebuke of Priscilla Tomboy, Young Cockney alludes to contemporary fears about the deleterious effects of a tropical climate on white settlers.[21] Writing about Jamaica in 1774, the planter Edward Long observed that "The effect of climate is ... remarkable ... in the extraordinary freedom and suppleness of [creoles'] joints, which enable them to move with ease, and give them a surprising agility, as well as gracefulness in dancing."[22] While agility and gracefulness alone may not have caused alarm, the belief that a tropical climate could forever alter an individual's disposition, behavior, and physicality led many to worry about the degeneration of the planter class and their settler counterparts. These fears spread so widely that many planters sent their children to London for both a "proper" education and an immersion in London's social life. Such training, they hoped, would equip their sons and daughters with the same social graces as their English-born relations and thereby ensure the continuation of "civilized" behavioral norms upon their return to the colony.[23] But Priscilla Tomboy has resisted social inoculation and its corresponding lessons in femininity and grace; she remains rough, violent, "unmannerly," and willful—a problem child.[24] Kicked out of school for beating her teachers and refusing to dance and speak as instructed, she has come under the guardianship of the business-minded grocer Cockney, who sees in the hoydenish heiress a potential match for his nephew, the very same Young Cockney who scolds Priscilla for her wayward ways.

This brief yet important revelation about Priscilla Tomboy's history points to the intersection of whiteness and blackness in the performance of eighteenth-century girlhood, especially within the context of British settler colonialism. This racial entanglement would continue to inform the performances of tomboys well into the next century. Yet compared with the tomboys of the 1840s and 1850s, whose rambunctious ways were seen as proof of their fitness to birth healthy babies, Priscilla's tomboyhood is depicted as aberrant and destabilizing—the direct manifestation of her creole status. It is her "breeding" on the plantation that has led her to reject the education, manners, and behavioral norms that would secure her marital success and subsequently stabilize white colonial relations. In Young Cockney's view, she has absorbed too much of the culture of the "blackamoors" to affirm her position as a respectable *white* British woman.

From a dramaturgical perspective, Priscilla's creole identity serves as a distancing device, inviting Bickerstaff's London audience (and audiences elsewhere) to delight in, rather than take offense at, her hoydenish acts. This delight has its limits, however, and Bickerstaff makes a point of distinguishing Priscilla's behavior from that of her friend Penelope, the grocer's niece. In one of the play's most disturbing scenes, Priscilla warns her slave Quasheba that if she discloses anything of her secret conversation with "Miss Penny," she will have the enslaved woman "horse-whip'd 'till there is not a bit of flesh left on your bones."[25] When Penelope cries out in horror at this threat, Priscilla responds, "Psha! what is she but a neger? If she was at home in our plantations, she would find the difference; we make no account of them there at all; if I had a fancy for one of their skins, I should not think much of taking it." When Penelope asks, "I suppose then you imagine they have no feeling?" Priscilla retorts, "Oh! we never consider that there," at once exposing her ignorance and unwillingness to contemplate the pain of (enslaved) others.[26] It is at this point that Priscilla swiftly turns the topic to her primary concern: avoiding an arranged marriage with Young Cockney. "I know very well your uncle Barnacle has a mind to marry me to him, but if he is left my guardian, and I am sent over to London for my education, I don't see any right he has to choose me a husband, though."[27]

Priscilla's abusive, threatening treatment of the silent Quasheba echoes the white supremacist logic of eighteenth-century slaveholders, which held that that black men and women lacked the capacity to experience pain.[28] Once again Bickerstaff hints that Priscilla's tomboyish rebellion and proclivity for violence are tied to her creole status and the degenerative effects of a tropical climate. He guides his audience to feel disgust at Priscilla's denial of Quasheba's capacity for pain and to share in Penelope's dismay at such gross incivility. Here too we observe the complicated dynamic between white freedom and black captivity:[29] it is only after Priscilla rejects the very notion of black feeling ("we never consider it there") that she articulates her desire for independence in matters of love. Confident in her whiteness and her status as the daughter of a plantation owner, she refuses to let a London grocer choose her husband for her. In this moment the colonizing white girl's dependency on the destruction and erasure of the enslaved black woman is painfully evident: white female self-determination arises not just alongside but *through* the fierce rejection of black female subjectivity.[30]

Such assertions of white liberty were hardly unique to a play like *The Romp*.[31] Thomas Southerne's *Oroonoko* (1695), an adaptation of Aphra Behn's 1688 novel about a slave revolt in Surinam and the horrendous death of its black hero, enjoyed immense popularity on the London stage for over a century. This success, Elizabeth Maddock Dillon explains, was due in no small measure to the way the play offered the urban audience "compensation for the tears it sheds . . . in the form of an optimistic vision of the bourgeois possibilities of colonialism for English men and women."[32] A London theatregoer could weep for Oroonoko and rail against the injustices of slavery while still anticipating the economic opportunities that awaited in the colonies.

The Romp is not *Oroonoko*, of course, and while some critics cite the farce as an example of anti-slavery drama,[33] Priscilla's unrepentant racism raises questions about Bickerstaff's political intent. Certainly he encourages his audience to share in Priscilla's exploits, to cheer in act 2 when she tricks the foolish Cockney into believing that her virtue has been compromised after an evening spent with Captain Sightly, her chosen amour, leaving her guardian with no recourse but to agree to her marriage with him instead of his nephew. The play concludes with a round of proposals in typical comedy fashion and preparations for Priscilla's return to Jamaica with her new husband—the captain—where she will presumably continue to enjoy the privileges of plantation life. Nevertheless, Priscilla's future marriage and return to Jamaica hint at the eventual containment (if not "taming") of her tomboy ways within the bonds and bounds of heteronormativity. Her removal from London (and the stage) will restore peace—if not wealth—to the Cockneys and thereby affirm white male authority.

The Romp opened to loud applause at Covent Garden in 1778 and subsequently crossed the Atlantic, playing in Philadelphia as early as 1790.[34] What ultimately secured the play's popularity in London was its adoption by Dorothy Jordan (1761–1816), an actress praised for her comic sensibility and natural charm. "You have made [*The Romp*] peculiarly your own, by your happy conception and admirable representation of its principal character," a contemporary declared of Jordan in

1786.[35] The writer Fanny Burney confessed that although her initial response to Jordan's Priscilla Tomboy was one of disgust, she revised her opinion as the play progressed: "afterwards she [Jordan] displayed such uncommon humour that it brought me to pardon her assumed vulgarity, in favour of a representation of nature, which, in its particular class, seemed to me quite perfect."[36] Jordan's naturalness and sense of humor helped smooth over Burney's negative first impression of the hoydenish character.

Jordan embodied the freedom and *jouissance* of the emerging Romantic movement, so much so that critics frequently referred to her as a "child of nature," nodding to her starring role in Elizabeth Inchbald's play of the same name.[37] Physically attractive with long curly hair that cascaded around her shoulders and sometimes obscured her face, the actress projected an air of youthful vigor and infectious mischief that struck audiences as delightfully natural.[38] Writing in 1815, the critic William Hazlitt enthused, "It was not as an actress, but as herself, that she charmed everyone. Nature had formed in her most prodigal humour; and when nature is in the humour to make a woman all that is delightful, she does it most effectually."[39] By insisting that Jordan did not perform but rather appeared "as herself," Hazlitt implied that she was untainted by the artifice and deception typically associated with the acting profession and theatre more broadly.[40]

Burney's and Hazlitt's comments offer a potent reminder of how an individual artist's interpretation of a role can affect whether or not that role is taken up by others. Jordan's attractively packaged Priscilla Tomboy made the vulgar character palatable to audiences like Burney and in so doing ensured the character's place in the repertoires of later Anglo-American actresses—girls and women alike. And as Priscilla Tomboy crossed from body to body, the figure of the rambunctious tomboy who refuses to adopt the modes and manners of a lady, who schemes to get what she wants and doesn't apologize, gained cultural legibility and grudging acceptance. Although it is perhaps going too far to suggest that the mid-nineteenth-century tomboys discussed by Abate and Sentilles owe their vitality and viability to Priscilla Tomboy, this Interlude's brief excursion through *The Romp* demonstrates that the project of tomboyhood, with all its white supremacist baggage, was well under way by the turn of the nineteenth century.

CHAPTER 2
The Spoiled Child

ON THE POLITICS OF TRAVESTY ROLES

He that spareth his rod hateth his son:
but he that loveth him chasteneth him betimes.
—*Proverbs 13, King James Bible*

Theatrical portraitist George Clint specialized in capturing moments of tension or surprise. That skill is evident in his 1823 painting (Figure 9) described by the *New Monthly Magazine* as "a clever composition, and not without character."[1] At first glance, the scene represents a conventional courting ritual: a man and a woman sit on a bench beneath a tree. Although seemingly past the first blush of youth, they adopt the gestures of young lovers. The man, dressed in a crimson frock coat, black satin breeches, and tricorn hat, extends his arm toward the woman's right hand as it rests in her lap. With his left hand he gestures toward his heart. The woman, dressed in a brown and gold silk gown, tilts her head toward the man in a bemused almost quizzical manner, neither enraptured nor dismayed by his advances. With her left hand she holds up her fan, erecting a mini-barrier between herself and her would-be lover. To the right of the bench, a petite, youthful figure, presumably a boy, spies on the couple from behind some foliage. A curly mop of red hair and a white ruff collar frame his cherubic features. But this is no cherub. This is Little Pickle, the central character in the two-act farce *The Spoiled Child*, and he is about to sew the lovers' clothing together in an act of vengeful naughtiness.[2]

The mischievous boy in Clint's painting is also Clara Fisher, the celebrated girl actress whose name became synonymous with Little Pickle in the early nineteenth century. As one contemporary observed, her

66

FIGURE 9. *George Clint's painting of* The Spoiled Child.
Courtesy of the Garrick Club, London.

performance of the prepubescent boy was "distinguished by so rare a combination of skill, humour, and good sense, that the applause she receives belongs less so to the *youth* than to the *merits* of the actress."[3] A writer in Bristol concurred, marveling at how Fisher managed to exhibit both natural talent and technical ability: "All was graceful, because natural—all was thoughtfully deliberate, both in speech and action; and no parent's sympathetic feelings could have been excited by apprehension for the undue exercise of physical powers so very tender."[4] Although Fisher was not the first girl to play Little Pickle, her success in the role inspired dozens of other girls in England and North America to add it to their repertoires. Louisa Lane (Mrs. John Drew) recalled that she made her debut as a child prodigy in *The Spoiled Child* in New York at the urging of her stepfather in the late 1820s.[5] Other Clara "wannabes," chief among them Jean Margaret Davenport (see Figure 12), followed a similar path to stage glory. Anne Varty lists eleven girls and boys who played Little Pickle between 1804 and 1866 in London, while T. Allston Brown's *History of the American Stage* identifies at least eight actresses who debuted in the role at various theatres in the United States during the 1830s and 1840s. These accounts do not include performers who introduced the role later in their careers and so there were likely many more Little Pickles traipsing across the Anglo-American stage in the first half of the nineteenth century.[6]

Yet for all its appeal to nineteenth-century girls (and their audiences), Little Pickle was originally written for Dorothy Jordan, a specialist in travesty and breeches roles, and the same actress who made Priscilla Tomboy palatable to London audiences. Jordan first appeared as Little Pickle in March 1790 at a benefit night showcase, and the character remained part of her featured repertoire for much of her career. The question arises: how did a role originally written for Jordan, a grown woman, become so closely associated with girls? The answer, I venture here, has as much to do with changing attitudes toward travesty and breeches roles as it does with the surge of interest in girls on the stage.

Most accounts of Romantic-era actresses overlook the relationship between girl and adult performers, except in cases when well-known actresses began their careers as children (a not uncommon practice) or in rarer moments when actresses like Sarah Siddons brought their own children onstage to perform with them.[7] This chapter insists that it is impossible to fully understand the rapid expansion of a theatrical repertoire for girls in the nineteenth century without analyzing corresponding shifts in the repertoire for women. Reading these histories together calls attention to the subversive potential of a travesty role like Little Pickle, both for Jordan and for the girls who followed her. Such a reading further suggests that the popularity of girl actresses in the nineteenth century was closely tied to critical anxieties about women usurping male privilege onstage and off. In fact, it would appear that certain travesty roles became the preserve of girls because they had become too dangerous or unseemly for women to continue playing. By the 1790s the long-standing delight in watching adult actresses in travesty and breeches roles was waning as critics worried aloud about the long-term consequences of women assuming male dress.[8] Such anxieties do not appear to have extended in the same way to girls, however, due in part to contemporary views of girls' physical and mental development, which held that they were malleable, plastic subjects, as yet unformed and therefore easy to mold.[9]

What makes the character of Little Pickle so fascinating is the particular kind of boyhood he represents—like his theatrical sibling Priscilla Tomboy, he embraces fun, resists authority, lives for pranks, and cares little about how his actions affect those around him.[10] In other words, Little Pickle embodies many of the tomboy's attributes but from the privileged position of *boy*hood. Analyzing Little Pickle's creation and eventual migration into the repertoire of the girl actress thus demonstrates how emergent notions of girlhood developed in tandem with shifting representations of women *and* boys. Just as many Victorian boys enjoyed a period of "girlhood" prior to assuming the mantle of manhood, so too, many nineteenth-century girls reveled in rambunctious boyhood.[11]

Full of jokes and pratfalls, melancholy songs, and joyful dances, *The Spoiled Child* is also a fascinating commentary on parent-child relations. Much more than a warning to parents about the risks of raising a willful child, the play presents a spectrum of competing pedagogies—from the "poisonous pedagogy" of John Wesley to the Romantic pedagogy of Rousseau—only to flip them on their head in a display of triumphant naughtiness. Rather than treat boys (and girls) as two-dimensional figures prone to goodness or badness, *The Spoiled Child* showcases their resourcefulness, humor, and resilience.[12]

The Spoiled Child revolves around Little Pickle's chaotic misadventures. Home from school for the holidays, he executes a series of cruel practical jokes that test the limits of his family's patience: he kills his aunt's pet parrot and places it on a roasting spit for dinner (offstage); he whips the groom trying to prevent him from riding an untamed mare (also offstage); he sets bowls of water on top of door frames to greet unsuspecting servants (onstage); he uses a string to withdraw a chair from his father (also onstage); and causes all manner of havoc. Rather than resort to more traditional forms of corporal punishment, his father, Pickle, decides to play his son's game. He discloses that Little Pickle is not, in fact, his son by birth but rather the son of his nurse Margery and must therefore leave the house. Devastated at first, and movingly so, Little Pickle soon realizes that his father is lying and disguises himself as a sailor boy to continue his reign of terror. He interrupts his aunt's intimate moment with her lover Mr. Tagg and enlists the aid of his sister Maria, who pretends that she is in love with the young sailor and desperate to run away with him. This revelation shocks and dismays their father, who fails to recognize his disguised son. In the midst of this action, Little Pickle dances a hornpipe, sings several cheery songs, and fantasizes about life at sea.

Mystery has surrounded *The Spoiled Child* since its March 1790 premiere.[13] According to Jordan's biographer James Boaden, "Pickle was ascribed to Mrs. Jordan herself, then to Mr. [Richard] Ford, whose Little Pickle was still younger, we know. The truth is, I suppose, the exile Bickerstaff, whose Sultan had been kept alive by Mrs. Jordan, still tried occasionally to be received under cover, and that the 'Spoil'd Child' might yet contribute to the support of its parent."[14] The "exile Bickerstaff" is a reference to Isaac Bickerstaff, the playwright, who fled from England to France in 1772 following the publication of salacious stories of a sexual liaison with a soldier at the Savoy Barracks.[15] Although Bickerstaff never returned to England, he continued to write and adapt plays for the stage. Boaden therefore assumes that the writer has sent *The Spoiled Child* to Jordan and dismisses the prospect that Richard Ford or Jordan herself wrote the play.

But later sources contradict Boaden. In the introduction to the 1831 publication of the play, the anonymous writer "D——G" asserts, "From certain hints in the Prologue, from internal evidence, and other circumstances, we should ascribe it [the play] to Mrs. Jordan."[16] The opening lines of the prologue, delivered by Jordan while "opening a Letter," offer compelling evidence to support this claim:

"Dear Madam—Disappointed by a friend—
"Promis'd a Prologue—at my poor wit's end—
"Ruin'd—unless so good—your laughing way—
"T'insinuate something for my luckless Play."
Poor Devil! what a fright he's in—but why—
Am I to help him—What can I supply?
I'm doom'd to speak but just what Authors say:
Dull, when they're dull—and sportive when they're gay;
Mere puppets here, obedient to their will,
We love or hate—are blest or wretched—kill'd or kill—
Mirth we put on, just as we put on graces—
And wit—that's sent home ready with our dresses.[17]

Jordan's exclamation over the plight of the "Poor Devil," presumably Bickerstaff, brings immediate attention to the actress's friendship with the playwright. In keeping with the metatheatricality of the prologue as a dramatic form, Jordan ponders the challenges of an actress writing her own material, describing herself as a "mere puppet" beholden to the "will" of the playwright, an agentless being waiting to be formed. Of course, writing her own material is exactly what she's done—or so the winking convention of the prologue implies.[18] Jordan's opening words can therefore be read as a declaration of support for Bickerstaff, as well as a sly acknowledgment of her own contribution to the "luckless Play."[19]

It is worth pondering why Jordan and Bickerstaff created the role of the naughty little boy at all, given the actress's specialization in romping girls, hoydens, and precocious innocents, most notably Peggy in *The Country Girl* and Rosalind in *As You Like It*. These breeches roles accentuated Jordan's charm and physical attractiveness, allowing her (and the characters) to experiment with masculine garb and mannerisms before returning to her "natural" (i.e., female) form and dress. Though Jordan occasionally crossed over into travesty roles—one of her most popular travesty roles was Sir Harry Wildair in *The Constant Couple*, which she performed twenty-eight times between May 1788 and October 1790—these performances ruffled feathers and pushed buttons.[20] Little Pickle represents something of a half-measure: a travesty role that allowed Jordan to experiment with a less threatening expression of masculinity in the fictionalized form of a twelve-year-old boy.

Tellingly, the prologue to *The Spoiled Child* emphasizes the play's relationship to Jordan's other celebrated roles, including Priscilla Tomboy:

> Brimful of mirth he comes—Miss Tomboy's brother
> We hope you'll think they're something like each other.
> To please his cause she'll try a sister's skill,
> I'd fain prevent her—but, "ecod you will."—
> Perhaps she may shock you, of precise prim air,
> But Lord! what then, she never minds that there.[21]

In this passage the actress casts the two characters as rambunctious siblings and warns those "of precise prim air" that they may be shocked by what they see.[22] Curiously, the phrase "she never minds that there" recalls Priscilla's dismissive response to Penelope when asked if she considers her slaves' feelings: "Oh! we never consider that there." The line's near repetition in *The Spoiled Child*'s prologue points to the notoriety of the original scene and to the writer's expectation of audience familiarity with *The Romp*. Yet for all their similarities, Little Pickle is *not* a tomboy. This change in the character's gender is critical: the transformation of the teenaged Priscilla Tomboy into the twelve-year-old Little Pickle strips away the most dangerous aspects of the tomboyish character—namely her refusal to accede to patriarchal expectations. This change facilitates a different, arguably safer, conversation about gender roles in that it naturalizes naughtiness as the "rightful" domain of boyhood and suggests that any girl who exhibits such behavior is doing so temporarily.

For all this, *The Spoiled Child* received a mixed response at its first performance. Audiences hissed at Jordan's debut performance as Little Pickle, and the play was "damned by nearly all the critics wherever it was performed."[23] Writing in 1822, the publisher P.P. makes no effort to hide his disgust for the "utterly despicable" and "completely worthless" play, identifying deficiencies in plot, character, and language. P.P. is baffled at the play's three-decade-long "career of popularity" before conceding that he felt compelled to publish it as part of a comprehensive series of *"acting-drama."*[24] P.P.'s criticism foregrounds the importance of acting (Jordan's and others) to *The Spoiled Child*'s long-term success. But *The Spoiled Child* is much more than a star vehicle. It is also a fascinating, deceptively complicated commentary on childhood education, punishment, and parent-child relationships.

Poisonous Pedagogy and *The Spoiled Child*

Little Pickle is every eighteenth-century parent's worst nightmare. Bored and overindulged, he rejects moral order and bourgeois manners; he manipulates others and ignores authority; he breaks rules, flouts taboos, and does as he pleases. And for all of this, he thrives. Even the threat of disownment does little to alter his behavior, and the play concludes with the boy's triumph over the adults in his life. As a case study of parent-child relationships, *The Spoiled Child* depicts the chaos that ensues when parents adopt an overly lax attitude toward their children's behavior. This theme is established in the first moments of the play when the unmarried Miss Pickle warns her brother that he must take a more authoritative position toward his misbehaving son: "Brother, unless he is severely punished for what he has already done," she cautions, "depend upon it this vicious humour will be confirmed into habit, and his follies increase in proportion with his years."[25] Paraphrasing the biblical verse from which the play takes its title—"spare the rod and spoil the child"—Miss Pickle urges her brother to intervene before his son's bad tendencies become habit and permanently alter his form.

Miss Pickle's perspective on child-rearing echoes a particular strand of "poisonous pedagogy," a term introduced by feminist scholar Alice Miller in 1983 to describe systems of punishment used by parents and authority figures to break the will of the child.[26] Such pedagogy flourished in the seventeenth and eighteenth centuries, fueled by the Calvinist belief that children were born stained with original sin and therefore required careful instruction in Christian morality to save their souls from eternal damnation.[27] In the mid-eighteenth century, John Wesley, one of the founders of Methodism, preached that "self-will is the root of all sin and misery, so whatever cherishes this in children ensures their after-wretchedness and irreligion."[28] It therefore fell to parents to "break the will, if you would not damn the child.... If you spare the rod, you spoil the child; if you do not conquer, you ruin him. Break his will now, and his soul shall live, and he will probably bless you to all eternity."[29] For Wesley, the unchecked will was a matter of concern for both this world and the next. Good parents were those who broke their children's wills and steered them onto a straight and narrow path to salvation. Of course, the concept of the "spoiled child" is not unique to Wesley. William Congreve's 1694 play *Double-Dealer* contains the earliest known uses of the verb "to spoil" to refer to a kind of injury to character "especially through over-indulgence or undue lenience."[30] In that play, the character Lord Froth warns Lady Froth, "I swear, my dear, you'll spoil that Child," when she insists on seeing her nine-month-old infant for the sixth time that day. Here, overattentiveness to a babe-in-arms is understood as an indulgence that will interfere with the child's moral and spiritual development.

Stories about the dangers of willful children, especially girls, pepper eighteenth- and nineteenth-century narratives.[31] In her study of willfulness, Sara Ahmed cites the Grimm brothers' tale about a young girl who refused to do her mother's bidding and so lost favor in God's eyes, which resulted in her early death of an incurable illness. Even after death, however, the girl continued to assert her willfulness, continually thrusting her arm out of her grave until her mother finally struck down the arm with a rod, after which "the child had rest beneath the ground."[32] For Ahmed, the image of the thrusting, unbending arm in the Grimm tale offers a vivid metaphor for the history of willfulness, especially as it pertains to children, women, persons of color, and LGBTQ2+ folks.[33]

On a first read, *The Spoiled Child* seems to fall in line with Wesley and other eighteenth-century pedagogues, warning parents about the risks of coddling the willful child. The pseudonymous D——G emphasized this reading in his prefatory "Remarks" to a later edition of the play:

> *Little Pickle*, the hero, is one of those anointed young urchins, denominated *Spoiled Children*, whose pranks are chargeable to that unlimited indulgence which certain *tender*, or, more properly speaking, *cruel* parents allow their offspring, from their earliest infancy: parents, who, when the error of their training discovers itself in a thousand irregularities, when the *lively spirit* and *diverting sullies* of my young master being to defy control, and

render him annoying to themselves, and insufferable to every one else, think themselves hardly treated by Providence, in sending them such a wayward and untractable disposition. . . . There is a power entrusted to parents, in the shape of restraint and admonition; which, added to a proper example, on *their* part, is sufficient to enforce parental authority, without lessening filial regard.[34]

For D——G, parents who yield too readily to the will of their children are performing acts of cruelty. Such parents refuse to take responsibility for their parenting "errors" and instead look for external reasons to blame their child's "wayward and untractable disposition." D——G concludes by promoting a counter-model of strong, loving parents who set their children on the path to moral uprightness through a combination of "restraint," "admonition," and "proper example."

In D——G's view, then, Mr. Pickle epitomizes the "cruelty" of the overindulgent parent. Despite his sister's warning, he is unconvinced that the "poisonous pedagogy" she advocates is the appropriate response to his son's behavior. He refuses to accept that Little Pickle "[has] actually some vice in him" and dismisses the "stumbling blocks" and water traps his son prepares for him as nothing more than whimsy: "I own there is something so whimsical in all his tricks, that I cannot in my heart but forgive him, and for aught I know, love him better into the bargain."[35] Mr. Pickle bridles at his sister's suggestion that he has lost control of his son and declares that he can "make a lord chancellor, or an archbishop of Canterbury of him, which ever I like—just as I like."[36]

Mr. Pickle's views on parenting represent a hodgepodge of eighteenth-century thinking. On the one hand, his bold assertion that he can shape his son into anything he chooses echoes John Locke, who depicted children as blank slates or *tabula rasa* waiting to be written upon by parents, teachers, and other influential figures. Refuting the belief that children were stained by original sin, Locke emphasized their dangerous plasticity, noting they could be "easily turned, this or that, as water itself."[37] Proper instruction was therefore necessary to prevent the malformation of the individual child. On the other hand, Mr. Pickle's unwillingness to see vice in his son gestures toward the idealized "child of nature" celebrated by Romantic poets like William Wordsworth, who depicted children as innocent beings born "trailing clouds of glory."[38] Although *The Spoiled Child* appeared on the English stage over a decade before Wordsworth published his "Ode: Intimations of Immortality from Recollections of Early Childhood," the notion that children were "naturally" innocent and should be left to their own devices was becoming a dominant theme in discussions about childhood education, influenced in large part by Jean-Jacques Rousseau's *Émile* (1762).

Like Locke, Rousseau rejected the tenets of "poisonous pedagogy" and advanced a model of childhood education that stressed adult mentorship. Where Rousseau differed from Locke was in his contention that children should learn through experience as well as instruction, which included the freedom to explore nature and develop an independent view of the world.[39] This did not mean that parents or teachers should let their charges freely assert their will but rather that they should gently guide them to see the error of their ways.[40] By way of illustration, the narrator in *Émile* describes how he redirected an especially "capricious" boy "who was accustomed not only to hav[ing] his own way, but to mak[ing] everyone else do as he please[d]."[41] Observing how the child's tutors would take him out whenever he wished, Rousseau's narrator proposes an alternative: he permits the child to go out on his own and then orchestrates several encounters with strangers who tease and taunt the child without harming him. The child asserts his will but learns through his unpleasant encounters that giving in to his will can have negative consequences. As Sara Ahmed concludes, Rousseau's pedagogy equates willfulness with unhappiness, leading the willful child to yield of his own free will to the wishes of his parent or tutor: "The child is made to will according to the will of those in authority without ever being conscious of the circumstances of this making."[42] Again, the "child" in question here is clearly a boy; although Rousseau doesn't ignore girls entirely, recalling the story of a girl who uses her "natural gift" of "cunning" to get sweets, he has very little time for such creatures.[43]

When Rousseau first published *Émile* in 1762, public reaction was mixed. Compared with the Wesleyan vision of the willful child beaten into submission, Rousseau's proposal seemed radical and risky. But during and in the immediate aftermath of the French Revolution, Rousseau's ideas gained traction and crossed borders of nation and genre. French playwrights like Mme. de Genlis incorporated *Émile*-like characters and scenarios into her play *Zélie*, which in turn became the basis for Elizabeth Inchbald's *The Child of Nature*, a play intimately associated with Dorothy Jordan, who in turn helped to popularize Rousseauesque notions of natural beauty.[44]

Given the adoption of Rousseau's ideas by theatre artists, it is no surprise to find Rousseau lingering behind the scenes of *The Spoiled Child*. The play's debt to *Émile* is most obvious in the complicated plan Miss Pickle and Mr. Pickle devise to teach Little Pickle, not through physical punishment or a lengthy lecture but rather through painful experience. Reluctant at first to "abandon [his] only child"—a peculiar statement that ignores the existence of his daughter Maria—Mr. Pickle eventually agrees to Miss Pickle's plan: he will inform his son that there was a mix-up at his birth and that he is not, in fact, Mr. Pickle's son but the child of his nursemaid Margery. Miss Pickle hopes that this scheme will lead the errant child to "reflect upon his bad behavior" and amend his ways. Like Rousseau's narrator, she anticipates that Little Pickle will learn through experience the problem with asserting his will. Mr. Pickle is concerned with his son's emotional well-being but he goes along with the plan anyway, motivated in part by the fear that his sister will vacate their home and take her considerable inheritance with her if he does not.[45]

But if *The Spoiled Child* is a commentary on *Émile*, that commentary is doused with skepticism. Indeed, Bickerstaff seems to have made the most of Jordan's "child of nature" associations to query some of Rousseau's core ideas—and the frequent pairing of *The Spoiled Child* with Inchbald's *Child of Nature* on Drury Lane playbills must have made this connection explicit.[46]

Pickle and Miss Pickle put their extreme parenting into action and for a short while it seems to produce the desired effect. Little Pickle responds with shock and disbelief when he learns of his "real" parentage: "I another person's child!—impossible!—ah! you are only joking with me now, to see whether I love you or not, but indeed—(*To Pickle.*)— I am your's [*sic*]—my heart tells me I am only only your's."[47] After first assuming (correctly) that he is the target of a practical joke intended to assess his love, Little Pickle turns to his father and insists that he is "only only your's." The double "only" here hints at both the boy's sincerity and his growing panic. Pickle remains unmoved by his son's declaration, though, and insists that the boy leave the house and return to his "real" parents. At this, Little Pickle speaks wistfully about how happy he has been in Pickle's home and begs forgiveness for "the faults

I have committed—you cannot, sure, in pity deny me that." He then sings a mournful song, "Since then I'm doom'd," and concludes the act with a melancholic declaration:

> Where'er I go, whate'er my lowly state,
>   Yet grateful mem'ry still shall linger here;
> And perhaps when musing o'er my cruel fate,
>   You still may greet me with a tender tear.
> Ah! then forgive me, pitied let me part,
>   Your frowns, too sure, would break my sinking heart.[48]

With this song, a sorrowful Little Pickle begs forgiveness and promises that he will never forget his father and aunt. If *The Spoiled Child* concluded here, the final image would resemble that of the repentant "capricious child" of *Émile*, who, upon venturing out into the world on his own, learns to temper his will through error and mishap. Not surprisingly, the pathos of this particular song was one of the play's emotional highlights, as a flourishing market in sheet music sales attests.[49]

But this is not where the play ends. By the opening of act 2, Little Pickle has discovered the plot against him (thanks to his nurse's confession) and has hatched a scheme of his own. Inverting Rousseau's lesson, he dresses as a sailor and introduces himself to Pickle as his (fictional) long-lost son. Following a rousing hornpipe, Little Pickle goes in search of his sister, Maria, whom he persuades to pretend to fall in love with the sailor to bring further distress to their father. Maria zealously agrees to play along, evincing the same naughty spirit as her brother. As expected, Pickle responds with horror at Maria's profession of love (and the implied threat of incest) and he locks her in her room to prevent her from further association with the dangerous sailor. So much for Maria.[50] Not long after this the errant father receives a letter from his outcast son (a trick letter, of course) announcing his departure from England "for ever." The scene ends with Little Pickle as the sailor singing about the joys of life at sea. Pickle's plan has imploded.

Miss Pickle does not escape her nephew's mischievous vengeance either. As described earlier, the sailor boy interrupts her romantic tryst with Mr. Tagg and forces the lovers to part ... but only after they have disentangled themselves from the clothing Little Pickle has stitched together. The boy then disguises himself as Tagg and reappears just as his aunt, Miss Pickle, returns with her fortune so the two can elope.

But before they can depart an enraged Pickle enters and tries to appre-hend Tagg for misleading his spinster sister. Delighted to have caused such chaos, Little Pickle finally throws off his disguise as Tagg and re-veals his true identity. A much-relieved Pickle embraces his son and up-braids him for his tricks, to which Little Pickle saucily responds, "Oh, sir, recollect you have kindly pardon'd them already."[51] Here the errant son invokes the performative power of his father's earlier act of for-giveness, but then asks for his father's assistance in seeking atonement with his aunt.

The final moments of *The Spoiled Child* feature further acts of repen-tance, forgiveness, and reconciliation. After cheekily suggesting that his father has nothing to pardon, Little Pickle asks in a more conciliatory vein whether he is willing to forgive him and "forget all my follies," to which Pickle replies that the happiness he feels in reconciling with his son is more than sufficient payment for any suffering the boy caused. "Kind, sir, my joy is then complete, and I will never more offend," Little Pickle vows.[52] The play ends with Little Pickle singing about the duty, love, and obedience a child owes to his father, followed by a plea to the audience to excuse the "childish pranks" of a schoolboy:

> Dear sir, once more receive me,
>> And take me to your arms,
> Nor drive me forth to wander
>> Exposed to rude alarms.
> His/my duty, love, obedience,
>> This penitence resuse [?]
> Then ne'er adopt another child,
>> For he/I alone is/am yours.
>
> *Chorus—My duty, love, &c.*
>
> Our/My joy is then completed,
>> Wou'd but each gen'rous heart,
> With partial favour smiling,
>> Applaud the artless jest.
> The object of these childish pranks,
>> Was barely to amuse 'em,
> Then censure not a school-boy's faults,
>> But laugh at, and excuse 'em.[53]

The Spoiled Child

Appealing to his father as well as the audience, Little Pickle presents himself as a prodigal son who has learned his lesson. Although skeptics may wonder how long it will be before the boy inevitably breaks his vow to "never offend," the final image of the penitent, loving son is ultimately hopeful, not unlike the story of the boy in *Émile* who learns to bend his will through harsh experience. As a satirical response to *Émile*, then, *The Spoiled Child* offers a sobering lesson to parents who do nothing to guide their willful children. Little Pickle may transgress again, but Pickle has also learned a valuable lesson about the importance of "restraint," "admonition," and "proper example."[54]

The Spoiled Child is notable for its representation of boys as psychologically complex individuals, by turns naughty, resourceful, cunning, diligent, playful, and loving. This perspective aligns with the work of Romantic female children's writers such as Anna Letitia Barbauld, Mary Wollstonecraft, and Maria Edgeworth, who collectively challenged the image of the innocent, "uncannily beautiful child"[55] so central to the writing of male Romantic poets. As literary scholar Judith Plotz asserts, these women wrote stories that "stag[ed] interactions among members of a family or other small communities in which children learn the life lessons that help them to function as self-regulated adults."[56] Such stories do not position parents as all-knowing and dominant but rather model the "interassimilation of adulthood and childhood"[57] in the interests of promoting healthy individuals capable of empathizing, collaborating, and negotiating with others. Although Little Pickle has much to learn before he becomes a mature, "self-legislating" adult, he demonstrates a capacity to collaborate through his interactions with his sister, and his final exchange with his father likewise suggests a willingness to learn and change.

This aspect of *The Spoiled Child* points to an important distinction between the image of Romantic childhood enshrined by Wordsworth and his peers and the more complicated image of boyhood that flourished on the Anglo-American stage in the bodies of performing girls. Whereas "male Romantics produc[ed] children not as integrated into the social realm but as a race apart,"[58] the girls (and boys) who appeared onstage were very much of this world—and audiences seemed to enjoy this. Tracing *The Spoiled Child*'s migration to the repertoire of the girl actress also stretches Marah Gubar's observation that later nineteenth-century audiences favored plays that allowed young performers to indulge in displays of precocity and naughtiness by showing how girls embodied the figure of the "artful" or cunning child in the early decades of the century.[59] But what prompted Little Pickle's migration from women to girl actresses in the first place?

"Barbarous, Injurious, and Unnatural"

In the final moments of the 1822 version of *The Spoiled Child* (presumably the version used by Clara Fisher), the actress playing Little Pickle steps out of character and speaks as herself. Addressing the "generous spectators" before her, she asks them to acknowledge their amusement and promises that a positive response will "tempt" her "once more to transgress."[60] The word "transgress" works doubly here to refer both to Little Pickle's many transgressions as well as to the actress's transgressions of gender and age.[61] This final moment points to yet another reading of *The Spoiled Child*—one that sees the play as a fierce rejection of patriarchal norms. More than a plot device, Little Pickle's strategic use of disguise to thwart his father's plot can be read as a deliberate nod to Jordan's own cross-dressing abilities and her performance of youthful masculinity. Significantly, *The Spoiled Child* is both a travesty and a disguise role, one that requires the actress to showcase her versatility by portraying three male characters: Little Pickle, the sailor boy, and the considerably older artist Tagg.[62] Written specially for Jordan, these roles provide numerous opportunities for rambunctious acts—practical jokes, dancing the hornpipe, making saucy remarks—all at the expense of a patriarchal figure.

Reading *The Spoiled Child* as both an enticement to romp and an allegory about women cross-dressing offers some explanation for the role's gradual migration from women to girls. By the early 1800s critical murmurings about certain actresses' proclivity for cross-dressing were intensifying. Such reservations characterized anxieties about shifting gender roles and fear about the social danger that might result from actresses assuming the guises, gestures, and vocabularies associated with men. This attitude toward cross-dressing stood in sharp contrast to earlier eighteenth-century perspectives, which looked favorably on cross-dressed actresses. Their "marketability," Katrina Straub writes, "had as much to do with a playfully ambiguous sexual appeal as with the heterosexually defined attractions of her spectacularized feminine body."[63] Eighteenth-century audiences not only tolerated but reveled in the "sexual confusion" represented by the cross-dressed actress. Helen E. M. Brooks attributes this openness toward and fascination with cross-gender performance to belief in the one-sex body, "in which sexual difference was a matter of degree and the humoural composition of the individual body." By the mid-eighteenth century, however, this model was supplanted by the "two sex model" of the body, which aligned gender and sexuality, seeing the differences between men and women as the product of the body.[64] Even with these changes, later audiences remained open to performances of gender fluidity as long as they were clearly marked as stage acting, "an illusion to be bought and kept within the marketplace of the theater."[65] This notion of cross-dressing as a contained and containable theatrical practice is discernible in James Boaden's biography of Jordan. Writing in 1830, Boaden attributes the actress's 1783 success in the opera *Rosina* to her "display of female not male perfections," insisting that the "attraction after all is purely feminine." Had she "really" appeared as a man, he insists, "the coarse *androgynous* would be hooted from the stage."[66] For Boaden, Jordan's cross-dressing was acceptable because it enhanced rather than detracted from the actress's femininity, thereby affirming gender hierarchies by privileging the male gaze.

Not all critics were as willing as Boaden to treat cross-dressing as a benign mode of performance. In an 1807 series of *Critical Essays* on the era's leading performers, theatre critic Leigh Hunt dedicates several pages to Jordan and to the question of breeches roles. He begins by commenting on Jordan's younger days when she was "the most natural actress of childhood, of it's [*sic*] bursts of disposition, and it's [*sic*] fitful happiness." He estimates that she would still be "the most natural actress" if not for the "increase of her person" (i.e., weight gain). Hunt expresses relief that "Mrs. Jordan, with much good sense, seems to have almost laid aside her *Romps* and her *Little Pickles* for younger performers."[67] But these roles have nevertheless marked the actress's body. Pondering why Jordan "should be so deficient" in the portrayal of ladylike characters, Hunt concludes that her many years of playing "broad and romping characters" have affected her gestures to such an extent that they "must in some degree unavoidably be bent." In other words, the decades spent playing naughty boys, romping girls, and

MRS JORDAN as SIR HARRY WILDAIR.
From the Rare Portrait of 1788.

FIGURE 10. *Dorothy Jordan as Sir Harry Wildair in* The Constant Couple.
© *National Portrait Gallery, London.*

other breeches roles have rendered Jordan incapable of playing a lady. Her body remains a living archive of the theatrical repertoire she has theoretically left behind.[68]

Concluding that Jordan's predilection for breeches roles has permanently bent her body out of shape, Hunt launches into a lengthy diatribe on cross-dressing as a theatrical practice:

> The male attirement of actresses is one of the most barbarous, injurious, and unnatural customs of the stage. . . . In all cases it is injurious to the probability of the author and to the proper style of the actress, for if she succeeds in her study of male representation she will never entirely get rid of her manhood with its attire; she is like *Iphis* of Ovid, and changes her sex unalterably. There is required, in fact, a breadth of manners and demeanour in a woman's imitation of men, which no female, who had not got over a certain feminine reserve of limb, could ever maintain or endure; and when the imitation becomes frequent and the limbs bent to their purpose, it is impossible to return to that delicacy of behavior, which exists merely as it is incapable of forgetting itself. Vivacity does nothing but strengthen the tendency to broadness by allowing a greater freedom of action; it merely helps the female to depart more from her former chaste coldness of character and the simplicity of her former mental shape; it is like attempting to straighten a curled lock by holding it nearer the fire. I cannot but persuade myself therefore, that Mrs. Jordan's inability to catch the elegant delicacy of the lady arises from her perpetual representation of the other sex and of the romping, unsettled, and uneducated part of her own.[69]

Hunt's deep anxiety about cross-dressing, particularly his belief that an actress who is too successful at playing male roles will forever be marked by "manhood," points to the emergence of a much more rigid view of gender and a corresponding desire to police aberrant female bodies. Hunt is not simply worried that cross-dressed women will exhibit the manners of men. He is scared that they will forever lose the "feminine reserve of limb" that makes their bodies legible as female and will ultimately be "unsexed" . . . or queered. The threat of a queer transformation is not simply physical but mental as well. Hunt's fear that displays of vivacity encourage women to dispense with their "chaste coldness of character and the simplicity of [their] former mental shape" speaks to the danger and unruliness of plasticity.

Hunt's use of words like "bending" and "bent" to describe Jordan's movement anticipates later uses of the term "bent" as a homophobic slur and the corresponding use of the word "straight" to represent heterosexual desire. "Things seem straight (on the vertical axis), when they are 'in line,'" writes Sara Ahmed, "which means they are aligned with other lines." Conjuring the image of drawing lines on tracing paper, she describes how perceptions of alignment rely on repetition and the use of "straightening devices that keep things in line, in part by 'holding' things in place." But when the straightening device is removed and "when even one thing comes 'out of line' with another thing, the 'general effect,' is 'wonky' or even 'queer.'"[70] Jordan's wonky, bent limbs, unruly curls, and questionable desires thus rendered her quite literally "out of line" with dominant modes of femininity. She was strange, bending and bendable, "romping, unsettled, and uneducated," and therefore a danger to herself and others.[71]

Hunt implicitly recognizes how performance can lead to new (for him, dangerous) behavioral modes that challenge or undermine accepted norms.[72] He frets that the more women like Mrs. Jordan move their limbs and indulge in the "freedom of action" accorded men, the less likely they will be to return to "[their] former chaste coldness of character and the simplicity of [their] former mental state." Performances like Jordan's, which played with androgyny and disguise, threatened the new gender order and thus required containment or rejection. Hunt's image of Jordan's bent limbs also resonates with this chapter's discussion of willfulness in children. "A willing child is bendy, or bendable in the right way," Ahmed observes; "the willful child is the wrong bent."[73] Throughout *Willful Subjects* she examines a range of "wayward parts: parts that will not budge, that refuse to participate, parts that keep coming up, when they are not even supposed to be" and concludes with a powerful "call to arms" that celebrates those who use their bodies to act differently and bend otherwise. If we apply Ahmed's theorizing to Dorothy Jordan's acting, we can see how the latter's portrayal of Little Pickle, Priscilla Tomboy, and many other "wayward parts" led the actress to bend away from rather than toward patriarchal expectations—to assert her right to form herself rather than slip easily into the form that others wished for her.[74]

What made an actress like Jordan even more threatening, however, was her reputation for naturalness and her close identification with the roles she played. "More than any actress on the stage," Jean I. Marsden writes, "Jordan created a bond of sympathy between herself and her audience through the strength of her identification with the characters she played."[75] The danger was not just that female audiences would see Jordan as an appealing masculine figure and desire her for themselves but that they would come to desire the freedom she modeled onstage because it seemed so natural and easy to achieve.[76] Such naturalness called into question what Kristina Straub identifies as the two foundational concepts of the modern sex/gender system: "1) the subjugation of a feminine spectacle to the dominance of the male gaze and 2) the exclusive definition of feminine sexual desire in terms of its relation to masculine heterosexual desire."[77] When Jordan performed romping roles or stepped into the shoes of Little Pickle, she modeled an alluring form of female masculinity that invited queer ways of looking and being.

The appeal and danger of female masculinity is immediately apparent in Samuel De Wilde's 1802 watercolor of Jordan's contemporary, Mrs. Mills, as Little Pickle (Figure 11). Mrs. Mills first assumed the role in October 1798, originally for one night only as a special arrangement between Covent Garden and the Drury Lane proprietors; however, the play was such a hit that it appeared at least a dozen more times on the Covent Garden stage that season—ten times between October and December alone, thanks in no small part to Mrs. Mills's charming performance.[78] Sporting short, curly hair and dressed in a form-fitting blue jacket and white breeches with a wide-collared shirt, she looks out of the frame with a confident, inviting expression. Her left hand rests saucily on her hip; her right hand grasps a riding crop with a black riding hat perched on top. The sexual imagery is potent: the phallic crop disappears into the black lining of the hat, while the crop handle directs the viewers' eyes down to the bottom of the drawing, where the artist has outlined Mrs. Mill's vulva against her white breeches. Although, as Gill Perry observes, portraits of actresses in breeches roles were typically "half- or three-quarter-length rather than full-length portraits, thus avoiding representation of the lower legs and ankles," there is no denying the eroticism of this particular image.[79] Unlike other portraits of sexually available actresses from this period, which likewise guide

FIGURE 11. *Mrs. Mills as Little Pickle.* © *Victoria & Albert Museum, London.*

the viewers' eyes to the actress's pelvic region,[80] De Wilde's portrait grants Mrs. Mills an assertive sexual agency; she is the one wielding the crop after all.

Compare this image with the one that opened this chapter (see Figure 9), in which a diminutive and bewigged Clara Fisher peers from behind a shrub at the two adults playing Miss Pickle and Tagg. The difference in scale between the performers offers visual evidence of Little

Pickle's charming cuteness. Whereas the portrait of Mrs. Mills projects confidence, control, and sexual knowingness, the image of Fisher appeals to viewers on the basis of her youth, size, and apparent vulnerability, as well as her close physical resemblance to a twelve-year-old boy. This representation invites tender feelings of care and longing, in keeping with the longstanding association of cuteness with the maternal.[81] Significantly, Fisher's cuteness is closely entangled with her portrayal of Little Pickle's naughty boyishness. Such boyish cuteness serves to contain, if not exactly erase, any association between Little Pickle and sexual desire. Clara Fisher as Little Pickle may not be an innocent, but she's certainly not the confident sexual creature that leaps from the portrait of Mrs. Mill.

In light of the anxiety that Jordan and her fellow actresses provoked in critics like Leigh Hunt, Little Pickle's gradual migration to girls' repertoire is hardly surprising.[82] This isn't to say that women stopped playing the role—the famed actress Mme. Vestris offered her version of Little Pickle in the 1830s, and Fisher herself continued to play the role well into her twenties.[83] But by the mid-nineteenth century, Little Pickle was widely recognized as an ideal vehicle for young girls, in large part because the most subversive aspects of the character were diminished when embodied by a prepubescent girl.

The Spoiled Child in a Girl's Body

Little Pickle crossed the Atlantic to North America in the mid-1790s. The adult actress Mrs. Thomas Marshall debuted the role in March 1794 in Philadelphia and actively asserted her right to play it for eighteen years.[84] In this, she was only partly successful. Her adult contemporary Mrs. Williamson also delighted Boston audiences with her interpretation of the naughty boy between 1796 and 1799.[85] Girls had greater opportunities to test their mettle outside the major cities, however. On December 20, 1796, nine-year-old Elizabeth (Eliza) Arnold introduced Little Pickle to audiences in Newport, Maine.[86] There, the local newspaper marveled at her astonishing powers: "Add to these her youth, her beauty, her innocence, and a character composed which has not, and perhaps will not be found on any Theatre."[87] This writer's surprise with both the actress *and* her character suggests that the role—and possibly the actress—was something of a novelty.[88] Four years later, Arnold returned to *The Spoiled Child* for the August opening of the United States Theatre in Washington, DC, supported by members of the Philadelphia Company.[89] That the play and the (by then) thirteen-year-old actress featured prominently in such an auspicious event attests to the popularity of both Little Pickle as a character and the girl playing him. Nevertheless, as Jeanne Klein has shown, girls were beholden to managerial preferences, which meant that they often had to watch from the sidelines as more experienced adult actresses played the naughty boy.[90]

Little Pickle's transition from adults to girls occurred later in England, possibly because of the role's longstanding association with Dorothy Jordan and actresses like Mrs. Mill. Bettymania changed all this when children (and their managers) unabashedly raided adult repertoire. In September 1805, Jane Fisher (Clara Fisher's older sister) performed a version of *The Spoiled Child* at Drury Lane on the same bill as Jordan. Her performance must have been greeted favorably because she kept Little Pickle in her repertoire, pairing it with Young Norval, Richard III, Rosalind, and Jane Shore, among others, during her provincial tours.[91]

Ultimately, though, it was Jane Fisher's younger sister Clara who secured the naughty boy's place in the repertoire of girl actresses, both in Britain and North America. Little Pickle was ideal for a performer of Clara Fisher's abilities because it allowed her to display her skill in singing, dancing, and acting, while indulging in boyish excess. Writing in 1821, a critic for the *Literary Chronicle and Weekly Review* described Fisher's Little Pickle as "the smartest little romp we ever saw in the character."[92] Another writer waxed poetic after seeing her play the role in Bristol:

It was, in sober joyousness, the complete triumph of Nature and Art most intimately blended, by a mistress in her profession of only eleven years old! We fancied we saw the beauties of all the *Little Pickles* that ever were, from the lamented Jordan down to little Booth, bound up, as "Beauties" generally are, in one pretty little volume. She sang both of the original songs with a degree of melodious feeling and musical propriety which, as we were not prepared to expect it, the more surprised and delighted us. The "Yeo! Yeo!" was encored, and so was a hornpipe, very fitly substituted for the customary exchange of the latter for a dancing song.

All was graceful, because natural—all was thoughtfully deliberate, both in speech and action; and no parent's sympathetic feelings could have been excited by apprehension for the undue exercise of physical powers so very tender.[93]

For this writer, Fisher's Little Pickle is an amalgam of all previous Little
Pickles, notably those presented by Jordan (who had recently died) and
Miss S. Booth, another adult actress, who had similarly played the role
to great acclaim.[94] Fisher not only sings beautifully, with "a degree of
melodious feeling and musical propriety" that surprised this writer but
also dances the hornpipe with aplomb, earning an encore. But it is the
girl's skill, her thoughtfulness and precision "in speech and action" that
distinguish her from her peers. The writer's reference to Fisher's naturalness and grace calls to mind earlier descriptions of Jordan, the celebrated "child of nature." As with Jordan, Fisher's distinct talent lies in
her ability to project naturalness even as she showcases deliberation in
movement and voice. The ease with which she assumes the character
of Little Pickle reassures the writer (or any "sympathetic parent") that
Fisher is not being overtaxed or unfairly asked to exercise her "physical powers." Naturalness, then, is invoked to divert questions about
child labor exploitation, even as it justifies casting a young girl to play
a child character.[95] It is Fisher's size and age, combined with her ability
to package "the beauties of all the *Little Pickles* that ever were" into "one
pretty little volume," that make her Little Pickle so attractive.

Such references to the girl's physical attractiveness might lead us to
doubt whether the subversive aspects of *The Spoiled Child*—specifically
its rejection of patriarchal expectations, its celebration of naughtiness,
and its invitation to transgress gender norms—carried over into the performances of Clara Fisher and the girls who followed her lead. Would
the sight of a little girl dressed as Little Pickle in "white trowsers and
waistcoat, little blue sailor's jacket bound with white, and white buttons"[96] have had the same unsettling effect as seeing a grown woman
in the same costume? This image of Jean Davenport as Little Pickle,
created in the late 1830s or early 1840s, is charmingly harmless (Figure
12). Her femininity isn't in dispute: we glimpse rosy cheeks and lips,
a tapered waist, and delicate shoulders. She looks more like a tomboy
than an actual boy, and her embrace of masculine dress and gestures
is visible *as* performance. For all their playing *at* being naughty boys,

FIGURE 12. *Jean Margaret Davenport as Little Pickle.*
MS Thr 158.1, Houghton Library, Harvard University.

the girls who performed Little Pickle were unthreatening because they were not yet women.[97]

This emphasis on the temporary status of the girl actress assuaged (male) concerns about female performers overidentifying with their roles or becoming masculine in the process. Instead, as the following excerpt from the *New-York Mirror, and Ladies' Literary Gazette* suggests, an actress's ability to wear male dress convincingly was seen as evidence of her talent: "Miss Fisher has rather a penchant for male attire, which is not to be wondered at, for it becomes her well: all other women whom we have seen wear the inexpressibles in public, cannot forget their sex, but betray throughout a smirking consciousness that they are feminine, and are of course for the most part awkward and embarrassed; she appears to forget her dress and all minor considerations in the character she is representing."[98] In this account, Fisher's unique abilities—her intense focus and commitment to character—explain her unselfconscious appearance in male dress. Unlike other girls or women who betray their femininity through a "smirking consciousness," Fisher "forgets" that she is anything but the character she is playing. This description recalls Leigh Hunt's account of Dorothy Jordan, especially his lament that the years of playing men have made such an imprint on her body that she is no longer capable of portraying a lady. Like Jordan, Fisher's "penchant for male attire" seems to disguise her femininity. Here, though, the writer treats this aspect of Fisher's cross-dressing as more of a virtue than cause for alarm. Unlike Hunt, he doesn't imagine that her limbs will be bent out of feminine shape or that her sex will be "unalterably" changed, because to him, she is still a girl, a subject in formation with limbs that have yet to set. As Mullenix concludes, "Cross-dressed actresses who played boys ultimately could not transcend their sex. . . . They would never grow up, both because the actress could not change her sex (or 'evolve' into a man), and because the dramatic boy was trapped within discourse."[99] Thus while the girls who played Little Pickle may have encouraged their juvenile counterparts to embrace the freedoms they modeled onstage,[100] those freedoms belonged to a (fleeting) stage of life. Consider the following 1831 joke published in *The Aurora Borealis or Flashes of Wit*: "A noble personage, enraptured with Miss Fisher's representation of Little Pickle, (in the Spoiled Child,) exclaimed, 'There is no girl of her age like her!' 'I engage, sir,' replied a friend, 'there is not a ladies' boarding-school in the kingdom that has not a *spoiled child* in it.'"[101] In this joke, the naughty little-boyishness of the spoiled Little Pickle is aligned with the silliness of spoiled little-girlhood, a passing phase of life that presumably will end upon graduation. The threat of spoiling is diminished by the very ephemerality of girlhood.

The Spoiled Child's teasing sentimentality may also have subsumed the more transgressive elements of Little Pickle. This dampening effect is notable in moments of song, such as the mournful ballad, "Since, then I'm doom'd," which the boy sings at the end of the first act when he fears that all has been lost. Cast out of his home by his father who asserts that he is another man's son, he sings:

> Since, then I'm doom'd this sad reverse to prove,
> To quit each object of my infant Care;
> Torn from an honored Parent's tender love,
> And driv'n the keenest, keenst Storms of Fate to bear;
> Ah! But forgive me pitied let me part;
> Ah! But forgive me pitied let me part;
> Your Frowns too sure, wou'd break my sinking Heart;
> Your Frowns too sure, wou'd break my singing Heart.
>
> Wher'er I go, whate'er my lowly State,
> Yet grateful mem'ry still shall linger here;
> And when, perhaps you're missing o'er my Fate,
> You still may greet me with a tender Tear,
> Ah! Then forgive me, pitied, let me part,
> Your frowns too sure wou'd break my singing heart.[102]

The lyrics depict Little Pickle's sorry state and urge the audience to forgive and pity him. But as much as the song is rooted in the particularities of the plot, the sentiment taps into the intensity of parent-child relations and the almost universal fear of abandonment. The song's subsequent publication, not once but six times between 1790 and 1806, offers compelling evidence of its lingering effect on audiences, as they brought it into their homes and sang it around parlor pianos.[103]

In some cases, audiences collectively wept as they listened to the song. Recalling Clara Fisher's 1829 performance of Little Pickle in Quebec City (when she was eighteen and more recognizably a woman than a girl), the author A.L.E. wrote:

In the evening we had our countrywoman, Clara Fisher, to play "The Spoiled Child" for us. I thought she never appeared to better advantage, singing her best and sweetest song "Since then I'm doomed from thee to sever:" her action was beautifully suited, and it being a country of emigrants, the effect upon her audience was really quite pitiable. Some young girls unaccustomed to stage representation sobbed, and cried aloud, and very few were there who could boast indifference. Our party tried to laugh off the feeling, but I never saw so ridiculous an attempt. The tears starting through the eyelids, notwithstanding all the exertions to absorb them, made us appear like the old simile of the sun, endeavouring to shine through a heavy shower, or rather like the very thing itself, which you may witness every day at schools, when boys receive punishments which, upon their return to their companions, they try to laugh at—yet, betray the full effect of, by an expression of feeling in which it is difficult to say whether the eye, lip, or chin cuts the most awkward figure.[104]

The writer offers compelling evidence of the emotional power of Fisher's performance. No one is immune: not the young girls new to the delights of the stage nor the company of seasoned theatregoers. Resist as they might, they are all reduced to schoolboys with tear-filled eyes and quivering lips. In this moment, the most transgressive aspects of Little Pickle's naughtiness are forgotten, replaced by collective sighs of (distinctly boyish) nostalgia. Such nostalgia could be especially powerful in colonial locales like Quebec City, where audiences looked for community in the performances of traveling performers like Fisher. In turn, this desire for communion profoundly influenced where and how girl actresses moved throughout the colonies, as the following Interlude shows.

INTERLUDE 3
DREW'S THREE SENTENCES

At the close of the second season at the "Warren"
we went to Halifax, Nova Scotia, to act with the Garrison
amateurs twice a week during the summer. We saw a good
deal of human nature there—all the petty strife of real
actors without their ability. However, it passed the
summer away very pleasantly.
—Mrs. John Drew

At an early stage of this project, I stumbled across three revealing sentences in the 1899 memoirs of Mrs. John Drew (née Louisa Lane), a doyenne of the nineteenth-century American stage.[1] I was fascinated by Drew's account of her experiences as a young girl when she and her family toured the West Indies and along the Atlantic coast in pursuit of theatrical glory. Flipping through the first few chapters of her "autobiographical sketch," I learned that her early years were filled with excitement, discovery, hardship, suffering, friendship, obligation, and boredom. Several pages after reading her account of her stepfather's death following the family's misguided trip to Jamaica, I came across her description of an 1833 visit to Halifax where she and her mother "act[ed] with the Garrison amateurs twice a week."[2] Fourteen years old at the time, Drew recalls that "we saw a good deal of human nature there [Halifax]—all the petty strife of real actors without their ability. However, it passed the summer away very pleasantly."[3] This description of a pleasant summer among "amateurs" surprised me, not only because I had assumed that garrison actors were exclusively male but also because I had read little about amateur actors performing alongside touring professionals in pre-Confederation Canada. How typical was this kind of engagement, I wondered? And what, if anything, did it have to do with her earlier experiences in the West Indies and United States? Had I completely misunderstood Halifax's contribution to the formation of transatlantic, hemispheric, and imperial theatre cultures? If so, was it just me or was my ignorance symptomatic of a broader cultural myopia?

Drew's three sentences about Halifax tripped me up and led me down a rabbit hole of historical (re)discovery that I retrace here. This act of tripping offers a prime example of what Terry Eagleton calls the "symptomatic point," an "apparently peripheral" word, image, passage, or other fragment in a text that catches the reader's attention and in so doing threatens to unravel "or dismantle the oppositions which govern the text as a whole."[4] It's not that Drew's memoir itself fell apart as I stumbled on her three sentences, but rather that the stumbling exposed lingering blind spots in my own thinking. Drew's three sentences complicated received histories about divisions between amateurs and professionals, men and women, and children and adults in 1830s Halifax, demonstrating that all participated in the formation of a distinctly transatlantic theatre culture. (Drew's name change poses a challenge for writing about her experiences as a girl. For clarity, I've opted to refer to her by her later professional/married name, Mrs. John Drew, which I truncate to Drew. I nevertheless recognize that this decision constitutes a partial erasure of Louisa Lane, the girl she once was.)

Let me start with three pesky questions that arise from Drew's account. If, as previous studies of garrison theatricals suggest, there was an "unwritten rule barring women from acting in garrison productions,"[5] what compelled Drew and her mother to play alongside them? And if women, and not just women but teenage *girls*, performed with the garrison troupe, why hadn't earlier historians acknowledged this anomaly—or had they? What led professional actresses like Drew and her mother to appear alongside the garrison amateurs in the first place?

I first understood Drew's reference to the garrison amateurs to mean that she had performed in a garrison theatrical—a fairly logical assumption, I think, given most historical treatments of garrison theatre. I remembered first reading about such entertainments in Eugene Benson and L. W. Conolly's *English-Canadian Theatre* as an undergraduate student so I returned to this source and other histories of garrison theatre to learn more. These texts reminded me that military officers garrisoned in Halifax, traveling on naval vessels, or stationed elsewhere frequently staged productions of popular British dramas to amuse themselves and strengthen ties with the local community.[6] Such productions served as important tools of empire, inviting male officers and their predominantly male audiences to affirm their connection to British culture and to consider themselves as part of a much larger "imagined community" of imperial theatregoers.[7] But where did girls like Drew and women like her mother fit into this narrative of homosocial imperial culture?

Help came from Alex Boutilier and his 2005 master's thesis, "The Citadel on Stage." Although Boutilier confirms that "female parts were always played by male officers," since Halifax society would have objected to the notion of women playing on stage, he acknowledges that "from time to time unmarried actresses from the United States would appear with professional troupes on the stages of Halifax."[8] Here was a significant piece of evidence. I realized that while women did not perform in garrison productions per se, they occasionally appeared alongside garrison actors *if* and when those men were needed to round out a professional company.[9] I came across further evidence of this practice in the online pages of the *Halifax Acadian Recorder*. For example, a June 1833 announcement for an upcoming production of *Paul Pry* and the farce *Soape Grace* informed readers that "The principal parts in both pieces by the Gentlemen Amateurs, of the Garrison, who have kindly consented to appear on the occasion."[10] This advertisement answered the question of the garrison amateurs—they had "kindly consented" to appear onstage with the professional company—but where was Mrs. John Drew (the former Louisa Lane) in all of this?

I turned to the *Oxford Companion to Canadian Theatre History* and to Patrick O'Neill's entry on Nova Scotia theatre. I noted his paragraph on Halifax's New Theatre, a dynamic performance space that welcomed numerous professionals onto its stage between 1829 and 1844, including William Rufus Blake, who performed for "two years ending in 1833."[11] I flipped to O'Neill's entry on Blake and retraced the steps that led the actor-manager-playwright to Halifax, discovering that he had "managed the opening seasons at Boston's Tremont Theatre in 1827 and the renovated Walnut Street Theatre in Philadelphia, before returning to Canada in 1831" to perform in Quebec.[12] O'Neill then mentions that Blake "later managed his own company of American actors at The [New] Theatre, Halifax, for which he produced and probably wrote *FITZALLAN*, the first play by a Canadian-born author produced in Canada."[13] This led me to ask whether Drew and her mother knew Blake from earlier contracts? Had they, for example, played at the Tremont Theatre or the Walnut Street Theatre under Blake's tenure as manager? I returned to my PDF of Mrs. John Drew's autobiography and typed in Blake's name. Bingo. There he was on page 66, identified as a member of the acting company at Boston's "Warren" Theatre.[14] I read on and realized that Drew had traveled to Halifax after her second season at the Warren when she was fourteen years old.[15] What Drew leaves out of her account, but which I'm now almost certain was the case, is that she and her mother traveled to Halifax at Blake's invitation for what would be his final season in the city. There, as members of Blake's professional acting company, they shared the stage with several garrison amateurs, and fourteen-year-old Drew observed "all the petty strife of real actors without their ability." Riddle solved.

Perhaps. But so what? At first glance, the story of Drew's visit to Halifax and her encounter with the garrison amateurs seems relatively insignificant, an interesting trivia item. On closer examination, however, Drew's recollections of Halifax pose key questions about the relationship between amateurs and professionals in colonial contexts that in turn might lead historians to rethink how they draw aesthetic, geographic, and temporal borders. Let's begin with Drew's own investment in professionalism.

Drew's brief but dismissive comments about the "Garrison amateurs" hint at ongoing tensions between "real" professional players and local performers in colonial Halifax. What is unclear is whether these comments represent *actual* tensions that Drew and her mother experienced in the 1830s or, rather (as I suspect), shifting attitudes toward professionalism in the 1890s when Drew wrote her memoirs. By the late nineteenth century, actors and actresses in the United States were finally gaining the respectability and social standing they had desired for decades. In an effort to perform their professional status, they established official clubs and associations, befriended society leaders, formalized actor training, and published articles and memoirs detailing the challenges of the acting life.[16] As one of the most widely respected actresses and theatre managers in nineteenth-century North America, Drew epitomized "professionalism." More than documenting her career, then, her memoir participated in a larger cultural project designed to secure a better social standing both for herself and for her fellow actors. Small wonder that she was so abrupt in her dismissal of the bumbling "Garrison amateurs."

Reading Drew's memoirs as a product of late nineteenth-century professionalism reveals new evidence about amateurs and professionals in colonial Halifax. For example, they show that William Rufus Blake's professional theatre company often performed with amateur actors out of necessity and that this mixing gave a girl like Drew a new perspective on "human nature" and the "personal strife" felt by these actors, as much as it informed her opinions of their acting ability. This account further complicates assumptions about the homosocial nature of garrison theatre, suggesting that the actors who performed in male-only garrison productions might have received training or drawn inspiration from the professional actresses with whom they occasionally performed. Intriguingly, a May 1833 review of Blake's production of *Fitzallan* concludes with the critic's hope that the professional company will continue to collaborate with the amateurs in staging Shakespeare, alluding to an earlier production of *Romeo and Juliet*.[17] This led me to wonder how frequently garrison actors played with Blake's company (among others) and whether such interactions influenced the amateurs' understanding of theatre. How "professional" were the garrison amateurs after all? Did their brief encounters with professional companies inspire dreams of becoming "real" actors? In what ways did the amateurs in turn shape touring actors' perceptions of local communities? What friendships, romantic liaisons, and other exchanges did this mixing of performers invite? Unfortunately, the scope of this project prevents me from pursuing these questions, but I'll leave the crumbs here and perhaps someone else might pick them up.

As I followed the clues left by Drew's three sentences, I found myself pulled back to earlier pages in her memoirs, where accounts of personal tragedy and forced mobility intermingled with character sketches of some of the era's most celebrated players. I realized that if I wanted to understand Drew's life touring along transatlantic and hemispheric theatre circuits, I had to pay closer attention to the experiences that had brought her to Halifax. In so doing, I also hoped to learn more about the colonial city's contribution to transatlantic and hemispheric theatre cultures. What follows then is a fairly typical biography of Drew's early years, but I recount it here as a way of getting at some of the complexities noted.

Drew was born into a theatrical family in 1820 in London and christened Louisa Lane. Her father, Thomas Frederick Lane, was "an actor of considerable provincial fame" and her mother, Eliza Lane (Trenter) was a "very pretty woman and a sweet singer of ballads."[18] Drew made her stage debut at twelve months of age, when her mother took her onstage to play the part of "crying baby."[19] Her earliest speaking roles at age five included the part of the "rightful heir" in the melodrama *Meg Murnock; or, the Hag of the Glen*, and the brother of Frankenstein in an adaptation of the Mary Shelley novel. Drew's graduation to speaking roles coincided with the death of her father, yet despite (or perhaps due to) this loss, mother and daughter continued to work in the theatre. When Drew was seven, John Hallam, the "accredited agent for Price & Simpson, of the old Park Theatre, New York," engaged mother and daughter to travel with him to North America along with other members of a newly formed acting company.[20] Drew recalls that the four-week journey onboard the packet ship *Britannia* was "exceptionally fine" and the company landed in New York in 1827, after which they traveled to Philadelphia for a stint at the Walnut Street Theatre.[21] During this period, the Lanes performed alongside and came to know most of the major US stars of the day, notably Junius Brutus Booth and Edwin Forrest.[22]

Not long after their arrival in the United States, Eliza Lane married her second husband, John Kinlock, "a stage manager, and a very capable actor and manager," who was always eager for new business opportunities.[23] Noting the popularity of juvenile actress Clara Fisher, who had herself just arrived in the United States, Kinlock decided to promote his stepdaughter as a second "Clara."[24] Drew made her debut as a "prodigy" in *The Spoiled Child* and "from this time to the latter part of 1830 [she] played as a star with varying success (financially)."[25] In late 1830, the entrepreneurial Kinlock, "bitten with the idea of management," partnered with a Mr. Jones with the goal of taking a company to Jamaica.[26] But his dream of theatrical gold quickly dissolved when the ship the company was traveling on struck a hidden rock, "a case of ignorant carelessness," Drew opines, "as it was a most beautiful moonlight night."[27] The boat was close enough to shore for the passengers to safely disembark but since they were nowhere near "any settlement," the com-

FIGURE 13. *Eight-year-old Louisa Lane as five characters in the protean farce*
Winning a Husband. *TC 58 olvwork10085, Houghton Library, Harvard University.*

pany had little choice but to "settl[e] ourselves to stay for some time," making strategic use of shingles and staves from the ship's deck.[28] For six weeks, the company remained in their makeshift shelter while the captain and another crew member traveled approximately forty miles to San Domingo for help. After a lengthy delay, the captain returned with help, and the company made its way to San Domingo and thence to Kingston, where they fulfilled their contract at the theatre, much to the delight of the local audience. But success was short-lived. Not long after arriving in Kingston, both John Kinlock and Drew's infant sibling contracted yellow fever and died. Drew's mother Eliza also became very ill, and the company retreated to Falmouth in the northern part of the island so she could recuperate. When "rumors of insurrection" in the region became "alarming,"[29] Drew and her mother returned with the company orchestra leader to Kingston, and from there continued to New York.

Though Drew says nothing further about the insurrection or its cause, she is clearly referencing one of many slave uprisings that rocked colonial Jamaica before the British abolished slavery in 1833—possibly the Baptist War (Great Jamaican Slave Revolt) of 1831–1832, a huge uprising that began on December 27, 1831, and continued for eleven days, drawing support from thousands of enslaved men and women before the British military forcefully intervened.[30] Here, memories of family trauma bump up against disturbing evidence of rebellion and colonial violence. Tellingly, Drew does not reflect on her own place within the broader colonial narrative or the eventual outcome of the "alarming" events. She remains safely in the realm of personal narrative and white privilege, avoiding political commentary and further reflection on the pain of anyone other than her own immediate family. Nevertheless the unacknowledged men and women who led the "insurrection" linger beneath the page, making their presence known in spite of Drew's careful omission.

Not long after their disastrous time in Jamaica, mother and daughter returned to the stage. For several years, they traveled along the Atlantic coast, performing with companies in New York, Boston, and Philadelphia out of financial need as well as (presumably) a desire for community and friendship. These needs and desires brought the two to Halifax in the summer of 1833 when William Rufus Blake hired them for his company.[31]

Drew's account of her extensive travels—from England to the United States, to Jamaica, back to the United States, and then to Nova Scotia—offers a reminder of how nineteenth-century theatre culture exceeded borders of colony and nation. This reminder in turn invites theatre historians to recognize Halifax's place within or along the evolving transatlantic touring circuit—to see it as one of a chain of colonial theatre cities that included Kingston (Jamaica), New Orleans, Charleston, Boston, and other major cities along the Atlantic coast.[32] Such recognition is important, not just for Canadian theatre history, but also for the history of transatlantic theatre culture more broadly. As historian Elizabeth Maddock Dillon observes of the Atlantic world, "the circuits of transportation that were in full-fledged operation in the eighteenth century were those developed and fine-tuned by the economic systems that sustained the colonial Atlantic world, linking Charleston, for instance, to London, the Caribbean, and Africa."[33] Yet despite her sophisticated mapping of Atlantic theatre cultures, Maddock Dillon overlooks Halifax, and indeed any British colony north of the US border. She is hardly alone in this geographic oversight; such definitions of the Atlantic world are symptomatic of larger gaps in hemispheric (and transatlantic) theatre studies.[34] Nevertheless, Maddock Dillon's framing of colonial cities as "nodes in a larger Atlantic/imperial network" presents new ways to think about theatre's role in Halifax *and* Halifax's place within the Anglo-American world.[35]

While previous research by O'Neill, Ed Mullaly, Denis Salter, and others has effectively traced the ebbs and flows of theatrical activity in Atlantic Canada,[36] new research might follow the hemispheric travels of those who visited Halifax, St. John's, and other Maritime towns and shed new light on the hemispheric circulation, transmission, and reception of performance repertoires, not to mention the intimate ties that united touring performers across vast distances.[37] Before becoming an actor-manager in Halifax and Boston, William Rufus Blake spent some time in Kingston, Jamaica, where he was called upon to "assume many of the leading roles" after a "senior actor died of yellow fever."[38] This detail raises the possibility that Blake felt a special affinity for Drew and her mother following their tragic losses in Jamaica and that his offer of employment was (in part) an act of empathy. A transatlantic focus might also account for the extensive travels of the garrison amateurs themselves. As hypermobile subjects, soldiers and touring performers experienced the British Empire in ways that settler-colonists did not.[39] Might this shared mobility have tightened emotional bonds or other forms of communal feeling between soldiers and touring actors? Or is the disdain evident in Drew's memoirs typical of the way professional actors looked upon members of the British military who tried their hand at acting?

While many of these questions remain unanswered (for now), the account of Drew's transatlantic travels invites historians to rethink how nations "claim" performers as *theirs*. Drew traveled extensively along the Atlantic coast throughout her early career yet she is frequently, if not exclusively, described as an American actress/manager.[40] What if instead historians identified her as an important player in the history of multiple nations, as someone who shaped these nations (in varying degrees) even as she moved through and across them? This acknowledgment might lead to investigations of why certain plays or actors have been deemed "Canadian" or "American" and thereby complicate dominant narratives of local, national, and transatlantic theatre cultures.

CHAPTER 3
Old and Young

ON "AGE-APPROPRIATE" ROLES FOR GIRLS

At Fisher, astonish'd the people all gaz'd
"'Twas wonderful" still they kept saying;
For my part, I own, I was not much amaz'd
At seeing a little girl playing.
— *"Impromptu on Miss Fisher" (1823)*

This anonymous poem invites readers of *The Mirror of Literature, Amusement, and Instruction* to reflect critically on their obsession with Clara Fisher. Everyone calls her astonishing and wonderful, the author observes, but to him she is no actress. He emphasizes Fisher's little girl-ness, effectively ignoring the longevity of her career (six years by 1823), and refuses to admit that her abilities might exceed those of the average girl. Instead, he attributes her success to her age and her gender; she charms because she is "a little girl playing," nothing more. Critics of child performers from Master Betty onward frequently called on the discourse of natural childishness to scold or tsk-tsk audience amazement, yet the timing of this poem is curious given the critical conversations that had encircled Fisher the previous year. By 1822 she had performed full-length and abbreviated versions of *Richard III* well over two hundred times, and her expanded repertoire included such diverse roles as the avaricious teacher Doctor Pangloss in *The Heir at Law*, the scheming Crack in *Turnpike Gate*, Little Pickle in *The Spoiled Child*, and all six characters of varying ages and nationalities in the farcical afterpiece *The Actress of All Work*.[1] Critics continued to laud her as wonderful, astonishing, surprising, and amazing, but in 1822 the language changed as some critics began to express discomfort watching the now-eleven-year-old Fisher perform.

In September 1822, a critic for *The Drama; or Theatrical Pocket Magazine* was one of the first to share reservations about the repertoire Fisher exhibited during her summer engagement at the English Opera House.[2] For him, the "vast difference of age between herself and the parts assumed ... frequently destroys the illusions of her talent."[3] The problem was not that Fisher was incapable of tackling such diverse characters. Assessed solely on the basis of her years, *The Drama* critic admitted that she was "most assuredly beyond all competition," a "brilliant little creature," and "a clever actress" capable of giving "extraordinary performances" that placed her among the professions greatest talents.[4] The critic for the *Theatrical Examiner* agreed, commenting that her performance of Doctor Pangloss was "fully equal to that which we are now entitled to expect from her."[5] The problem was one of decorum. For all Fisher's abilities, the *Theatrical Examiner* averred, "we cannot bring ourselves to dilate upon a representation so *outré* and ludicrous. ... We wonder, and must wonder, for the child extorts it, by her very astonishing aptitude; but here our pleasure ends."[6] The question is why. Why did critics who had been writing for years about Fisher's "astonishing" talent suddenly feel uncomfortable watching her perform? What prevented them from taking pleasure in her impersonations of eccentric male characters like Doctor Pangloss and Crack? The most obvious answer is age ... and the unsettling experience of watching a maturing girl offer travestied interpretations of roles originally written for men.

This chapter explores the cultural anxieties and shifting perspectives that fueled the critiques of Fisher and ultimately led Drury Lane's manager Robert William Elliston to contract her to play "Children's Characters only" for the forthcoming 1822–1823 season. More than an attempt to placate the critics, this micro-event can be understood as a response to growing demand for idealized representations of children in visual art, literature, and other cultural arenas. Images of beautiful boys and girls in natural settings, isolated from the struggle, hardship, and cruelty of adult life, enjoyed incredible popularity in Britain, Europe, and North America for most of the nineteenth century, thanks in no small part to developments in the mass production of inexpensive prints and the circulation of illustrated newspapers and periodicals.[7]

FIGURE 14. *Clara Fisher as Madame Josephine in*
The Actress of All Work, *print published by T. & I. Elvey, London, 1822,*
Harry Beard Collection. © *Victoria & Albert Museum, London.*

The circulation of these images also coincided with increased efforts to
visibly gender boys and girls before the onset of puberty.

The new custom-created roles that Elliston commissioned for Fisher
were not only "age appropriate" but also foregrounded her status *as a
girl*.[8] Yet the most successful of these plays, John Poole's *Old and Young:
Or, the Four Mowbrays*, can also be read as a compelling counter-
commentary on Romantic notions of childhood, the naturalization of
gender binaries, and the performativity of age. "As with gender," Valerie
Barnes Lipscomb and Leni Marshall write, "age may be socially constructed and performative, but that performativity is in tension with
the undeniable ongoing change of the body as it physically ages. With

each performative iteration, a person's age changes ever so slightly, and the performance must accommodate the shift."[9] In other words, how a body performs age changes over time, as does the way others perceive that body as aged, which can necessitate further adjustments in appearance or behavior. Or, in the case with Clara Fisher, the introduction of new repertoire simultaneously accentuated her identity as a girl and challenged assumptions about the differences between girls and boys.

This chapter argues that *Old and Young* allowed Fisher to address anxieties about her maturing female body by performing *as a girl*, without sacrificing her talent for cross-dressing. In so doing, she skillfully overturned stereotypes of age and gender; encouraged audiences to rethink their definitions of girlhood and boyhood; and paved the way for later generations of child performers—boys and girls—to embody the contradictions and fluidity of identity in a charming, nonthreatening way.

The Trouble with Travesty

It is perhaps unsurprising that the greatest source of anxiety for Fisher's critics was her skillful portrayal of travesty roles. As the previous chapter outlined, actresses who ventured into the male repertoire tended to ruffle more feathers than actresses who performed breeches roles wherein a female character compelled by love or intrigue dresses (temporarily) as a man before resuming her feminine clothing and "proper" gender. For the travesty actress, there is no reassurance of a gender return; she remains in character and male garb for the duration of the play. This, it would seem, was part of the problem with Clara Fisher.

By 1822, Fisher was eleven years old and no longer the petite little girl who had burst onto the Drury Lane as Lord Flimnap five years before. The previous September a writer for the *British Stage and Literary Cabinet* had observed that she was "shoot[ing] up apace towards woman's stature,"[10] a euphemistic statement hinting that the actress's body was becoming legible as a *female* body. In fact, a *Drama* critic whispered, rumor had it that the girl was "considerably older in reality than appearance" and that her "friends" deliberately used the "artifices of dress" to make her look even younger than her biological age. While I have found no further evidence to corroborate this claim,[11] it seems possible that what made the critics anxious about Fisher's "*outré* and ludicrous" roles was the *visibility* of her physical maturation. Tellingly, the *Theatrical Examiner* critic concludes his review with the hope that the "little girl would make haste to grow tall, and fall into that line of spirited female gentility, for which we think nature has more particularly designed her."[12] What this critic avoids saying is that the girl's "age transvestism"—meaning her performance of older male characters—is unnatural and unnerving because it is *out of line* with models of female gentility. It is not just Fisher's age per se but her "in-betweenness" (what we would today describe as her "tween" status) that stalls his enjoyment of her performance.[13] Fisher's skillful portrayal of adult male characters wasn't a problem when she was a child—but now that she was nearing puberty and not yet aligned with the scripts, gestures, and costumes of femininity, her performance of masculinity was deeply troubling to those around her.[14]

The *Drama* critic likewise found Fisher's repertoire jarring and distasteful. For him, though, the primary issue was one of verisimilitude: "The distinction between childhood and youth is much more strongly defined than that between youth and age."[15] It was one thing for Edmund Kean at the age of fifty-five to play Hamlet, quite another for a child of ten or eleven to play the Danish prince: "the voice, the form, the features, are all too powerfully opposed to such an occasion."[16] Again, the problem is not that Fisher lacks the skill or intelligence to play Hamlet, but that her child's body and voice prevent *the critic* from accepting her in that role. Ironically, it is the "very perfection" of her acting that amplifies the gap between her physical appearance as a preadolescent girl and the adult roles she portrays: "the more correctly she plays such characters as *Crack* [in *Turnpike Gate*], the more we are struck by the violent discord of the assumed part with the tones and figure of the child."[17] It is only time that will "give a *vrai-semblance* to the conception and execution of [her] talent," the critic concludes.[18] In the meantime, he hopes that she will find roles more suited to her age and thereby avoid acts of "violent discord."

I want to return to the *Drama* critic's observation that "the distinction between childhood and youth is much more strongly defined than that between youth and age," because it offers insight into early nineteenth-century conceptions of childhood as a life stage, for both boys and girls. As Dennis Denisoff has shown, while the "age demarcating childhood from later life was not stable" and hinged on a range of factors, not least of which were an individual's class, region, and gender, "there remained a relatively persistent view throughout the nineteenth century that a person's early years were the most formative."[19] This view owed much to the teachings of Jean-Jacques Rousseau, as discussed in the previous chapter, as well as to the ruminations of Romantic poets like William Wordsworth and William Blake, who depicted children as pure and natural beings "trailing clouds of glory."

British painters likewise shaped late eighteenth- and nineteenth-century conceptions of childhood as a period of sweet innocence, introducing "the vision of a disembodied childhood, a cute childhood, a miniaturized childhood."[20] Typical examples include Joshua Reynolds's hugely successful painting *The Age of Innocence* (1777–1778), which depicts a calm, beautiful girl with glowing white skin seated against a natural backdrop, and Thomas Gainsborough's *Blue Boy* (1779), which celebrates the charm and insouciance of apple-cheeked boyhood. By the end of the nineteenth century, *Blue Boy* was "the single most popular image of childhood," Anne Higonnet observes, thanks to the mass production of inexpensive prints, which middle-class families purchased for their homes.[21] So dominant was the *Blue Boy* image of childhood that mothers continued to dress their sons in his image late into the nineteenth century.[22]

Blue Boy's popularity offers evidence of the tendency to equate childhood with boyhood and to treat girls differently than their male counterparts. Whereas most boys in middle-class and elite families received a formal education with an emphasis on science, mathematics, language, and political economy, girls learned art, music, sewing, and other domestic skills in anticipation of the day when they would run their own households. While boys learned to value their intelligence and navigate the complexities of public life, girls learned to value their ability to care for others, to cultivate good manners and a pleasant physical appearance. For Mary Wollstonecraft, the limitations of female education stood as one of the greatest impediments to the emancipation of women. She lamented that girls were not taught in the same way as boys and so never fully developed the ability to think and act independently of men. "It is a farce to call any being virtuous whose virtues do not result from the exercise of its own reason," Wollstonecraft declared in 1792. "This was Rousseau's opinion respecting men: I extend it to women."[23] Despite Wollstonecraft's powerful call, most parents continued to treat their daughters as intellectually inferior to their sons, to whom they granted greater opportunities for personal growth and self-discovery.

Artists further emphasized gender binaries in their depictions of children. As Higonnet observes, "Boys, especially at play, were represented learning to control the world around them," she writes, "while girls were represented more passively, as the objects of admiring adult gazes."[24] Sara Holdsworth and Joan Crossley concur, going so far as to suggest that the "imagery of desirable behavior for young girls is remarkably unchanging in paintings from seventeenth century to the mid-twentieth century."[25] Early nineteenth-century American artists mirrored their British counterparts, juxtaposing images of young girls picking flowers, dressing up, or undertaking domestic tasks with "pictures of boys shown out and about sampling a variety of occupations— on the decks of seagoing ships, behind grocery store counters, stalking prairie game, and starting out in the newspaper trade."[26] Such images equated girls with stability, reliability, and stasis, while celebrating the mutability, dynamism, and freedom of boys.[27]

Given the popularity and influence of such imagery, it is hardly surprising that Clara Fisher's portrayal of raving kings, scheming merchants, and working-class blokes struck the *Drama* critic as both exhilarating and troubling. Although clearly a girl herself, Fisher projected an image at odds with the sweet, innocent "child of nature" idealized by Romantic artists and writers. Critics also seem to have been alarmed by Fisher's status as a child prodigy, as evidenced by her uncanny ability to "posses[s] a thorough idea of the humour and nature of whatever part she assumes."[28] Despite celebrating children's delightful precocity, Romantic authors tended to treat child prodigies as strange and sad creatures who had been robbed of the natural child's innocence and therefore deserved pity.[29] The exception was the child who appeared convincingly childlike in the midst of their prodigious displays.[30] In sum, Romantic observers were willing to accept certain displays of uncommon ability as long as the prodigy behaved in an "age-appropriate" manner in other contexts. The *Drama* critic's anxious analysis of Clara Fisher suggests that he shared this view. The issue with Fisher, he implies, is that she is *too good* at playing adult roles, such that she appears strange and almost freakish. Although possessing the biological traits of a young girl—voice, facial features, physical size and characteristics—

her technical skill and the ease with which she embodies adult characters leave spectators bewildered. A writer for the *Literary Gazette* went even further, declaring that he looked at Fisher as he "would at a flea in a chariot team, or a learned lobster, or the automaton chessplayer, wondering how the deuce the thing could be taught." The problem is not simply that she is a curiosity or a freak of nature but that her performances "destro[y] all the illusion of the drama—and not only of the drama in which she takes part, but of the drama generally, for whenever we see a clever actor afterward, the impression is strong upon our minds, 'This is trick and not intellect, mere traditional imitativeness and not original talent.'"[31] In other words, Fisher's prodigious abilities threatened to destabilize the acting profession by exposing the artifice of the actor's craft.

Though Fisher was the focus of their criticism, most writers acknowledged that the ultimate responsibility for the girl's repertoire lay with the adult managers who surrounded her. Writing in 1823, John Finlay empathized with the girl and the roles she was obliged to play:

> It is a pity, and therefore can give pleasure to no one, to see a highly gifted being like this harassed unnecessarily, or burlesqued or caricatured by her own talents; it is a pity that exertions so rare should not be placed in lights the most advantageous; that a glass so well formed to reflect the beauties, should be charged with the representation of the most revolting characters of the drama. The bravo's mustachio, the old man's wig, the paunch of Falstaff, the hunch back of Gloster, the sabre, helmit [*sic*] and coat of mail, are not of the costume of Clara Fisher. Why should her managers make her travestie [*sic*] herself? the cast of her characters should be in reference to her own character; her large stock of means to instruct and amuse should be in no respect mismanaged, for they deserve the best management.[32]

Finlay charges Fisher's managers with failing to recognize the girl's talent and requiring her to wear costumes that are distinctly *unlike* her. Tellingly, the objects he finds most troubling are those associated with masculinity—the mustache, the wig, the paunch, the saber, the helmet, and the coat of mail. These objects mar the critic's enjoyment of Fisher's performance because they conceal the young girl's beauty and instead transform her into "the most revolting characters of the drama." Finlay fails to consider that Fisher may have enjoyed disguising herself with an "old man's wig" or "coat of mail" or delighted in playing adult male characters who were nothing like her.

Writing decades later, Fisher claims that when she was a young girl she "cared nothing for the papers" and "heard little or nothing of their praise or blame." What mattered most was her parents' opinion, and that of her sister Jane. She was nevertheless aware of the "extravagant praise" that greeted her performances and admits that it "spoiled" her somewhat. Fisher describes hearing from a fellow Drury Lane company member that "a paper had spoken harshly to my playing parts like *Sir Peter Teazle* and *Dr. Pangloss* and *Dr. Ollapod*." To this she retorted "rather saucily for a twelve-year-old child: Well, they don't know what they're talking about!"[33] But Drury Lane's manager Robert Elliston did not dismiss the critics' concerns so quickly; instead, he proposed a solution.

New Repertoire: "Children's Characters Only"

On September 10, 1822, the *Kaleidoscope; or Literary and Scientific Mirror* announced that Fisher had just "obtained an engagement at Drury-lane, on the very extraordinary terms of 500 pounds and a half-benefit (about £200 or £300 more) for 4 months' performances annually. This engagement is for three years."[34] The length of Robert Elliston's commitment to Fisher was notable, as was the promised salary, especially for a child. What compelled the actor-manager to make such an arrangement? Finally, in late November, a playbill revealed more details about Fisher's forthcoming appearance: "Miss Clara Fisher (who is engaged for Children's Characters only) will make her first appearance in the course of a few days, in the part of Little Pickle, in THE SPOIL'D CHILD."[35] The notice seems fairly straightforward: it informs audiences of Fisher's performance as Little Pickle and further assures them that she will be playing a range of children's roles.[36] What the notice does not mention is that her forthcoming engagement would mark her triumphant return to Drury Lane after six years. The notice is likewise silent on the adult male roles that had become something of Fisher's hallmark since her last appearance there.

By publicly declaring the terms of Fisher's contract, Elliston sent a clear message to the critics who had agonized about the girl's "inappro-

priate" repertoire.[37] There would be no more juvenile Richards and Pan-
glosses and Shylocks at Drury Lane. Of course, Elliston had more than
the critics to manage. In restricting Fisher to children's roles, he also
signaled a clear demarcation between his adult company and his child
star.[38] As Fisher later recalled, the decision for her to play *The Spoiled
Child* and *Old and Young* "as afterpieces, only every other night" was
informed by a kind of benevolent paternalism, in that Elliston wanted
to prevent her from being "tired out by performing more than three
or four times a week."[39] Though I do not doubt that Fisher's health
was a factor, I expect that concern about wavering audience tastes, not
to mention the patience of his adult company, informed Elliston's repertorial and scheduling decisions. By limiting Fisher's appearances to
three or four times a week, Elliston protected her from overexposure,
while tapping into the growing characterization of children as innocent, dependent beings in need of adult support—emotional, physical,
financial, and otherwise.[40] In so doing, he addressed critics' fears about
her strangeness as a prodigy and instead emphasized the girl's youth,
vulnerability, and dependency. First, though, he had to find suitable
plays that also accentuated her talent.

When Elliston signed Fisher to a three-year contract, he committed
to developing her repertoire. This was no small gesture. If managers
had learned anything from Bettymania, it was that promising child performers rarely developed into excellent adult actors. "It is generally the
case, that the children who have been distinguished for their dramatic
precocity have not improved as they grew up," the *Literary Chronicle
and Weekly Review* observed in May 1822. In fact, most prodigies "de-
clined and s[a]nk into the rank of ordinary performers."[41] But Clara
Fisher was different.

In the summer and fall of 1822, Elliston commissioned John Poole
and George Colman to write new plays "for the special purpose of
bringing into operation the versatility of Miss Clara Fisher."[42] Both
men were experienced comic writers who understood how to accentu-
ate individual abilities. Poole was known as a writer of farce and Shakespearean travesties, who achieved his greatest success with *Paul Pry*
(1825). Colman was a widely respected writer of comedies, operas, and
various adaptations of French plays and farces, among them *Heir at
Law* and *The Actress of All Work*, both of which had been part of Fisher's
repertoire at the English Opera House. Writing a play for a young girl

should have been an easy commission for both men, but Colman appears to have balked at the prospect of having his name publicly associated with Fisher's. In December 1822 when rumors that he had been hired to write one or more pieces for Fisher began circulating, the playwright publicly denied that he had any involvement with her. "She is, I am told, a very clever little child, but I neither have written, nor INTEND to write, any thing for this precocious little lady," he declared in a letter sent to the London papers.[43] This was a bluff: Colman's play *Stella and Leatherlungs; or, the Star and the Stroller* premiered in October 1823 with Clara Fisher in the starring role. It ran for a single performance and then seems to have disappeared from Drury Lane altogether.

The *Stella and Leatherlungs* debacle exposes some of the challenges Elliston encountered while developing a repertoire for Fisher. Colman's play failed for several reasons, not least of which was its "uninviting" name and the playwright's inability (or unwillingness) to find a creative solution to the task Elliston had set for him. Rather than "bringing into operation the versatility" of the girl actress, Colman seems to have used *Stella and Leatherlungs* to debate the merits of child performers more broadly. Set in "the Green Room, then the Stage, of a Theatre, in a Country Town," the play opens with a manager in crisis. He has sold all the boxes in his theatre for the final night of the season but his actors are deserting him because they have just learned that he has contracted "a little Luminary newly from Nurse—scarcely out of her milking way,—and posted about the Town in letters larger than herself."[44] The leader of the actors' uprising, a man named Leatherlungs, rails against the emerging star system, which displaces local talent for the novelty of the latest innovation from London. When the manager, Mr. Barebench, declares that the "Little Star is a Comet," Leatherlungs ruefully notes that the company has no interest in "hold[ing] up her tail." Ultimately, Barebench convinces Leatherlungs to serve as a "second" to the "little Heroine" by enjoining him to "put your patriotism, with this [bank] note, into your pocket," and to "leave your brother conspirators to shift for themselves." A Call Boy, played by Fisher, briefly enters to announce the arrival of the star, and Barebench departs to greet her, leaving Leatherlungs alone on the stage to sing a satirical song about his life as a player. He exits and the play concludes with "a few imitations with Clara Fisher."[45] And that is it.

It is difficult to read *Stella and Leatherlungs* as anything but a thinly veiled attack on Fisher and the phenomenon of the child star. Colman's resentment and anger—presumably with Elliston, Fisher, and his own financial situation—leap from the page. The playwright shows no interest in developing a substantial character for Fisher to play—he gives her two lines to speak as the Call Boy. Instead, he directs audience sympathy toward the frustrated Leatherlungs (an obvious avatar for the playwright), who only yields to Barebench's pleas to perform with the "star" when promised a considerable sum of money. The play concludes with Fisher's imitations and offers no opportunity for the actress to appear as herself. Intriguingly, the manuscript submitted to the Lord Chamberlain's office makes no reference to specific imitations, although a subsequent review in the *New Monthly* names Shylock, Pangloss, Falstaff, and Young Norval as some of the characters presented.[46] This is a curious list given Elliston's insistence on "children's roles." However, as the *New Monthly* critic explained, "the young lady did not at all act the parts which are so unsuitable to her sex and age, but merely declaimed the speeches, as any forward child would do who had been well instructed."[47] Here the critic returns to the question of suitability according to gender and age and reassures readers that Fisher did not step beyond the bounds of "children's roles." Instead of embodying Shylock, Pangloss, Falstaff, and Young Norval, she stuck with declamation, maintaining an appropriate child-like distance from such "unsuitable roles" for girls.

Stella and Leatherlungs offers no further opportunities for Fisher to demonstrate her range, a less-than-subtle clue that Colman wanted the play and the actress to fail. Elliston confirms as much in his memoirs, when he writes that "the affair [i.e., the play] was altogether unworthy [of] George Colman, and was rendered still more discreditable to him, as he had only a short time before disclaimed all intention of writing for 'the precocious little lady.'"[48] *Stella and Leatherlungs* retreated quickly from the Drury Lane stage with most critics echoing Elliston's assessment.[49] "They say the piece is Colman's," a writer noted in the pages of *Blackwood's Edinburgh Magazine*. "A dull affair, whoever may be the author."[50] Audiences agreed, rejecting Colman's "attempt to foist the ridiculous upon them."[51]

Old and Young succeeds where *Stella and Leatherlungs* fails. Adapted by John Poole from one of French playwright Eugène Scribe's many works,[52] the play opens with "Old Wilton," a "Bachelor of Sixty," awaiting the arrival of his nephew Charles Mowbray and his family of nine boys and one girl, none of whom he has met. Regretting his childless life, Old Wilton plans to leave his inheritance to the family and invite them to live with him on his estate in Richmond. What he doesn't know is that Mowbray has no sons, only a young daughter named Matilda. When Mowbray and Matilda arrive at Old Wilton's home, the girl plots to convince her uncle that she is a worthy heir. With the help of his servants, Peter and Peggy, Matilda disguises herself as three of the nine irksome Mowbray brothers, each with distinct behavioral traits that disrupt their uncle's carefully curated life. With these character creations, Matilda embodies extremes of boyish masculinity—aggression, militarism, gluttony, pomposity—offering Old Wilton an all-too-real glimpse of the fantasy family he envisions. By the end of the play, the man is so exhausted from his interactions with the Mowbray boys that he is relieved to learn that it has all been an elaborate hoax.

Old and Young is tailormade to Fisher's abilities. It delights in her youth and versatility, most notably her comic timing, facility with language, and ability to portray numerous character types in rapid succession, all without stepping beyond the bounds of age. But more than this, the play celebrates Fisher's abilities *as a girl*, even as it critiques stereotypes of gender and age.[53] As Aparna Gollapudi notes, in the eighteenth century "a girl acting" often involved watching a girl play a *boy* since there were relatively few opportunities for girls to act *as girls* onstage: a girl acting was quite different from a girl acting as a girl.[54] The critical anxiety surrounding Clara Fisher's age transvestism in the early 1820s fundamentally changed this equation by creating a demand for plays that allowed girls to play girls. *Old and Young* met this demand without (entirely) abandoning the fun and subversive potential of cross-gender casting; unlike *Stella and Leatherlungs* it did so without offending audience sensibilities.

Old and Young is best described as a "protean farce," a genre that emerged in the early nineteenth century to demonstrate a performer's acting range. As theatre historian Jane R. Goodall describes it, protean farce is "characterized by a plot in which multiple-identity switches showcased the capacity of the leading performers to cross the categories of gender, race, nationality, age and class."[55] The celebrated actor and solo performer Charles Mathews popularized the genre in 1817 with George Colman's *The Actor of All Work*, in which he portrayed seven wildly different roles in the span of fifteen to twenty minutes. (Colman's previous success with the genre makes his refusal to write a compelling play for Fisher even more curious.) Not to be outdone, in 1819 the actress Mrs. Edwin introduced *The Actress of All Work*, playing "a country gawkey, a first rate London actress, a deaf old maid of 80, a literary fop, and a French dramatical lady" and "herself," all in a bid (within the metatheatrical frame of the piece) to convince a "country manager," the "father of her lover," to hire her for his company.[56] Other protean farces soon followed, often built around complicated love plots in which a doubtful woman tests her lover's loyalty by appearing before him in multiple guises representing a range of female types.[57] Originally written for adult actresses, these plays eventually crossed over into girl actresses' repertoires as well, delighting audiences on both sides of the Atlantic. For example, as an eight-year-old, Louisa Lane performed five different characters in the farce *Twelve O'Clock Precisely*.[58] Caroline (Caddy) Fox (Caroline Howard) did likewise in 1844 at the age of fourteen with *Winning a Husband; Or, Seven's the Main*, playing roles ranging from Jenny Transit, "a young lady who exemplifies the mutability of human affairs," and the literary spinster Miss Clementina Cornelia Clappergo to the pork butcher's widow Mrs. Deborah Griskin and Ensign O'Transit, "Of the Kilkenny Flamers."[59] Such roles honed girls' comic timing and emotional range, preparing them to assume more substantial parts as they matured.

The popularity of the protean farce for girls and women gains political significance when we consider the still-dominant casting practices of the early nineteenth century, whereby most performers specialized in character types, or "lines of business." The logic of the time held that some actors were naturally predisposed toward certain character types and should therefore refrain from playing outside that range. Actors became known professionally through the roles they played, so much so that by the beginning of the nineteenth century, most professional companies included a male juvenile lead, female juvenile lead (or ingénue), a high tragedian, low comedian, old man, old woman, and various other specialized actors depending on the size and needs of the company.[60] This suturing of type to actor posed a major challenge to emerging talent, many of whom were compelled to wait in the wings (often quite literally) until a vacancy in the company opened up. Within this ecosystem of hyper-specialization, protean farces pushed against the narrow parameters of traditional casting, inviting actors and actresses to stretch themselves and their repertoire by experimenting with behavior that defied norms of gender, class, and nationality.[61] As exercises in flexibility, if not quite plasticity, protean farces also encouraged performers, especially women (and girls), to model new ways of acting *off* stage. Writes Jane Goodall in her study of the genre, "actresses began to freely display qualities of volatility, exhibitionism and knowing humour that made women dangerous as social adventurers capable of traversing the divisions of the class system."[62] It is no coincidence that Jenny Transit, the heroine of *Winning a Husband; Or Seven's the Main*, is described as "a young lady who exemplifies the mutability of human affairs."[63] More than provoking laughter, protean farces "call[ed] into question the extent to which physical characteristics were really the determining factors in human life"[64] and invited performers to delight in their plasticity. In other words, by playing with types, actresses also learned to critique these types and question the hierarchies that defined the industry.

The protean farce was ideally suited to Clara Fisher's abilities. In 1821, a year before her Drury Lane contract, she introduced into her repertoire *The Actress of All Work*, through which she ably demonstrated her "quick intelligence, a bounding hilarity of voice and manner, and a prodigality of animal spirits."[65] The critic for the *Literary Chronicle and Weekly Review* enthused about her ability to play six characters "varying from gawkish childhood to decrepid [*sic*] old age ... with a truth and nature which was astonishing."[66] But not all critics were as impressed with Fisher's performance. Dismissing her as a "little monster," the critic for the *London Magazine* declared that those who saw "her performance of the *Country Girl* in *The Actress of All Work*, will find that it is not (what it ought to be) a delineation of bashful hoydenry, but of childish awkwardness; not the grown-up ignorance of a rustic maiden, but the *apple-eating* simplicity of a child."[67] For this critic, the problem wasn't the play but the girl playing it. She was too young, too awkward, too simple, too much of a *girl* to convincingly portray women of varying ages and life experiences.

By adopting the form but not the full character ranges of the protean farce, *Old and Young* offered the perfect answer to such gripes — simultaneously addressing concerns about the "appropriateness" of a girl playing adult male roles, while showcasing Fisher's considerable singing, dancing, and acting talents.[68] The critics responded with praise and enthusiasm. Following the play's November 30, 1822, opening, the *Mirror of the Stage* declared that it was "one of the most amusing pieces the stage has produced for a long time" and praised Fisher for "the ease with which she changed her manner and voice.... We were delighted beyond expression at her performance."[69] The *Literary Gazette* concurred, proclaiming that *Old and Young* "afforded by far the best opportunity we have seen for the display of Miss Clara Fisher's extraordinary talents," and congratulating the Drury Lane management for its good taste and judgment in engaging Fisher for "child's parts."[70] The piece was so delightful, in fact, that it was enough to (briefly) "reconcile" the *Literary Gazette* critic "to Lilliputian prodigies." Audiences seem to have felt much the same way. On December 7, 1822, a playbill announced that Fisher would perform the play "Three Nights in each Week till further Notice." By the end of December, she had performed *Old and Young* thirteen times and would go on to appear as the Four Mowbrays another twelve times before the end of the season in May 1823.[71]

For her part, Fisher seems to have accepted the Drury Lane arrangement with relief. Looking back from late adulthood, she claims that she "always preferred plays suited to my age" and didn't especially enjoy playing "the eccentric parts, as I called them, —*Shylock, Richard, Sir Peter Teazle, Goldfinch,*—and men's characters generally ... although of course, they drew best, and were a great curiosity to the audiences, who seemed to think a child's performance of such characters a wonderful thing."[72] Reflecting on the critics who worried about her portrayal of such roles, Fisher acknowledges that the "paper or magazine was right" and that her managers and father were most interested in showcasing her "wonderful memory and a facility for study" without (necessarily) taking her age or gender into consideration. Her own preference, she confesses, was for "the children's parts, the *Mowbrays*, and *Little Pickle*, and the really juvenile parts more suited to my years."[73] Such a confession must, of course, be taken with a grain of salt, recognizing that an elderly actress writing in the late 1890s might well have had a reason for distancing herself from her childhood dalliances into the repertoire of men and siding with the critics (as suggested in the previous interlude). Intriguingly, Fisher echoes John Finlay in attributing her continued performance of "eccentric" men's characters to audience tastes and, by extension, managerial preferences. And just as Finlay argued that "the cast of her characters should be in reference to her own character," Fisher asserts that her "favorites" were the plays that allowed her to share her talents in an age-appropriate way.[74]

Old and Young certainly fit this bill. However, as the following section details, what is most fascinating about the play is its subversive commentary on the performativity of gender and age.

Old and Young—Executing Stereotypes and Remaking Familial Bonds

Like *The Spoiled Child*, *Old and Young* demonstrates that girl actresses were essential for the theatrical representation of naughty boyishness. So too the play stages a kind of reverse pedagogy in which older adult characters rethink their perspective on age and gender through the comical instruction of a cunning child. Where *Old and Young* pushes the lessons of *The Spoiled Child* further is in its representation of girlhood. Unlike Maria Pickle, who has relatively few opportunities to demonstrate her capacity for clever scheming, Matilda drives the action of *Old and Young*, teaching Old Wilton the value of girls by overturning his perception of boys. It is not simply that Old Wilton cannot imagine life with a girl but rather that girls do not exist in his narrow vision of the future. Matilda destroys this false dream of homosocial tranquility through her impersonation of the three Mowbray boys, offering in exchange companionship and support. *Old and Young* is significant in the way it allows a girl actress to appear onstage *as a girl*.

But more than this, *Old and Young* enlists the plasticity of the girl actress to query emerging binaries of age and gender, "executing" stereotypes by demonstrating how Romantic notions of childhood place greater restrictions on girls' behavior, activity, and physical appearance. As Brian Eugenio Hererra articulates, "executing the stereotype" refers to situations "wherein the effective enactment of a particular stereotype (or constellation of stereotypes) eviscerates the apparatus of the stereotype's construction, thereby revealing how the charismatic familiarity of the stereotype works in service of a particular cultural mind-set."[75] Here we might recall Catherine Malabou's remarks on the destructive potential of plasticity—"the annihilation of all form (explosion)."[76] *Old and Young* simultaneously pulls on stereotypes of gender and age in order to explore, critique, and ultimately turn them on their head. Much of the play's humor derives from the interactions between the stereotypically slow, weak, balding Old Wilton and the rambunctious, physically active, young Mowbrays. This juxtaposition of old and young (made obvious in the play's title) invites audiences to view age as both a state of mind and a physical state and to see the boundaries between children and adults as porous and flexible.[77] *Old and Young* executes stereotypes of aging as a process of inevitable loss, decline, and loneliness by celebrating the bonds between old and young.

Though readers today might balk at the Mowbrays' treatment of Old Wilton, Fisher's audiences seem to have enjoyed watching the old man get his comeuppance at the hands of a young girl and her fictional brothers. As the pseudonymous D——G cheekily observed in an introductory note to the 1831 edition: "'Tis good sport to play off the young against the old,—to make age ridiculous, and its whims and infirmities a matter of mirth. We have only to give an old gentleman the gout, invest him with certain odd peculiarities, and send him a youthful tormentor, and the farce is done. The more he hobbles, the more we laugh; every twinge produces a roar; and, if he be fairly driven crazy, our satisfaction is complete."[78] While it is difficult to ignore the ageism that underpins D——G's note, his comments offer a revealing glimpse of the physical and behavioral characteristics of aging that would have been familiar to early nineteenth-century audiences. Old Wilton is physically weak and given to "odd peculiarities." His ailments include hearing loss, nearsightedness, bad teeth, and, perhaps most significantly, gout, a disease associated with the rich and indolent and frequently used by eighteenth- and nineteenth-century writers as an "image of excess and corruption."[79] Although he shows few signs of moral corruption, Old Wilton is prone to behavioral extremes, evidenced by his meticulous arrangement of furniture; his negative attitude toward his nephew's marriage; the ritualistic aspect of his relationship with the unmarried (and presumably pining) Miss Julia Somers, who sends him a partridge pie each year in exchange for his gift of lamb's wool and Welsh flannel; and his insistence that he will only leave his fortune to the Mowbray family if all ten children come to live with him. Doddery, intransigent, and in a state of physical deterioration, Old Wilton is a source of ridicule and Matilda's ultimate foil *because* of his age.

In many ways, *Old and Young*'s representation of Old Wilton's weakened state is consistent with the "decline narrative" of aging, the belief that "we reach the peak of our physical, emotional, and intellectual development sometime in young adulthood," and that everything that follows is one long decline with our "actions ... simply echoes of our former selves."[80] Images of failing and falling are especially potent within decline narratives. As Andrea Charise observes, "Decline ideology is quite literally the fear of falling: the belief that one will fall—chronologically, physically, perhaps even morally—with all that implies of personal failure."[81] Old Wilton's first entrance, "walking with a crutch-stick, and leaning on the arm of a servant," emphasizes his weakness and vulnerability, and also prepares the audience for a literal and figurative fall of some kind. And yet, while *Old and Young* flirts with the decline narrative, Matilda's clever reeducation of Old Wilton challenges this narrow view of aging. While seemingly set in his ways, Old Wilton learns to think and act differently thanks to his interactions with the young Mowbrays.[82]

When the play opens, Old Wilton has become obsessed with building a family for himself. Driven by Romantic fantasies, he despairs that his bachelor life has deprived him of the joys of fatherhood and so he has taken to inviting the neighbor children over to stage theatricals in his library.[83] So eager is he for a family that when he learns that an English merchant in Lisbon by the name of Mowbray has lost his wife, Old Wilton assumes that this Mowbray is his nephew, whom he had previously disowned for marrying against his wishes. Regretting his earlier actions, he resolves to invite the man, his nine sons, and young daughter to live with him. Of course, Old Wilton's dream of familial happiness rests on a misunderstanding: the widower Mowbray is not his nephew, but another Mowbray altogether. His nephew's wife is alive and well and together the couple has only one child, a daughter. When Charles Mowbray arrives at Old Wilton's place and learns of his uncle's expectations, he fears that he and Matilda will be cast out once the truth of their situation is revealed. But Matilda has other plans. Assuming the guise of three Mowbray boys—with assistance from Old Wilton's servants and the costumes left behind by the neighbor children—Matilda exposes the shortsightedness of the older man's Romanticism, offering in its place a nightmarish vision of naughty, destructive, egocentric boyhood.

Old and Young trades aggressively in gender stereotypes, representing boys as rowdy, loud, obnoxious, violent, reckless, rude, gluttonous, and fun, while showing girls as sweet, quiet, delicate, sensitive, polite, caring, helpful, and also somewhat boring. Matilda, observes D——G in the introduction to the 1831 publication, is "the reverse of her brothers. She is mild and intelligent, and charms the old bachelor with the gentleness of her manners."[84] Beneath the surface, however, the play actively disrupts obvious gender binaries by marking the ease with which Matilda (and the girl playing her) assumes varying forms of boyish masculinity. It is no coincidence that the play gains political significance through cross-dressing and the deliberate juxtaposition of the three fictional Mowbray boys with their savvy real-world sister.

With each invented Mowbray boy, Matilda explores different, albeit highly stereotypical, facets of boyish masculinity. Hector is obsessed with all things military. He enters Old Wilton's library, "a drum before him, a sword at his side, and a feather in his cap," singing loudly about his desire to abandon his education and enlist as a soldier to fight for the king.[85] He quickly sets about disrupting the calm and order of his uncle's library, first by skipping rope and then by stacking chairs on top of one another to reenact the storming of a fortress. "Come on, my brave fellows, follow me—victory or death!" he cries, before "overturn[ing] tables and chairs with a great clatter."[86] Distressed by the noise, not to mention the destruction of his furniture, Old Wilton begs the boy to occupy himself otherwise so that he can finish writing a letter. Eager to comply, Hector begins throwing around a ball, which inevitably ends up toppling the inkstand on the table and ruining the old man's letter. At his wit's end, Old Wilton calls for his servants to take the boy away. Hector exits with a triumphant cry: "Victory! Victory! I've put the enemy to flight!"[87]

Hector's military fantasies and his general disregard for his uncle's pleas challenge Romantic notions of the pure, intuitive child of nature. Obsessed with his violent, role-playing fantasies, Hector is unable (or unwilling) to recognize how his actions affect others. This less-than-flattering representation is unsurprising in the decade following the Napoleonic Wars; Hector's hypermasculine embrace of the "martial spirit" appears dangerous and chaotic. For later audiences, however, this representation of "boyish aggression" was not unwelcome. To the contrary, art historians Sara Holdsworth and Joan Crossley assert, images of rowdy, sparring boys were "frequently treated as evidence of the martial spirit needed in business and Empire."[88] *Old and Young*'s representation of boyhood as loud, aggressive, and destructive anticipates the work of visual artists like Thomas Webster, who saw boyhood as a period of necessary "conflict and competition" in service to the imperial project.[89]

The characters of Gobbington and Foppington likewise celebrate the behavioral excesses of boyish masculinity. As his name implies, Gobbington is overcome by intense hunger and thinks only of his next meal. His gluttony leads inevitably to painful indigestion, not to mention the destruction of Old Wilton's favorite pie. By contrast, Foppington is a miniature version of the stage fop,[90] a teenaged "exquisite" obsessed with fashion, horses, and his own appearance. He refuses to be called a child, informing Old Wilton that he is thirteen and that "a—at a—my age there are no—a—children. . . . Children of that age have a—long been out of fashion."[91] This sly, metatheatrical comment nods toward Clara Fisher's own age and the fear of waning audience interest, even as it acknowledges the performativity of age itself. Foppington assures Old Wilton that he has reached a state of sophisticated maturity by highlighting his talents as a rider and boxer, his ability to "ti[e] a devilish good cloth [i.e., an intricate cravat]," and his daily shaving ritual—all repetitive acts that collectively naturalize Foppington's distinct performance of adolescent masculinity.

Together, Hector, Gobbington, and Foppington dismantle idealized notions of sweetly precocious boyhood, appearing by turns as wild, aggressive, gluttonous, overcultivated, and driven by base desires. In conjuring this terrifying vision (one that hearkens back to older Calvinist models of the child as a monstrous being) Matilda educates Old Wilton in the ways of the world—or at least in the ways of *boys*. In this she is largely successful. By the end of the play, Old Wilton is so overwhelmed by his previous encounters with the three Mowbray boys that when Matilda enters as herself with the good news that order has been restored to his home he is easily won over by her charms.

Playfulness aside, the stakes are incredibly high for Matilda, since failure to convince her uncle that she is worthy of sharing his home and inheriting his money will result in poverty and homelessness. Deploying a kind of "strategic essentialism,"[92] she contrasts the gendered stereotypes associated with boys with displays of sweet girlishness. Whereas her rowdy fictional brothers disregard Old Wilton's needs,

Matilda deferentially asks him to help with her lessons. Wilton defers, gesturing to his gouty foot, but the girl persists, painting a future of love and happiness.[93] Not long after this, Matilda's father enters and the truth about the Mowbray children is finally revealed, much to the older man's confusion. Seizing the moment, Matilda declares: "Why uncle, all that I have done, —all that I wished to do, —was to convince you that you have a better chance of happiness with one little girl who will love and obey you, than if surrounded by a dozen boys, who would vex and torment you."[94] A much-relieved Old Wilton promises to accept the Mowbrays into his home and the play concludes with a scene of familial harmony.

Old Wilton's willingness to revise his thinking and embrace Matilda demonstrates his capacity for emotional and psychological growth, despite his physical ailments, aging body, and fossilized daily rituals. Indeed, to the extent that *Old and Young* relies on stereotypes of old age for much of its humor, it ultimately executes these stereotypes to present a more complicated view of aging and the relationship between old and young. Old Wilton may never regain his full physical strength, but the play offers him a very different future than the one he imagined for himself. In the Larpent manuscript version of the play, the final moments are suffused with sentimentalism as the rift between nephew and uncle is mended and Matilda secures happiness for all. "My Uncle is cured of his Mania for children," Matilda declares, characterizing his Romanticism as a kind of illness that her "tough love" treatment has expelled from his body.[95] In exchange for this cure, he has "promised to protect"[96] her and her parents, forging a family unit grounded in love and respect. This representation of family harmony offers yet another example of the "interassimilation of adulthood and childhood"[97] that Judith Plotz observes in the work of female children's writers from this period. Old Wilton is not all knowing, but neither is Matilda. She needs his help and instruction. Both will learn and grow together.[98] Curiously, the final moments in the 1822 publication printed by J. Tabby of Theatre Royal, Drury Lane offer a variation on this scene of familial harmony, concluding instead with a *tour de force* monologue wherein Matilda briefly returns to each Mowbray boy to showcase her (and Fisher's) versatility. The play ends with Hector's rousing command—"Follow, my brave fellows; fire away! we've taken the fortress—huzza! huzza!"[99]— prompting (I imagine) a similar response from the audience.

In both versions of the play, *Old and Young* firmly pushes against the representation of girls as weak and needy by showcasing Matilda's intelligence, cunning, and influence over adults. In the place of Old Wilton's imagined future of innocent boys romping about, she imagines a future of familial camaraderie free from any illusions about the "wonder" and innocence of children. It is Matilda who devises the scheme to secure her family's future. In fact, by the end of the play, everyone owes their happiness to Matilda: she has guaranteed her family's financial stability, enchanted Old Wilton, and arranged Peter and Peggy's marriage. *Old and Young* thus presents a much more nuanced view of its old and young characters, celebrating intergenerational friendship, love, and mutual dependency.

Playing Boys Outside the Theatre

Yet in celebrating the bonds between the young girl and her uncle, *Old and Young* accomplishes a clever reversal of gender binaries. The Matilda who shows deference toward Old Wilson is the same Matilda who "conjured" the Mowbray boys to trick him.[100] She may have cured her uncle of his "Mania for children," but there is no proof that *she* has been cured of her love of adventure or her penchant for playing boys. And after watching Matilda/Fisher assume a variety of masculine guises, the audience may well have wondered whether her performance of girlhood was also a construction.

Outside the world of the play, Drury Lane playbills reminded audiences that *all* four Mowbrays were, in fact, Clara Fisher's creations. In a playbill from Fisher's 1822 engagement, the character names appear in a column on the left followed by the names of the individual actors portraying that character. At the center of the bill, Fisher's name appears four times, once for each of the four Mowbray characters:

Hector.... CLARA FISHER!
Gobbington .... CLARA FISHER!
Foppington ... CLARA FISHER!
Matilda ... CLARA FISHER!

Mirroring the playfulness of the protean farce, the playbill accentuates Fisher's virtuosity and prepares the audience for a performance of gender fluidity. Such billing was typical of the protean farce, which rejected the narrow parameters of traditional acting practices, encouraging actors and actresses to try on roles that fell outside their narrow "type" and to bend understandings of gender, class, and age. This billing further reminds audiences that all four Mowbrays, including sweet Matilda, are *performances*—clever creations to suit the artistic range of a very talented girl.

An 1823 illustration achieves a similar effect, depicting Fisher as all four of the Mowbrays (Figure 15). The boys appear in varying states of animation: Hector stands legs akimbo as he beats his drum, his feet crushing the spines of Old Wilton's books; Gobbington strides toward him, his right hand raised in front of his protruding belly; and Foppington peers through an eyeglass, his legs artfully arranged in a balletic fourth position. By contrast, Matilda looks demurely at the viewer, clasping her hands in front of her. She seems sweet, demure, passive, the antithesis of the loud, gluttonous, obnoxious boys who surround her. While the image appears to support emerging distinctions between boys and girls, the caption reminds spectators that Clara Fisher represents all four characters. Like the *Old and Young* playbill, the image encourages audiences to recognize and question the representational practices that naturalize gender stereotypes.

This image also invites reflection on the conventions of the breeches role. Unlike *The Spoiled Child*, which requires the female performer to appear in breeches for the play's duration, *Old and Young* stages the donning and doffing of different forms of male garb "as a feature of the narrative, and as a decision by the character"[101] and concludes with Matilda's final return to feminine form and dress. This kind of play is fairly typical of the breeches genre, which as Felicity Nussbaum notes, "heighten attention to the constructedness of gender categories in the real world."[102] But what makes *Old and Young* so unique within the genre is the way it foregrounds breeching as a rite of passage for boys, one that visibly distinguishes a male child from his female counterparts.[103] As literary scholar Chantel Lavoie has shown, breeching was a significant event in a boy's life, "an irrevocable ritual that demonstrated—and thereby enacted—the signs of both adulthood and masculinity."[104] Before donning breeches, boys were almost indistinguishable from girls: both wore long frocks, which granted them ease of movement and also simplified toilet training procedures.[105] Although, Lavoie notes, girls' "frocks, fripperies, and undergarments"

MISS CLARA FISHER,
as
The Four Mowbrays.

FIGURE 15. *Clara Fisher as all four Mowbrays in* Old and Young.
By permission of the Folger Shakespeare Library.

changed as they matured, alongside further changes in hairstyle, these changes were gradual and relatively minimal compared to breeching. By contrast, breeching was "a more drastic sartorial sign of crossing a threshold"[106]—a turning point in the entwined performances of boyhood and age that invited new ways of physical movement that would lead through repetition to the naturalization of gendered effects.[107] Once a boy was breeched, there was no returning to the frocks and blurred gender of early childhood: "breeching was for life."[108]

All three Mowbray boys are breeched, as evidenced by the 1823 image, but the style and cut of their breeches vary, as do the gendered performances that arise from them.[109] Hector's loose soldier's breeches serve a practical function, permitting him to climb chairs, reenact battles, and cause havoc. The gluttonous Gobbington wears his breeches high on his waist, presumably for comfort when eating. In keeping with the fashion of the period, his jacket is cut at the waist, further accentuating his round midsection. Breeches are critical to Foppington's performance of sophistication and elegance; his striped, tapered breeches show his legs to advantage, while his elegant tailcoat and buttoned waistcoat or vest highlight a slim waist. Matilda, of course, is unbreeched. Her ankle-length skirt conceals her legs and the style of her dress and her relatively short hairstyle make it difficult to guess her age—she could be six or sixteen. Here we might recall the critics' comments that the "artifices of dress" made it possible for Fisher to pass for younger than she was. Yet each time she disguises herself as one of her fictional Mowbray brothers, Matilda (and, by extension, Fisher) enacts a kind of self-directed breeching, calling attention to the performativity of age and gender for both boys and girls. This performance of breeching becomes more significant when considered alongside Fisher's Drury Lane contract and Elliston's efforts to limit her repertoire to "children's" roles. Appearing onstage as three recently breeched boys, Fisher paradoxically marked her status as a young girl, reminding audiences that she was acting in an age-appropriate play.

* * *

Clara Fisher performed *Old and Young* at Drury Lane an impressive twenty-two times between December 5, 1822, and February 22, 1823.[110] Shortly after her first appearance as Matilda Mowbray, playbills informed theatregoers that she would be appearing in the role "every

Tuesday, Thursday, and Saturday until Christmas,"[111] a clear indicator of the play's popularity with London audiences, including (I assume) those with young families. In fact, Fisher's performance was so widely admired that the four Mowbrays remained in her repertoire for years, even after she had comfortably crossed the threshold of womanhood.[112]

Fisher's success soon prompted other child performers to enter the theatrical arena and adopt the four Mowbrays for themselves. Of special note is a November 1826 account from the *Quarterly Oriental Magazine Review and Register*, which tells of an amateur production of *Old and Young* at an "impromptu theatre" in Dinapore, India. According to reports, the play owed its staging to a young man who had "taken [it] down from memory" and "acted the principal characters" with considerable vim.[113] Although the report makes no reference to Fisher, the young man's knowledge of the play and his ability to (re)perform it from memory suggests that he had more than a passing familiarity with her performance. Decades later a boy named Percy Roselle appeared in an adapted version of *Old and Young* in Dundee, in which all four Mowbray children were boys.[114] Evidence of the play's popularity with male performers raises fascinating questions about the simultaneous development of repertoire for boys as well as girls. For the most part, however, *Old and Young* was associated with girls, chief among them Louisa Lane (Mrs. John Drew), the Bateman sisters (Ellen and Kate), Matilda Heron, and Jean Margaret Davenport.[115]

Clara Fisher's Drury Lane engagement "for children's characters only" marks a turning point in the way managers and playwrights approached theatrical girlhood and the figure of the girl actress. Impelled by conservative anxieties about the impropriety of girls playing naughty men, managers like Robert Elliston commissioned new plays and expanded the range of roles available to girls specifically.[116] But while such plays can be read as reactionary responses to patriarchal anxieties, they achieved considerably more in performance. By challenging and stretching—if not entirely exploding—normative ideologies of gender and age, *Old and Young* demonstrated the subversive potential of plays "for children," allowing Fisher and the many other girls who followed her to play *as a girl*, while still delighting in the freedom, tricks, and revelry that some observers felt should be the exclusive domain of boys.

INTERLUDE 4
CLARA FISHER EVERYWHERE

In 1827, at the age of sixteen, Clara Fisher traveled to the United States with her family, including her sister Jane (the future Mrs. Vernon) and her brother C. J. B. Fisher, who would go on to edit *The Spirit of the Times*, one of the era's most popular weeklies. Following a triumphant American debut at the Park Theatre in New York City, Clara Fisher's name and likeness spread swiftly up and down the East Coast and beyond through news reports, imagery, and celebratory objects. By this time, her repertoire had expanded to include comedies like John Poole's *Paul Pry*, Hannah Crowley's *The Belle's Stratagem*, and Susanna Centlivre's *The Busy Body*; she also reprised roles like Crack in *Turnpike Gate*, which had so concerned her London critics.[1] Throughout, she continued to delight audiences with her mimetic plasticity, seen most vividly in *Old and Young* and *The Actress of All Work*.[2] Audiences clamored for more. On her last night in Boston in December 1827, theatregoers issued a rousing and "Unanimous call ... for a Re-engagement," to which the Boston Theatre managers obliged, but only for two nights "and positively no longer" because she was due for her next engagement in New York.[3]

Fisher seems to have found special favor with American men, according to the reminiscences of Walter M. Leman, who fondly recalled the "archness of manner ... buoyancy of spirits, ... [and] taste in costume" with which she "captur[ed] the young men (the old boys of today) who thronged to see her." Leman's words imply that men were not just enchanted by Fisher's spirited appearances in male dress but also appreciated her talents as a performer: "The mere mention of her name will resuscitate in the breast of every surviving Old-boy reminiscences of her versatility and ability," he concludes.[4]

But Fisher counted women and children among her fans as well. Her

FIGURE 16. *Portrait of Clara Fisher by Henry Inman, Esq.*
Image published by G. M. Bourne in New York on December 8, 1829,
Harry Beard Collection. © Victoria & Albert Museum, London.

rapidly growing popularity with US audiences led to the widespread dispersal of her name and image, resulting in a kind of semiotic excess that resembled her protean performance style. "Turn over any rubbishy lot of old plays in a second-hand bookstore and the odds are that you will find her portrait in character," journalist Charles T. Congdon quipped. "She outlived her girlish glories."[5] Though less than flattering, Congdon speaks to the persistence and ubiquity of Fisher's image: she is inescapable. Further evidence of her popularity comes from the vast number of objects that circulated with her name: plays, portraits, sheet music, and all manner of branded goods.[6] Recalling her effect on the US theatregoing public in the late 1820s and early 1830s, actor-manager Joe Cowell observed that "nothing could exceed the enthusiasm with which this most amicable creature was received everywhere. 'Clara Fisher' was the name given to everything it could possibly be applied to: ships, steamboats, racehorses, mint juleps, and negro babies" (more on this last reference later).[7] A Colonel Tom Picton similarly described Fisher as

> the talisman of fame, the idol of popular worship, whose name was attached to every imaginable contrivance dependent upon popular patronage. We wore Clara Fisher garments, ate Clara Fisher cakes, rode in Clara Fisher vehicles; in a word, nothing could go up or down, animate or inanimate, without having the name of the precocious comedienne couple with it, even to the race horse, whose contests with Bonnets o' Blue, Fashion's dam, derived extra interest from the favorite having been christened after the theatrical divinity.[8]

This broad and peculiar assemblage of clothes, cakes, horses, vehicles, alcoholic drinks, and even children offers evidence of the elastic scope of Fisher's celebrity and the commercial, aspirational, and even political deployment of her name and image. The more these objects circulated, the more Fisher's name and image became known and the more distinctive she seemed. In *The Drama of Celebrity*, Sharon Marcus astutely observes how the multiplication of a celebrity's name and image does not diminish that celebrity's individuality but rather increases it through a phenomenon she describes as the "halo of the multiple." "Copies do not dim the celebrity's halo;" she writes, "they brighten it."[9] This is one of the central paradoxes of celebrity culture.

Yet in their seemingly endless variety and dispersal, the garments, cakes, animals, and objects named after Clara Fisher worked collectively to detach the actress's name and image from her body, turning her protean virtuosity inside out by dispersing it across a multiplicity of forms. Together, these animate and inanimate entities exploded the notion of ever containing a single human in one time or place, of freezing, holding, or immobilizing that human through casting practices, scientific or theatrical. Instead, each entity carried a trace of the actress—or what Rebecca Schneider refers to as an "affective stain"—ensuring that she would continue to "*pas[s]* between bodies and across time."[10] In other words, a little bit of Fisher existed in all who witnessed and admired her performances or dreamed of escaping the constraints of race, class, and gender.

The brightness of a celebrity like Fisher made her particularly attractive to those seeking some shine of their own. Cowell's casual reference to the popularity of Fisher's name among African American families (the "negro babies" who appear in his list of "everything" named after her) suggests that for some fans she represented the promise of a better future. According to an 1893 *Cosmopolitan* article, African American families "proudly christened" their daughters Clara Fisher in the same way that they gave their sons "the honored names of George Washington or Benjamin Franklin."[11] This source (if accurate) offers compelling evidence of black audiences' cross-racial identification with Fisher and their desire to pass something of her charm, talent, and plasticity onto their children.

A similar impulse shaped the fandom of middle-class white girls, who not only collected commodities named after Fisher but also modeled their physical appearance and manner of speaking after hers. In *Records of the New York Stage*, John Norton Ireland writes: "Appearing, as she constantly did, in the characters of boys and striplings, [Fisher] had her fine hair closely cut on the back of the head, while on the brow she wore the then fashionable rolls or puffs, a style that was immediately adopted by all fashionable ladies under twenty-five, and by some of more mature age; while an imitation of her delicate but natural lisp was considered equally indispensable."[12] Ireland's account hints at the subversive potential of Fisher's cross-dressed performances and the subsequent performances of the girls (of all ages) who remade themselves—their hair, their clothing, their voices—in her image. If, as Susan Honeyman has suggested, reading books about boys' adventures inspired girls to dress as men,[13] did the experience of seeing Fisher play young boys on the stage have a similar effect? And what of those who were "of more mature age"? Was Fisher just a "talisman of fame," or was she also an appealing model of female masculinity for those eager to avoid "tomboy taming" and find alternatives to marriage and mother-hood?[14]

I want to return briefly to Schneider's image of the "affective stain," which she invokes to describe how traces of past performances continue to resonate in spectators' bodies long after the performance event has concluded. A stain is a persistent, if not permanent, mark left by a substance after it has passed from body to body, object to object. As a stain spreads, sets, and hardens, it becomes a reminder of a moment of touch. Its presence speaks to the vulnerability of the material it marks, highlighting its susceptibility to outside influence, to its permeability, its porousness. In other words, a stain offers evidence of a body's plasticity—of its capacity to change and change others in return. As such, staining is akin to Diana Taylor's "acts of transfer" or Marvin Carlson's "ghosting,"[15] except that there is something more tangible about the notion of a stain. Where ghosting implies that individuals can never fully avoid the past and must therefore resign themselves to living in the shadow of the dead, the concept of staining leaves open the prospect of freeing oneself through some process of *stain removal*. It points toward possibilities for resistance and refusal, for erasing the evidence of earlier contact.

The following chapter explores this potential.

CHAPTER 4
The Manager's Daughter

ON FIXING AND OTHER PERFORMANCES
OF MIDDLE-CLASS DOMESTICITY

When I was a young One, no girl was like me.
—"Child of Nature"

In May 1836, a notice in a London paper informed readers that a "clever little girl (about eight years of age), named Davenport, daughter of the manager of that name" had been rehearsing *The Spoiled Child* at Drury Lane. The notice said nothing about whether an official performance would follow the rehearsal, though it described the child as "a second Clara Fisher."[1] This reference to Clara Fisher nineteen years after her own Drury Lane debut offers further proof of her enduring influence on practices and perceptions of theatrical girlhood. By 1836 Fisher had married and retired from the stage, but her name and image continued to circulate in print on both sides of the Atlantic, extending to street-cars, race horses, babies, and, phrenological studies. As Fisher's reputation grew and word of her success spread throughout Britain and North America, so did the desire to imitate her. And yet the multiplication and dispersal of Clara Fisher's repertoire across the bodies of other girl actresses differed in subtle ways from the multiplication and dispersal of objects carrying her name. The career of Jean Margaret Davenport powerfully suggests that the girls who presented themselves (or were presented by others) as the second and third and fourth Clara Fishers did so in the hope that enough of her shine / stain would rub off to allow them to eventually emerge as unique individuals in their own right. For these girls, imitation was the starting point for invention. Or, to return to the concept of plasticity, the girls who molded themselves after Fisher first took her form and then found ways to break out of it.

To explore the complexities of such plastic performances, this chapter leaps forward by several decades and considers how Clara Fisher's dynamic embodiment of theatrical girlhood shaped the career of Jean Margaret Davenport. This is not to dismiss the careers of the other girl actresses who crossed Anglo-American stages in the 1820s and 1830s—among them Emily Mestayer, Louisa Lane, Caroline Fox, and Anna Cora Mowatt[2]—but rather to zero in on the most obvious and far-reaching effects of Fisher's legacy. Alongside Lane, Davenport was one of the first truly transatlantic girl actresses of the 1830s and 1840s, and she carried with her Fisher's repertoire. Rather than merely reproduce herself as a clever double, however, Davenport and her father Thomas worked hard to surpass Fisher.

To achieve this goal, the Davenports pursued four seemingly contradictory strategies. First, and perhaps most obviously, they encouraged audiences to recognize Jean Davenport as the second coming of Clara Fisher by demonstrating that she had the talent and range to perform the same repertoire.[3] It would appear that Thomas Davenport not only appreciated the affective power of theatrical "ghosting" but also understood the politics of what Joseph Roach terms "surrogation," a process whereby a community attempts to fill "the cavities created by loss through death and other forms of departure" with "satisfactory alternates."[4] In presenting Jean Davenport as Clara Fisher's surrogate, Thomas Davenport presumably hoped that his daughter would gain something of the status and acclaim previously accorded to Fisher. Second, he expanded Jean Davenport's repertoire to include roles that Fisher had never performed, thereby demonstrating that his daughter had the capacity to exceed her predecessor's range. Third, Davenport engaged in another form of surrogation, not with Clara Fisher but with the recently deceased actor Edmund Kean who, Davenport claimed, had recognized his daughter's talent and blessed her with a gift. Finally, once he had proven that Jean Davenport was plastic enough to fit into the cavity vacated by Fisher, he endeavored to break her out of Fisher's mold by offering audiences something different—*The Manager's Daughter*, a new protean farce that celebrated Jean Davenport *as* Jean Davenport.

A metatheatrical "interlude in one act,"[5] *The Manager's Daughter* transports the real-life Davenports into a fictional scenario wherein the character of "Jean Margaret"[6] assumes the role of six other characters to help her father (the eponymous manager played by Thomas Davenport himself) navigate a professional crisis. When the company's supporting players refuse to perform at the manager's benefit, Jean Margaret proves that she has the talent and range to replace them all, appearing by turns as a Yankee actor, French minstrel, Scottish lass, Irish rogue, English girl, and old woman. The play concludes on a happy note when Jean Margaret reveals her true identity to her father and the disgruntled actors finally agree to the manager's terms for fear of being replaced by the girl.

The Manager's Daughter delights in the performance of mimetic plasticity that is central to the dramaturgy of the protean farce. Like *Old and Young* and *The Actress of All Work*, the plays centers around a single body's ability to continually reproduce itself as other bodies through voice, gesture, and costume. But the play accomplishes considerably more than this through its explicit staging of the Davenports as an ideal family and in its implicit celebration of normative social values. Anne Varty reads *The Manager's Daughter* as a "drama of containment," which holds at bay a series of social and political threats, ranging from the fear of the precocious child to the risk of other nationalities.[7] While the play works hard to eliminate such threats, the metaphor of containment doesn't fully account for the central action of the play—namely Jean Margaret's use of performance to fix her father's business crisis. Instead, this chapter contends that *The Manager's Daughter* is best understood as a drama of fixes, fixing, and fixity. Fixing is about holding firm or securing an object, person, or situation. It is about hardening, preventing change or vacillation, giving "constancy to (the mind, thoughts, affections, purposes)."[8] It is also about solving problems, removing stains, and mending or repairing broken objects. Fixing is the opposite of plasticity. Both *The Manager's Daughter* and the manager's daughter fix matters onstage and off and, through these acts, they themselves are fixed.

In reading *The Manager's Daughter* as a drama of fixity, this chapter also highlights one of the shortcomings of the protean farce as a vehicle of social transformation. In Chapter 3 I followed Jane Goodall in arguing that protean farces like *The Actress of All Work* and *Old and Young* gave women and young girls greater opportunities for experimenting with gender, age, and class identity. Such farces celebrated human plas-

MISS DAVENPORT of the THEATRE ROYAL HAYMARKET, only 10 Years of Age

As the SEVEN CHARACTERS in the MANAGER'S DAUGHTER _ performed by her with extraordinary success.

ticity and the versatile performer, challenging the logic of fixity underlying nineteenth-century casting practices by presenting all human
identity as distinctly performative. This reading becomes more complicated, however, when we observe how protean farces like *The Manager's Daughter* reinforce rather than critique stereotypical depictions
of gender, race, class, and nationality. Jean Davenport's on- and offstage
performances flirted with fluid identity categories and the potential to
reject old forms yet ultimately reassured audiences that the little girl
they saw onstage was the "real" Jean Davenport and that her skillful
portrayal of characters of varying ages, genders, and nationalities was
simply child's play. Davenport's performances of little girlhood outside
the theatre, often in the company of a large doll, not only affirmed her
billing as an "infant phenomenon," promising audiences that she *was*
her advertised age (even if she wasn't), but also warded off suspicions
of child exploitation and gender transgression. Thus in *The Manager's
Daughter* the potentially destabilizing figure of the plastic girl promotes
a comforting image of idealized femininity consistent with the patriarchal values of the mid-Victorian era. Although Davenport's celebrity
arose in part from her ability to transition seamlessly from "real world"
performances of white, middle-class girlhood to fictionalized representations of adulthood, masculinity, and ethnic otherness, the message
was clear: Jean Davenport's aptitude for cross-dressing was a testament to her talent, not evidence of secret masculine desires to disrupt
the social order.

Inventing the Phenomenon:
Competition and Surrogation

Jean Margaret Davenport's birth year is something of a question mark.
Anecdotes from actors who worked with the family suggest that she
was most likely born in the mid-1820s, possibly as early as 1823, although the date listed on her gravestone in Washington, DC, is May 3,
1829.[9] The uncertainty surrounding Davenport's birthdate leaves open
the very real possibility that her family artificially prolonged her childhood to impress audiences.[10] Certainly this kind of tinkering is in keeping with the domineering management style modeled by the actress's
father, the lawyer turned actor-manager Thomas Donald Davenport,
who looms large in this chapter as a proto-Svengalian figure.

Thomas Davenport was the driving force behind his daughter's career. Educated as a lawyer at Dublin University—a profession he later abandoned for a life on the stage—he was keenly attuned to the rhythms of nineteenth-century celebrity culture. One of his most successful promotional strategies involved submitting letters to the editor of local newspapers when the Davenport company was on tour. In October 1838, for example, he wrote to the editor of the *Boston Daily Advocate* to address a false report that his daughter was American. "She is a Scotch Lassie—England, Ireland and Scotland bound her infant brow with laurel, with which America has entwined new wreaths," he asserted, using the excuse of the minor correction to tout his daughter's successes.[11] Through such letters Davenport represented himself as a caring father and educated gentleman. At a time when many upstanding, middle-class men and women continued to treat actors as social outcasts,[12] his public presence in the pages of local newspapers in England and throughout the British Empire made him, and by extension his family, familiar and respectable. Such carefully managed performances of accessibility would define Jean Davenport's juvenile career.

Unlike Clara Fisher, who became an overnight sensation after her 1817 appearance in *Gulliver's Travels*, Jean Davenport's rise to stardom was gradual. She made her first recorded stage appearance in March 1830 as a "Child" in her father's production of *The Stranger or, Misanthropy and Repentance* at the Crediton Theatre in Devon.[13] Five years later, while her family was touring the Chichester circuit, she played the role of the Duke of York in *Richard III* and Rob Roy in a dramatic interpretation of the popular Sir Walter Scott novel, a production that gave Thomas Davenport and other members of the troupe an opportunity to showcase their "facility with the Scottish dialect."[14] These roles offer early evidence of Davenport's efforts to stretch his daughter's range while keeping it within the bounds of audience familiarity, a promotional technique Sharon Marcus identifies as "historical competition."[15] This scheme became explicit the following year with the announcement of Jean Davenport's rehearsal in *The Spoiled Child*.[16]

In fall 1836, several months after Jean Davenport's appearance at Drury Lane, the Davenports leased the King's Theatre in Richmond, complete with the "dwelling house" where the famed actor Edmund Kean had died three years prior. From here, Thomas Davenport's promotional efforts intensified, as the following from a March 1837 playbill attests: "Great and Astonishing Success ... the most celebrated JUVE-NILE ACTRESS of the day MISS DAVENPORT! Who was received with Cheers of Applause!"[17] Behind the scenes, Thomas Davenport stretched his daughter's repertoire further in imitation of the "first" Clara Fisher. In addition to playing farces and comedies, Jean Davenport attempted several tragic roles, including Richard III, Shylock, and Young Norval, and assumed many of the other characters that had defined Fisher's career, notably Little Pickle, the Four Mowbrays, and all six characters in *The Actress of All Work*.[18]

But surrogacy is an imperfect process. As Robin Bernstein writes, "no act of surrogation fully succeeds in restoring the half-remembered, imagined original, but different bodies partially succeed and yet fall short in importantly different ways."[19] Such failure is, in fact, critical to surrogation as a process, since "each *ill fit* compels yet another performance,"[20] thereby guaranteeing the continued circulation of specific values, ideas, or repertoires. Surrogation's perpetual incompleteness invites variation and innovation—repetition with a difference. Like plasticity, surrogation is about taking and giving form; it's about allowing creativity to slip through the cracks.

Jean Davenport's failure to fit seamlessly into Clara Fisher's mold afforded greater opportunities for her to distinguish herself in roles that Fisher had never attempted. In other words, by inviting historical competition, Davenport (and her father) prepared audiences to see the girl as more than Fisher's copy. Thus, a January 1838 playbill declared that the young actress would "appear as SIR PETER TEAZLE! This difficult and arduous character was never attempted by MASTER BETTY, MASTER BURKE, MISS CLARA FISHER, or any other juvenile performer."[21] Referencing three of the century's most celebrated child performers, only one of whom (Burke) was Davenport's immediate contemporary, the playbill implies that the role is too "difficult and arduous" for other children to attempt. Those who see Jean Davenport as Sir Peter Teazle will therefore witness a wondrous feat of precocity.

In addition to positioning his daughter as Clara Fisher's superior successor, Thomas Davenport made the most of her connection to Edmund Kean. Although Kean was dead by 1833, Davenport used his new position as manager of the Richmond Theatre to invoke a different kind of surrogation. According to the actor William Pleater Davidge, Davenport "impressed the public in every town he visited, with the be-

FIGURE 18. *Jean Margaret Davenport as Young Norval.*
MS Thr 158.1, Houghton Library, Harvard University.

lief that Edmund Kean had, in a burst of admiration for his daughter's ability, presented her with what, in theatrical parlance, was called a battlefield hat."[22] Framing the gift exchange as an intimate gesture that traversed generations and even death, Thomas Davenport tapped into the era's fascination with death relics—belongings associated with deceased loved ones.[23] In fact, the "Kean hat" was not the original but a copy of a hat worn by Kean, another kind of surrogate that Davenport or one of his cronies had found in the property room.[24] Jean Davenport's own recollections suggest that the gift was more of a tribute to the deceased actor. Writing in an 1899 letter to the editor of the American journal *Shakespeareana*, she explains that in 1836 her father had taken over the lease of the Richmond Theatre and the "dwelling house attached," where Kean had died three years prior. "I was then seven years old," she writes, "& many friends of Kean were interested in a childish attempt to follow the Great actor & there I made my debut as a child actress."[25] From this account, it seems likely that Kean's friends viewed Davenport as a surrogate for "the Great actor" and enjoyed watching her try on his roles as though they too were objects of clothing. For my purposes, I am less concerned with the hat's provenance than with the way it allowed Thomas Davenport to access audience memories and present his daughter as Kean's surrogate, forever entangling their names.

What ultimately set Jean Davenport apart from both Fisher and Kean was a play that celebrated her singularity as a performer. In 1836 Thomas Davenport commissioned E. R. Lancaster to write *The Manager's Daughter*, a farcical afterpiece that required the lead actress to portray seven different roles (including herself). Since Clara Fisher had only ever played a maximum of six characters in *The Actress of All Work* (and only four in *Old and Young*), the new farce gave Jean Davenport the perfect vehicle for proclaiming her artistic superiority.

The Manager's Daughter plays
The Manager's Daughter

The Manager's Daughter opens on Mrs. Davenport sitting at a table waiting for her husband to return from rehearsal. She frets that he has been working too hard and laments that local audiences do not appreciate "the pains we endure for their pleasure—the expense, the anxieties and the frequent losses."[26] When Mr. Davenport arrives, he shares the troubling news that the actors in his company have refused to play at his upcoming benefit night unless they receive double salary. Without their participation, Davenport will be forced to cancel the performance and forego his chance of recovering the losses he has sustained throughout the season. Upon hearing the news, Mrs. Davenport "retires to [a] table and weeps."[27] Enter young Jean Margaret "singing with a large Doll in her arms":

> Oh my doll! pretty doll what a darling you are
> How I doat on those pretty blue eyes
> Such a head lips so red. It was dearest Mama
> Who gave you to me for a prize
> And I will keep you all my life
> And you shall be another doll's wife
> Oh my doll! pretty doll what a darling you are
> How I doat on those pretty blue eyes.[28]

Delighted to see her father, she invites him to "look at my new Doll!!" but stops short at the sight of her weeping mother. "O Mama, mama, what's the matter?" she cries, but her mother demurs, explaining that Jean Margaret is "not old enough to understand the cares of this life." Jean Margaret insists on knowing the cause of her parents' distress: "You and Papa are always so happy that I am joyful that when I see you grieved I almost think it a duty to be sad too." Reluctantly Mr. Davenport informs his daughter of the family's precarious situation, to which she responds: "Is that all? Oh never mind papa. Let the actors go if they please. I will supply their places."[29] In addition to taking on one of the roles herself, she proposes getting up a company of her school friends to replace the professional acting company. Mr. Davenport rejects this idea, citing the inexperience of the juvenile actors: "My dear Child I should not dare to bring anything but genuine and well tried talent before the Public."[30] Jean Margaret presses him, promising that her friends are clever and capable, but he reminds her of her duties as a daughter—"You should never say you should go against your father's wishes"[31]—and departs with Mrs. Davenport to the theatre.

Alone yet undeterred, Jean Margaret devises a plan that will allow her to fix her father's managerial crisis without betraying her promise to him: "Ah! I have it. I can represent them *all* myself. Papa did not forbid *that*—and if I can deceive *him* there is a probability of deceiving the company also, who will then be frightened into remaining with him, lest they lose their salaries—I shall thus be enabled to repay the debt of gratitude which I owe my parents—Let me hasten to the wardrobe." What follows is a series of entrances, exits, and quick changes as Jean Margaret appears before her father as six different characters, each seeking a place in his company. First to arrive is Hector Earsplitter, "an American Boy with stick and bundle"[32] who insists that he is a "perfect star" capable of dancing "anything from Jim Crow to a Spanish Fandango."[33] Next is Effie Featherblossom, a Scottish lass who performs a Highland Fling, followed by Fergus O'Botherwell, an Irish lad who "can play everything Tragedy, Comedy, Dancing, Singing."[34] The remaining characters are the French boy Paul, an orphan of the 1830 French uprisings; Sapinella Thespis, a fashionable English girl who offers cutting imitations of her schoolmates and their failed performances; and an unnamed old woman with a "hobbling gait ... for ever deprived of the elasticity of youth"[35] (unlike the girl playing the old woman who *must* possess considerable elasticity in order to take on the many shapes required of the play). Charmed and bemused by the flow of would-be performers (of course, he does not recognize them as his daughter's creations), Mr. Davenport gradually warms to the idea of hiring a company of juvenile actors. By the time Jean Margaret throws off her old woman costume to reveal her true identity, she has convinced her father that she can more than replace his actors at the benefit performance.[36] When the adult company returns to the theatre, she reprises five of the characters to showcase her skills. Dumbfounded, the actors realize that they are in danger of losing their jobs and pledge to play for Davenport's benefit on his terms.[37] Problem solved!

In the final moments of the play, Jean Margaret appears *in propria persona*, a Latin legal term meaning "for one's own person or character" or one's own representative.[38] What is unclear is who exactly the "self" is supposed to be: Jean Margaret, the character, or Jean Davenport, the actress playing the character Jean Margaret? For several lines, the actress speaks as her fictional self as she explains her plot to the befuddled actors. And then she turns, advancing toward the audience to deliver the final monologue as her "real" self:

King's Theatre, Richmond.

ASTONISHING SUCCESS

OF

Miss DAVENPORT,

She having been called before the Curtain in RICHARD by one of the most numerous Audiences of the Season,

CONGRATULATED, and RECEIVED with CHEERS,

A Compliment that has never been paid an Actor by a

RICHMOND AUDIENCE,

In consequence of which, will be repeated for the last time,

RICHARD III.

A Character never attempted in this Kingdom by a Child of her Age. The Hat worn by the greatest Richard of modern times has been presented to, and will be worn by Miss DAVENPORT.

ON WEDNESDAY EVENING, NOVEMBER 23, 1836,

Will be presented Shakspeare's celebrated Tragedy called

RICHARD III.

OR

THE BATTLE OF BOSWORTH FIELD.

Richard the Third .... Miss DAVENPORT,

A Child only Nine Years of Age.

King Henry ...... Mr. DAVENPORT,		Duke of Buckingham ...... Mr. SPENCER,
Earl of Richmond .... Mr. CURLING,		Lord Mayor of London .... Mr. WARREN,
Lord Stanley .... Mr. BROOKS,	Duke of Norfolk .... Mr. BENNETT,	Catesby .... Mr. EDMUNDS,
Earl of Ratcliff .... Mr. COPPIN,	Tyrrell .... Mr. BELVILLE,	Tressell .... Mr. SMITH,
Prince of Wales ...... Miss ROLAND,		Duke of York ...... Master DAVENPORT,
Queen .... Mrs. DAVENPORT,	Duchess of York .... Miss AUBREY,	Lady Anne .... Miss GRAYE.

A COMIC SONG, BY MR. WARREN.

To conclude with the admired and Laughable Farce called

Matrimony.

Sir Charles Courtall .... Mr. SPENCER,		Sharp .... Mr. WARREN,
John ...... Mr. BENNETT,	Thomas ...... Mr. BROOKS,	Labroche ...... Mr. EDMUNDS,
Lady Courtall .... Miss ROLAND,		Grace .... Miss GRAYE,

☞ That the Younger Branches of Families may have an opportunity of witnessing Miss DAVENPORT's Performance, all under Twelve Years of Age will be admitted at Half Price. Also Schools at Half Price. For this Night only.

BOXES, 4s.	PIT, 2s.	GALLERY, 1s.

Tickets and Places to be had of Mrs. B. BUDD, Housekeeper, at the Box Office, from Eleven till Four o'Clock, and at Mr. F. H. WALL's Public Library, Hill Street.

F. H. WALL, ENGRAVER AND PRINTER, HILL STREET, RICHMOND.

FIGURE 19. *Playbill for Jean Margaret Davenport in* Richard III. *TCS 72, Houghton Library, Harvard University.*

But what will my patrons say?—Ah I fear not them—My efforts
were to save a father.

And never yet in such a holy cause,
Did kindly hearts hands withhold that sweet applause,
Then which more joyous naught the ear can bless,
For ah! it carries tidings of success.[39]

In keeping with the convention of the epilogue, Jean Margaret begs indulgence for her deceitful ways (i.e., her acting), explaining that it had all been for her father's benefit. Through direct address—a mode of public intimacy between actor and audience that dissolves the fourth wall—she reassures the audience that her transgressions were temporary and that the "rule of the father" has been safely restored.

The Manager's Daughter as "Backstage" Protean Farce—Fixing the Status Quo

The Manager's Daughter borrows its central conceit from earlier protean farces, including George Colman's *The Manager in Distress* (1780), *The Actor of All Work* (1817), *The Actress of All Work* (1819),[40] and, somewhat surprisingly, *Stella and Leatherlungs*, Colman's ill-fated commission for Clara Fisher. These plays offer access to the backstage world of the theatre and profile the at times tense relationships between actors and managers, simultaneously exposing, celebrating, and critiquing the profession. In *The Actress of All Work*, a London actress performs six different female characters in a bid to convince the manager of a country theatre—who also happens to be her lover's father—to hire her for his season. In *Stella and Leatherlungs*, a group of disgruntled actors walk out of the theatre to protest the impending arrival of a precocious child performer, leaving the country manager to scramble to fill his bill. Both plays feature an easily duped yet authoritative paternal/patriarchal father/manager figure and celebrate (or fantasize about) the potential for performance to undermine existing power hierarchies: the actress finds employment; the frustrated actor is rewarded with better roles. Yet these victories hinge on the characters' willingness to accept other aspects of the status quo, especially where labor is concerned: the London actress will remain in the country and marry a man who cannot stand up to his father; the frustrated actor will perform alongside the girl actress who jeopardizes his employment. As such, these plays trade in what theatre historian Lisa A. Freeman describes as "antitheatrical theatricalism," a dramaturgical "technique whereby [playwrights] critiqued the insincerity, that is, the disguised performances of other forms, while locating their own sincerity in the admission that they offered and celebrated nothing more than a performance."[41] In pulling back the curtain on theatrical labor relations, *The Actress of All Work* and *Stella and Leatherlungs* expose the artifice and exploitation of the theatre industry, while delighting in the virtuosity of individual performers and the political potential of the art form more broadly.

The Manager's Daughter likewise reveals the "hidden" world of theatrical labor relations and centers on the adventures of an eager performer who portrays characters of varying ages, genders, and classes in an effort to persuade a skeptical theatre manager of her talent. But *The Manager's Daughter* departs from previous backstage farces in several ways. First, most obviously, the play is distinct in its explicit celebration of girl *qua* girl (*Stella and Leatherlungs* is hardly a celebration). Second, the central characters in *The Manager's Daughter* represent their real-life counterparts: Jean Davenport plays Jean Margaret; Thomas Davenport plays Mr. Davenport; Mrs. Davenport—a talented actress in her own right—plays Mrs. Davenport; and so on. Such strategies may seem eerily familiar to twenty-first-century readers accustomed to the addictive delights of reality television and the tactics of "theatre of the real," where the line between reality and fiction, true and false is always blurry.[42] Yet metatheatrical casting was hardly new to the nineteenth-century British stage—several eighteenth-century plays featured actors or actresses "playing" themselves, while actresses like Sarah Siddons and Anne Oldfield occasionally brought their children onstage with them to mark their status as respectable mothers.[43] What was new about *The Manager's Daughter* was its representation of the backstage lives of an entire theatrical family. This fusion of the real with the theatrical served multiple purposes, one of the most practical being resistance to imitation: only the *real-life* Jean Davenport could play Jean Margaret.[44]

This performance of self points to the third way *The Manager's Daughter* departs from previous protean farces: by dissolving the boundaries between onstage and offstage worlds, the play refuses to engage with antitheatrical theatricalism and indulges instead in a kind of hyperreal metatheatricality that undoes much of the farce's progressive potential. Rather than destabilize notions of gender, age, and class through an emphasis on the performativity of all identity categories, Jean Davenport's autobiographical performance in *The Manager's Daughter* secures her identity as a sensitive, middle-class daughter.

It is here where we can see "fixing" as a performance strategy operating on multiple levels within the world of the play and beyond. Within the fictional world, Jean Margaret, the character, fixes (i.e., solves) her father's professional problem, and she fixes (i.e., corrects) his opinion of her talents. The actors' refusal to play at Thomas Davenport's benefit exposes the manager's vulnerability. As representatives of specific lines of business—Principal Low Comedian, First Tragedian, Leading Actress—the actors assume (quite literally) that the show cannot go on without them. It is only when confronted by a superior performer, one capable of crossing many lines of business and standing in (surrogating) for any of them, that the actors yield to Davenport's request. Jean Margaret's fix, then, is not just a domestic fix but an economic one as well. Her performance of flexibility affirms patriarchal norms by undermining the adult actors' talent as well as their attempted labor disruption, thereby restoring her father/manager's authority in the private sphere of the home and in the public realm of the theatre. This emphasis on fixing foregrounds the important work of the girl actress as real-life performer and fictional character—without ignoring how the play exploits her labor to achieve larger ideological goals.

Beyond the internal logic of the play, *The Manager's Daughter* also labors to fix the audience's attention onto the real-life Jean Davenport. This dramaturgical gesture offers yet another example of how displays of "public intimacy" fueled the development of celebrity culture in the early nineteenth century. As noted earlier, "public intimacy" is produced when celebrated figures produce a feeling of closeness in their admirers.[45] By making themselves publicly available while maintaining a certain emotional or physical distance, such individuals hold audiences firmly in their grasp. As Roach insists, the "very tension between their widespread visibility and their actual remoteness creates an unfulfilled need in the hearts of the public."[46] Here readers might recall the crowds that gathered outside the home of Master Betty when he became ill and their avid consumption of any and all details related to his physical health (see Chapter 1). While the response to Betty was (presumably) unscripted, *The Manager's Daughter* can be understood as a calculated exercise in public intimacy. In celebrating the ideals of bourgeois domesticity, the play exceeds its function as a star vehicle, inviting audiences to observe the "real" dynamics of the Davenport family with Jean Davenport at its center. The play's explicit emphasis on public intimacy fixes (i.e., firmly positions) both the fictional and the actual Davenports as ideal representatives of middle-class values, reassuring white middle-class audiences that the family onstage holds the same values as they do.

The Manager's Daughter as a Comedy of Bourgeois Family Life

The Manager's Daughter exemplifies a relatively new vision of the daughter's role within the middle-class family. Social and economic historians have shown that families in the preindustrial era functioned as complete economic units. "Members of the household, which likely included not just mom, dad, and kids, but extended family members and possibly servants or others, were seen as assets for the household's productive activities," writes the historian Steven Horwitz.[47] Children were valued primarily for what they could contribute to the family's income, and their economic usefulness fostered large families and extended family units. With the Industrial Revolution, the structure and function of the family changed dramatically as new flows of capital and the reorganization of industrial labor brought greater wealth to many homes, improved standards of living, and diminished the need for large families. This move toward the "nuclearization" of the family fostered a corresponding shift in attitudes toward marriage and children. Marital unions became less about forging a successful economic partnership and more about forming a loving emotional bond. This change likewise affected parent-child relations. Parents moved away from seeing their children as "economically useful" little adults capable of contributing to the family's coffers and toward treating them as "economically useless" yet "emotionally priceless" beings to love and protect within the sanctity of the home.[48] This heightened emphasis on emotional labor affected the socialization of girls within the family unit. Young girls learned to care for others, especially their fathers and other adult male family members, and were expected to offer love and affection in exchange for economic stability and a pat on the head.[49]

In *The Manager's Daughter*, E. R. Lancaster skillfully blends auto-biographical detail with aspirational elements to create a flattering representation of the Davenports as an ideal bourgeois family with an economically useless girl-child who acts out of love rather than economic need. The play opens with an intimate scene of family life: we glimpse the hard-working father, the emotional mother, and the devoted daughter. We quickly learn that Jean Margaret is not a regular member of her father's acting company and has never performed on the professional stage. She attends school, like many middle-class girls of the era, and enjoys the company of other children her age. While her decision to appear before her father in multiple guises is motivated by familial duty, her student status situates her performance within the broader repertoire of at-home theatricals—tableaux and short plays staged by middle-class children during the holidays for no reason other than to amuse family and friends.[50] Such performances called attention to the significant leisure time that was available to "economically useless" middle-class children and showcased their pricelessness within the family home.

By representing Jean Margaret as a "regular" middle-class girl, Lancaster dodges the thorny issue of child labor exploitation and the distressing figure of the stage child. Although it would take another four decades before the campaign against the employment of child actors gained critical steam, theatre critics and other social reformers had long expressed concern about the life of the stage child. According to Marah Gubar, these concerns generally followed a binary logic, simultaneously insisting that child performers were "incompetent naïfs shoved into the limelight by greedy parents and managers," while dismissing any display of talent or the premature knowledge of complex human emotions as morally reprehensible and "disgusting."[51] In light of these anxieties, Lancaster's representation of the fictional Jean Margaret as a nonprofessional or amateur player deliberately emphasizes both her economic uselessness and her emotional pricelessness. Of course, audiences watching the play would have been aware of the girl actress's professional status and her economic value, not least because Thomas Davenport's promotional campaigns continually reminded them of this. Yet the fictional framework of *The Manager's Daughter* distances the girl from the world of the professional: she performs because she is having fun and because she loves her parents. This, Viviana Zelizer argues, is the "curious paradox" of the stage child, an economically valuable professional who labored to "portray the useless child" in fictional scenarios that deliberately obscured their work.[52] Within the fictional frame of *The Manager's Daughter*, Jean Margaret's performance is no performance at all but an act of love. She is an economic innocent, not an exploited professional—a dutiful daughter, not a sexualized commodity.[53]

Jean Margaret's portrayal of an economically useless child stands in sharp contrast to one of the era's most (in)famous examples of a dutiful daughter forced to take to the stage to rescue her family from debt: Fanny Kemble. Born into the famed Siddons/Kemble theatrical family, Kemble initially hoped to avoid going onto the stage and spent her early girlhood traveling and pursuing an education in Paris. In 1829, however, her father Charles Kemble ran into significant financial difficulties in his capacity as the manager of Covent Garden and appealed to his twenty-year-old daughter to make her theatrical debut as Juliet. Kemble's first appearance was very much the "ultimate family affair," as her mother played Lady Capulet and her father performed as Mercutio.[54] The young actress's striking physical appearance and appealing embodiment of Shakespeare's thirteen-year-old heroine delighted audiences and brought much needed financial stability to her father's theatrical management. For Kemble's part, the debut not only marked her "initiation into acting" but also her "initiation in sexual expression," both of which, Catherine Burroughs argues, "were strongly associated with her nuclear family, especially with her father."[55] It is here where the differences between Fanny Kemble and Jean Davenport are most pronounced—for while the latter would go on to play Juliet later in her career,[56] she (and her family) eschewed any association with sexual expression, emphasizing not just her economic innocence but her sexual innocence as well. To accomplish this feat, the Davenport family made strategic use of costuming and props, the most significant of which was a doll.

Playing with Dolls

There is nothing accidental about Jean Margaret's first entrance in *The Manager's Daughter*. Her appearance with a doll clasped in her arms indexes her economic innocence, age, and gender, as well as the Davenports' disposable income—consistent with new perspectives on children and toys. At the turn of the nineteenth century, parents and educators began to think differently about how, with whom, and with what middle-class children spent their time at home. The writer Maria Edgeworth disapproved of expensive "fashionable toys" such as gilt chairs, horses, and china dolls that invited children to play with miniature versions of objects "consumed by 'fine' adults."[57] The best thing a child could do with such toys was break them, Edgeworth claimed, and she urged parents to opt for durable toys that engaged the mind. Encouraging indoor play likewise supported the larger project of bourgeois domesticity by intensifying children's relationships with their parents and siblings.[58] Toys kept children at home and offered a suitable replacement for other forms of play that led impressionable young ones away from surveilling eyes. (Of course, Jean Margaret's declaration that her new doll will make her the envy of all her school friends suggests that not all toy acquisitions promoted positive sociability.)[59] Toys marked children's class status as well as their status *as* children through an embrace of cuteness. By playing with cute toys, Daniel Harris observes, the child learns "the dual roles of actor and audience, cootchying as much as he is cootchy-cooed,"[60] and comes to appreciate "the nature and value of cuteness."[61] Playing with toys was therefore critical to the formation of the privileged, white child who learned to embody and leverage the cute charms of the toy as a distinct kind of emotional capital.

Although these broader social developments affected the lives of all white, middle-class children irrespective of gender, differences in play distinguished boyhood from girlhood, especially where the performance of cute innocence was concerned. Dolls enjoyed a privileged place in the nurseries and imaginations of many white middle-class girls from the 1830s onward, which in turn supported the proliferation of "doll literature." Such stories and novels about the fictional world of dolls entertained their juvenile readers while imparting moral lessons about "appropriate" gendered behavior. As Eugenia Gonzalez writes, "the increasing role of surveillance in nineteenth-century theories of education influenced the generally didactic and formative purposes of . . . doll tales."[62] These tales naturalized the repertoire of benevolent motherhood for girls, equating doll play with tenderness and care. But not all girls followed the gender script. Some actively rebelled against the patriarchal emphasis on female domesticity embedded in doll play, "smashing, mutilating, or even arranging funerals for the perfect little bodies with which they were intended to have tea."[63] Robin Bernstein has similarly shown how some dolls, especially black dolls made of rubber or gutta percha, invited white American girls to engage in rough play, scripting actions that defied gender norms even as they reinforced white supremacist logic.[64]

Within *The Manager's Daughter*, Jean Margaret's onstage interactions with her prized *new* doll position the fictional daughter (and therefore the real one) as a sweet, sexually innocent girl who has absorbed the ideals of gender conformity.[65] As she sings to her doll— her "darling"—she rehearses the language of maternal devotion and heterosexual inscription, praising her doll's prettiness ("those pretty blue eyes / Such a head, lips so red"), and her marriageability—some day she will become "another doll's wife." The song invites audiences to see the actress Jean Davenport in the same light—as a pretty little "doll" put on display to entertain adult (male) admirers.[66] This initial marking of Jean Davenport's attractive girlishness casts audiences as (sexual?) consumers and reassures them that for all her protean ability, she remains a delightful little girl.[67] At the same time, any inkling of audience desire is mitigated by the doll's presence, which marks Jean Davenport's distance from motherhood and foregrounds her vulnerability, innocence, and cuteness.[68] More than a charming moment, then, Jean Margaret's cute interactions with the doll purposefully redirect any misplaced sexual longing, inviting audiences to feel affection (but no more).

The doll also reminds audiences that both the character Jean Margaret and the girl actress Jean Davenport are still young enough to play with dolls (the play never discloses her actual age). By so quickly signifying "girl," Varty suggests, the doll "sets up the possibility of audience astonishment at the contrast between the display of innocent juvenility and the subsequent proficiency of her performances."[69] The need for a doll as testament to Jean Margaret's juvenility seems to have intensified as the actress matured. "The onset or approach of menarche made the continued suppression of girlhood uncomfortable" for cross-dressing girls,[70] Shauna Vey observes and required new techniques of "juvenation." The term "juvenation" comes from the work of media studies scholar John Hartley, who defines it as "the creative practice of communicating with a readership *via the medium* of youthfulness."[71]

Film studies scholar Gaylyn Studlar usefully extends Hartley's term in her study of girlhood in classical Hollywood cinema, focusing on the "construction of girls and girlhood in and through Hollywood stars and their film vehicles."[72] Although the specific practices of juvenation—casting choices, costuming, hairstyles, publicity materials—varied from one actress to another depending on biological age and physical appearance, the end goal remained the same: persuading audiences of the performer's youthfulness.[73]

The following reminiscence from William Davidge, who toured with the Davenports circa 1837, identifies some of the strategies the family deployed to "juvenate" Jean Davenport: "The infant phenomenon was a buxom English lass of twelve or fourteen with stout legs and a florid complexion. She was always dressed in short dresses and pantalettes and neat slippers. Her hair was in braids down her back, and she wore the large, flapping hat of the period. Her head was large and her beauty small, looked nine years old, and was a good actress in certain heavy lines—indeed, quite remarkable in some heavy characters."[74] Here, girlish clothing (short dresses and pantalettes) and a youthful hairstyle ("braids down her back") draw attention away from the actress's sexually maturing ("buxom") body to give her the appearance of a nine-year-old girl. Likewise, her appearance onstage with a large doll redirects questions about the actress's biological age and extends her surrogation of childhood. "The juvenile body is a naturalistic effigy through which to surrogate childhood," writes Bernstein, "but that body continually grows, incrementally and inevitably losing the state of childhood." When the maturing juvenile body can no longer "contain that surrogation ... [it] overflows into other effigies, including ... nonhuman things such as dolls."[75] As an effigy of childhood, a doll stabilizes girlhood as a concept and helps to fix (albeit temporarily) the problem of the maturing female body.

In Jean Davenport's case, the doll (or dolls) was integral to her performance of young girlhood *offstage* as well. As Davidge recalls, when the company toured the provinces, Thomas Davenport would select "a lodging which all the churchgoers would have to pass on Sunday morning. He would dress up the infant phenomenon and make her sit dancing a big doll where she could be seen in the window, and the people would stand in groups open-mouthed in wonder at the baby who played with her doll in the morning, and trod the boards at night as Macbeth."[76] Playing into the public's desire to "know" the actors behind their stage personas, Davenport effectively restaged the opening of *The Manager's Daughter* by placing his daughter in the window of the family's private dwelling. In fact, the "big doll" Jean Davenport danced with in the window was likely the same doll she sang to onstage. This deliberate collision of real and fictional worlds stimulated "open-mouthed" wonder at the babylike actress capable of portraying vicious kings. Davidge's account implies that much of the pleasure audiences experienced watching Jean Davenport came from observing the huge disparities—of gender, age, class, nationality—between the performer and her roles. But in order for provincial audiences leery of the moral ambiguities of theatrical representation to take pleasure in the spectacular plasticity of Jean Margaret (the character), they had to know that beneath it all was a little girl. In other words, the "large doll" was key to safely promoting Jean Davenport (the actress) as a talented girl who could convincingly portray masculine energy and desires—as she did in her portrayals of Macbeth and Richard III—without abandoning her girlish innocence.

The public intimacy of the window scene also reassured passersby that the Davenports' onstage depiction of bourgeois domesticity in *The Manager's Daughter* was not just "for show"—but was rather an accurate reflection of the actual Davenport family. Tellingly, as Davidge recalls, the window scene was but a prelude to a collective performance of respectability, in which the "family formed in procession with prayerbooks in their hands and the vanity of early joys in their faces and went to church," arriving "just after everybody was seated, and marched up the aisle to the communion table in a style of pure melodrama, thus attracting the attention of all to the phenomenon."[77] Once again the boundary between the fictionalized and the real Davenports collapses, as churchgoers (and would-be theatregoers) stare at the tiny wonder and the family gathered lovingly around her.

The Davenports would continue to project this image of idealized family life as they embarked on a lengthy tour of British North America, the United States, and the British West Indies. As the following chapter shows, Jean Davenport's performances of devoted daughterhood took on additional meaning when played before settler audiences, with mixed results.

INTERLUDE 5
OBJECT LESSONS FROM JEAN DAVENPORT'S SCRAPBOOK, C. 1840

It's 2010 and I'm in the Library of Congress Manuscript Reading Room looking at papers that once belonged to Jean Margaret Lander (née Jean Margaret Davenport). Lander negotiated the awkward transition to adult stardom in the middle of the century through her portrayal of such tragic heroines as Marguerite in *La dame aux camélias* and Hester Prynne in the theatrical adaptation of *The Scarlet Letter*. But it is through her status as the widow of a Civil War general that she entered the Library of Congress; her personal papers are enfolded within the much larger collection of papers belonging to her husband General Frank W. Lander.

I turn to a scrapbook.[1] At first glance, it looks much like any other scrapbook from the nineteenth century. I am aware that it's special only because a thoughtful archivist and an intriguing finding aid have directed me here. The bluish leather cover is mottled with cracks and spots of decay or rot—thankfully none of the hand-staining red rot I've encountered in other scrapbooks from the period. The brown binding is torn and the words "Scrap Book No. 2" run up the side of the cover in faded black ink, presumably inscribed by the book's original owner. The broken spine exposes fibers of blue and yellow, reminding me to take care when turning the pages to avoid further damage. From beneath the cover, a few newspaper clippings escape containment and invite me to follow their trail. I'm not sure what I'll find beneath the cover but am eager to find out.

I open the book. A playbill pasted onto the inside front cover announces the forthcoming appearance of "La celebrada señorita Davenport del Teatro Real de Drury Lane," in the title roles of "Ricardo Tercero

[*Richard III*]" and "La hija del Empresario [*The Manager's Daughter*]."
In flowery language typical of the genre, the playbill presents Davenport as a well-traveled global performer, noting that despite her age—
"trece años [thirteen years old]"—she has played to "infinitos aplausos"
in London, Dublin, Boston, and New York. In fact, the name-dropping
playbill continues, the celebrated British actor Edmund Kean was so
impressed with the young señorita that he bestowed upon her one of his
very own "sombreros." Tellingly, the playbill does not identify *where* the
young wonder will perform, which may mean that it was used to reach
Spanish-speaking audiences in multiple locations.

On the facing page, a handwritten note pasted into the scrapbook
confirms the playbill's creation for colonial audiences and yields important clues about the scrapbook's purpose and provenance. The words
"Scrap Book" appear again at the top of the page, beneath which the unidentified author—possibly the celebrated señorita herself or another
family member—details the itinerary of the Davenport company's
Caribbean travels:

> West Indies 21st May 1840
> We sailed from Barbados 21st May about 3 o'clock P.M.
> —The sun set upon this little Paradize [*sic*], and we lost for
> ever in night the Island of Barbados.—23rd Anchor'd at Tortola—
> sail in from thence about 10' A.M. beach at [?] St. Thomas about
> 12.—Left Mail Boat for Tartarous [*sic*] steamer same Evening for
> Jamaica About 8 o'clock next morning anchor'd at Porto Rico
> —28th St. Domingo—29th—1st Iago de Cuba 1st of June landed
> at Kingston Jamaica—Theatre not finish'd—compelled first to,
> *open at*
> Spanish Town
> Monday 8th June 1840

Though sparsely written, the note conveys something of the Davenports' frequent movement throughout the Caribbean in the spring of
1840 and the author's eagerness to document their travels. Their attention to the specific timing of the company's departures and arrivals
suggests that they wrote the introductory note shortly after the journey
had ended, not months or years later. The description of the book as a
"Scrap Book" also implies that its creator planned to use it for collecting
and preserving articles, editorials, and related print matter from local

newspapers over the course of the Davenports' tour. Unlike a diary, the scrapbook contains very little of the collector's own writing, yet when viewed as "a multi-lens telescope," it reveals much about the Davenports' (accidental?) involvement in colonial politics.[2]

I keep coming back to Scrap Book #2. I've visited it twice in the Library of Congress Reading Room, and as a dutiful twenty-first-century historian, I've digitally photographed all of its pages. I revisit the scrapbook now (in its digital format) in an effort to learn about the person/family who glued the articles to its pages. Although I consider the content of the articles and related "scraps," my primary focus here is on the materiality of the scrapbook. I am interested in the arrangement of the clippings—many of them critical attacks on Davenport and her manager father Thomas—and the maker's use of handwritten notes to reach imagined readers. Returning to Robin Bernstein's concept of the "scriptive thing," an approach that acknowledges the various ways that objects shape, direct, and script human actions, I argue that the individual (or individuals) who assembled Scrap Book #2 used the scrapbook format to contextualize the printed words and influence the way future readers flipped through its pages. If, as Rebecca Schneider suggests, "archives are, first and foremost, *theatres* for repertoires of preservation, leaning toward and into a promise of the coming 'liveness' of encounter,"[3] then scrapbooks are also simultaneously scripts and theatres that direct readers along a specific path and offer access to hidden repertoires.

When I began this project, I assumed (and desperately wanted to believe) that Jean Margaret Davenport had pasted the articles into Scrap Book #2. I reasoned that the book's inclusion in her official papers meant that she *must* have created it. But over time, I had to admit that I didn't have enough evidence to support this assumption. Though frustrated, I contented myself by reasoning that *if* the scrapbook collector was *not* Jean Davenport, it was likely one of her parents. Since then, I have opted to read the scrapbook as a kind of family album, an archive created to document the transatlantic adventures of an exceptional family and promote a specific version of colonial confrontation and intercultural exchange.

Scrapbooks defy straightforward classification: historians have described them variously as "filing systems,"[4] "diaries of sorts,"[5] "multilayered expression[s] of individual sentiment enunciated through objects that carry an emotional association," "material artifact[s] [that] symbolize[e] both personal and cultural identity,"[6] and "paper museum[s]" built by "otherwise anonymous individuals who extracted mass-produced items from one context and provided them with a new different setting."[7] Differing in size and content, scrapbooks are best understood as books that invite their owners to assemble and paste newspaper clippings, cards, images, and other small objects onto their blank pages.

Scrapbooks first gained popularity in the early nineteenth century as a variation on the commonplace book, a form of life writing that generally included selections of poetry and passages from the owner's favorite sermons, novels, and related texts.[8] By mid-century most scrapbooks fell into one of two categories: books bursting with "brightly colored chromolithographed images known as scraps" and keepsake albums filled with a mix of texts and engravings.[9] The proliferation of print media in the mid- to late nineteenth century fueled the craze for clipping and pasting printed text and attractive images into personal scrapbooks. In this respect, cultural historian Ellen Gruber Garvey argues, "scrapbooks merge the *practice* of saving with the *record* of saving."[10] Through scrapbooking, men and women not only participated in the production, consumption, circulation, and preservation of print culture but also used the form to tell histories about themselves. The scrapbook can thus be understood as a unique form of life writing, different from but comparable to the diary or memoir, all of which "materialize the collector's vision of herself."[11]

Theatrical scrapbooks constitute a unique sub-genre of the scrapbook form. Such scrapbooks, writes Sharon Marcus, have much to "teach us about the history of performance" including the "economics, geography, and sociology of theatre spectatorship" as well as insight into historical enactments of gender, race, sexuality, and nationality.[12] Scrapbooks created by theatrical *performers* likewise offer lessons in the cultural politics and professional dynamics of a given period. Garvey identifies actors and actresses as "particularly avid scrapbook makers." Alert to the form's promotional capacity, many nineteenth-century performers pasted reviews, playbills, and related ephemera into personal scrapbooks, which they occasionally used "as a job-hunting aid to show to theater managers."[13]

Scrap Book #2 may have served as a promotional aid, but its value for historians lies in the fascinating narrative that rises from its pages.

Like most scrapbooks it includes dozens of carefully clipped and pasted newspaper articles arranged into two or three columns on each page. In cases where an article extends beyond the edge of the scrapbook, the creator has carefully folded the clipping to prevent ripping. The length and content of the articles vary, giving each page its own distinctive design. Some pages present a uniform appearance, with three columns of neatly clipped articles, while others adopt a more haphazard look, with groups of short clippings more or less aligned in a row or arranged in a geometric pattern. On many of the pages, brief notes written on horizontal strips of white paper provide context for the articles that follow. Most of the articles are reviews of Davenport's performances, but editorials attacking the young actress and her father are prominent exceptions, as are several "Letters to the Editor" written by Thomas Davenport himself.

Reading through the scrapbook, the contemporary reader tracks Jean Davenport and her family from Spanish Town to Kingston, eventually to Montego Bay and back to Kingston; later pages take the reader forward in time to Nova Scotia, Newfoundland, Dover, and the Hague. The scrapbook's structure and organization script the reader's movement through its pages, supporting a linear temporal journey. "In a scrapbook, the order of the materials on the page remains the same and uses the language of juxtaposition," Garvey writes.[14] She distinguishes scrapbooks from newspapers or clippings files: "Scrapbooks declare that they are something other than files of clippings; the framework and arrangement of materials they embody are works in themselves."[15] Readers cannot reorder the clippings in the scrapbook without destroying the book itself and must therefore follow its organizational structure and the path laid out by its creator (though, of course, a reader might choose to flip ahead). Put differently, scrapbooks make manifest the collector's point of view and work on behalf of that collector to promote a particular interpretation of the material pasted within.[16]

If the reader follows Scrap Book #2's script and reads the articles in sequence, a most peculiar story of colonial anxiety emerges. As I detail more fully in the following chapter, the Davenports arrived in Jamaica during a time of rapid social and political change following the 1838 emancipation of the enslaved population. For years, as Errol Hill documents in *The Jamaican Stage*, theatre in Kingston had "waned" with the exception of "local amateur productions" as the white settler population waited to see how abolition would affect their communities.[17] Following emancipation, the citizens of Kingston once again sought theatrical amusement, only to realize that the existing theatre was in a state beyond repair. In May 1838, a petition to build a new theatre was forwarded to the Kingston Town Council, followed by public subscription to raise funds for the construction. However, Robert Hancock, the man first contracted to build the theatre, was ill equipped for the job— apparently he had never been in a theatre other than the dilapidated old one in Kingston. When his first attempt failed, the Council decided that major renovations were needed to produce a functional theatre and invited John T. Dias, a dentist by trade and the manager of the Kingston Amateur Association, to oversee the theatre's construction and raise money to cover the cost of interior decorations. Nicknamed "John Kemble Macready Dias" after the famous English actor-managers John Kemble and William Macready, the dentist took his responsibilities seriously and construction of the new theatre resumed.[18]

The note on the first page of Scrap Book #2 indicates that the Davenport company was originally scheduled to perform in Kingston in May 1840 but that the theatre was "not finish'd" on time, and so they were "compelled first to, *open at* Spanish Town." Beneath this note, several short clippings from Kingston newspapers enviously discuss the actress's forthcoming appearance in Spanish Town. "The Spanish-tonians ought to esteem themselves as highly fortunate in having the first '*peep*,'" a writer for the *Kingston Dispatch* wrote, "however, we are led to hope that *our* Theatre will be finished, and then we shall have the pleasure of seeing this 'wondrous little lady's' performances."[19] After a successful visit in Spanish Town, documented in the scrapbook by several pages of glowing reviews, the company returned to Kingston in late August or early September and prepared for their performance in the newly completed theatre.

A writer for the *Kingston Dispatch* saw Davenport's forthcoming performance as an important moment in Kingston's cultural history. "It is gratifying to think, that the first impression the lovers of Drama will have, in the new Temple, will be that of this extraordinary Young Lady," the writer remarked. "It would have been unfortunate indeed, if strollers, destitute of talent, had given the stamp of their buffoonery to the Kingston Theatre."[20] This disparaging reference to "strollers" and buffoons alludes to internal divisions within the Kingston community

FIGURE 20. *Theatre Royal in Kingston, Jamaica,*
possibly drawn by Jean Margaret Davenport during her visit to the city.
Library of Congress.

over who should have the honor of appearing first in the new theatre
(I am reminded of Mrs. John Drew's dismissive comments about the
amateur performers of Halifax; see Interlude 2). This author is relieved
that an accomplished actress not a talentless amateur will bless the
"new Temple." Other Kingstonians felt differently and used the public
platform of the Kingston press to lambaste the Davenports for attempt-
ing to fob off mediocre talent on the colonial audience. The details of
that struggle appear in the following chapter.

For now, let me conclude with a brief description of the only image
that appears in Scrap Book #2: a drawing of the newly constructed
theatre in Kingston, Jamaica, created by a juvenile hand, possibly Jean
Davenport's. Pasted sideways into the scrapbook, it records the new
theatre's impressive façade, its prominent front steps, support columns,
large windows, and balcony. The image also records the artist's presence . . . standing or seated in front of the theatre in its earliest days.
They have documented the new theatre in as much detail as possible,

as though aware that by passing through its doors they are making history and may wish to remember their time in that building.[21] From its pasted place on the page, the drawing folds time, joining past and present, actress and historian. I turn the book to get a better look at the drawing, directed by its sideways placement. I take a photo. I take another photo, and another, trying to capture the drawing's simplicity and beauty, trying to follow the script of the scrapbook and to recover something of its repertoire.

CHAPTER 5

A Daughter of the Empire

ON THE LIMITS OF REPRESENTATION

On July 30, 1841, readers of the *Newfoundland Public Ledger* learned that Jean Margaret Davenport, the "First Juvenile Actress of the Day," would be making a brief visit to St. John's before returning home to England. The announcement, likely written by Thomas Davenport, took pains to remind readers of the young girl's many international successes: "Miss Davenport is so well known as to almost render it unnecessary to state that she was presented with the late Mr. Kean's Hat, after her performance of Richard III, in London—with a splendid Gold Watch and Chain by the citizens of New York—and that lately when on a rapid tour to the West Indies her receipts clear of expenditures mounted to the unusual sum of One Thousand Dollars per night!!!"[1] The subtext was clear: the forthcoming arrival of the "juvenile actress" would transform Newfoundland from a lonely island colony into a privileged member of an imagined community bound by imperial and affective ties. Through an explicit reference to the recently deceased actor Edmund Kean and an implicit promise that Davenport's presence would unite the people of St. John's with audiences in London, New York, and the British West Indies, the announcement appealed to colonial desires for cultural achievement and cosmopolitan affiliation.

In the previous chapter, I argued that *The Manager's Daughter* can usefully be understood as a domestic drama that reflects emerging bourgeois ideals and in many ways anticipates the sacralization of the innocent little girl—a cultural phenomenon that would remake adult-child relations in the second half of the nineteenth century.[2] This chapter looks beyond domestic circles to read *The Manager's Daughter* against the backdrop of British imperialism, taking into account the play's apparent popularity with white settler audiences in North America and the British West Indies. Thanks to advances in steamship travel and the expansion of intercontinental railways in the 1820s and 1830s, it became economically feasible for British performers like the Davenports to undertake extensive tours of the colonies. Such companies contributed to the formation of a "national performance culture," which, in the words of historian Kathleen Wilson, united "widely-dispersed and amalgamated" groups of people, "exposing, eliding, or superseding regional and provincial identities—Irish, Scottish, Jewish, East or West Indian—in favor of a more anodyne 'British' allegiance as it did so."[3]

Touring from colonial city to colonial city, girls like Jean Davenport modeled the peculiar entanglement of theatre and empire,[4] serving as ambassadors of British culture who encouraged colonial audiences (primarily, if not exclusively, white settlers) to see themselves as part of the empire's "imagined community."[5] Davenport's performance of daughterly duty and clever fixing in *The Manager's Daughter* found special favor among white settler audiences in the British West Indies as they contended with the abolition of slavery and its effects on their financial and emotional well-being.

But not all colonial subjects were receptive to the instrumentalization of young girls for imperial objectives. Some outright refused to be coerced by the loudly proclaimed charms of "astonishing" girls and accused the Davenports of trying to dupe them with clever words and puffery. These critics took special exception to the pubescent girl's embodiment of masculinity onstage, and their angry reactions prompted debates about masculinity within colonial settings more broadly. To explore these tensions, the second half of this chapter focuses on the controversies that played out in the pages of colonial newspapers: the first in the island colony of Jamaica in September 1840, the second in the island colony of Newfoundland in August 1841. Although the sociopolitical, economic, and geographic conditions of 1840s Jamaica differed considerably from those of 1840s Newfoundland, a comparison of responses to Jean Davenport reveals that white settlers in both locations were deeply concerned with questions of civility as it related to masculinity and colonial identity, especially when that masculinity was embodied by a girl. This chapter demonstrates that one of the advantages of tracing a theatrical performer or company's movement from one colonial location to another is the way it reveals striking commonalities; these become even clearer when they emerge from Jean Davenport's personal scrapbooks in newspaper articles separated by only a few pages.

The stories that arise from Davenport's scrapbooks attest to the tug-of-war that has always characterized celebrity culture as performers, fans/critics, and the media vie for attention and influence.[6] Thomas Davenport excelled at promoting his daughter but even he was incapable of controlling the discourse surrounding her in Jamaica and Newfoundland. In both locations, colonial theatres and newspapers became the staging ground for heated debates about the girl's proclaimed virtuosity, notably her portrayal of male characters like Richard III and her supposed resemblance to Edmund Kean. These debates quickly extended beyond the realm of repertoire and acting, however, to include discussions about the responsibilities of audiences and critics, definitions of gentlemanly behavior, and settler treatment of traveling players. Set eleven months apart, the twinned debates over whether to accept the girl as a representative of British culture on par with the "*masculine* acting" of Kean brilliantly foreground the disruptive power of girls playing across colonial and gender lines.

The chapter concludes with a very different critique of the Davenport family, one offered by the novelist Charles Dickens in the pages of *Nicholas Nickleby*. Although Jean Davenport would insist in later years that she was *not* the inspiration for the pathetic figure of Ninetta Crummles, a talentless girl actress forever trapped in a juvenile state by frilly costumes and alcohol, the evidence suggests otherwise. Ultimately Thomas Davenport's grand scheme to fix his daughter in the minds of readers succeeded all too well, but not in the way that he or Jean had anticipated.

National and Ethnic Stereotypes in *The Manager's Daughter*

Like other protean farces of the period, *The Manager's Daughter* offers a sampling of the national and ethnic stereotypes that dominated the British cultural imaginary in the 1830s, chief among them Scottish, Irish, American, and French types.[7] Jean Margaret even veers briefly into a parody of African Americans with a rendition of the hugely popular minstrel song "Jump Jim Crow."[8] While these stereotypes showcase the actress's dancing and singing ability, not to mention her facility with accents, they also reaffirm the cultural superiority of the British, while highlighting the imperial ties (and hierarchies) that bind the English to the Scots and Irish. It is no coincidence that the American Hector Earsplitter is an overconfident braggart and that the Irish Fergus O'Botherwell is a hotblooded "firebrand," or that the Scottish Effie Featherblossom is delicate and lovely (Thomas Davenport was a Scot). And it is certainly no coincidence that the manager shows charity toward an impoverished French child, a victim of revolutionary turmoil. Moreover, as Anne Varty observes, all but one of the characters: "represent national identities with which the English either had or continued to have relationships of sovereign conflict. The American War of Independence (1775–1783) was not a distant memory, the Napoleonic Wars (1803–1815) had ended merely some twenty years before the play was staged, while the Scots and the Irish exhibited longstanding restlessness under the yoke of Westminster, not subdued by the Acts of Union of 1707 (Scotland) and 1800 (Ireland). Each type presented poses a potential threat to the hegemonic stability of the era."[9] *The Manager's Daughter* effectively handles these "potential threat[s]" by filtering them through the doubled bodies of a girl—Jean Margaret the character and Jean Davenport the actress. Here we see a different kind of surrogation at work than that discussed in the previous chapter, one in which the girl performer absorbs abstracted national types into a single, harmonious performance in order to assuage English anxieties. As such, *The Manager's Daughter* not only stages the British Empire's allies, rivals, and internal threats but also functions as an allegory of British cultural and military supremacy. In this reading, the title of the afterpiece refers both to the specific daughter and to the many daughters (and sons) required to sustain the empire. This aspect of the play offers some explanation for the enthusiastic response it received from colonial audiences when the Davenports embarked on a transatlantic tour of North America and the British West Indies.

British acting companies had toured the Atlantic for over a century by the time the Davenports decided to cross the ocean. The gradual expansion of the transatlantic theatre circuit, which included Kingston, Jamaica; Bridgetown, Barbados; New Orleans, Charleston, Virginia, New York, and Boston, in the United States; and Halifax, Nova Scotia meant that by the end of the eighteenth century colonial audiences along the Atlantic coastline consumed a broad and dynamic theatrical repertoire, everything from Shakespeare to the latest London comedies.[10] These settler audiences kept abreast of new fashions in theatrical entertainment through newspapers, correspondence with friends and family, and their own transatlantic travels. Going to the theatre thus became a way for white settlers and their offspring to assert cultural knowledge and demonstrate that their sophistication and taste was equivalent to that of their London counterparts.

As noted, advances in steamship travel, the expansion of intercontinental railways, and the intensification of the colonial project meant that by the mid-1830s it was much easier for growing numbers of British companies to venture abroad.[11] Motivated by a desire for social and financial gain, touring companies actively participated "in the spread of British hegemony," which, as Richard Foulkes notes, "could be both an advantage and a disadvantage depending on their destination and the time of their visit."[12] This increase in theatrical touring coincided with major changes in British imperial governance, most notably the abolition of slavery in 1833 and acts granting greater autonomy to the British North American colonies following the Durham Report of 1839. As a result, itinerant performers often found themselves caught up in local political debates about sovereignty and colonial rule.[13]

Curiously, a 1903 clipping in the *Dramatic Mirror*, published shortly after Jean Davenport Lander's death, asserts that the Davenports initially journeyed to North America on a whim: "It chanced that while the family was playing an engagement in Cork the steamer *Sirius*—one of the first steam vessels in the transatlantic trade—entered the harbor. Without any preparation, attracted perhaps by the novelty of the ship, the family embarked upon her to come to America."[14] While later rumors of Thomas Davenport's managerial limitations complicate this cheery post, implying that the Davenports boarded the *Sirius* in May 1838 for reasons other than "novelty," the journey undoubtedly marked a major turning point in Jean Davenport's life and career. Following a successful engagement at the National Theatre in New York, the family remained on the continent for close to a year, with stops in Boston, Philadelphia, Baltimore, Washington, New Orleans, Kingston (Upper Canada), and Montreal. The tour was a success, and so in the summer of 1840, the Davenports undertook a second lengthy tour of the colonies, this time with additional stops in the West Indies and the British Maritime colonies.

On both tours, *The Manager's Daughter* featured prominently in Jean Davenport's repertoire, as did the travestied roles of Richard III, Young Norval, Rob Roy, and Shylock.[15] Throughout their travels, settler audiences responded with great feeling to the metatheatrical afterpiece with its cornucopia of national representations. In August 1839, for example, a "most respectable" Montreal audience in what was then Lower Canada offered up "universal and unanimous applause" for *The Manager's Daughter*. The critic for the English-language *Montreal Royal Gazette* described Jean Davenport's imitations as "perfect": "They displayed a wonderful versatility of talents of the highest imitative order." What most delighted this critic, however, was the girl's Scottish dance (in the character of Effie), which reminded him of home: "Every Caledonian who retains a veneration for the joyous amusements of his country, must witness Miss Davenport's Highland Fling; and sure we are, that he will never forget the impressions made upon his mind, and his affections for his native hills."[16] Here the homesick (for Scotland) critic interprets Jean Margaret's dance as an affective bridge between colony and homeland. Deeply moved, he directs others to seek her out so that they too might imaginatively traverse time and space and return to the "native hills" of home. Curiously, this account complicates earlier historical work on the hegemony of Englishness within the colonial realm, suggesting that touring performers supported assertions of ethnic and regional pride.[17]

The Caledonian's emotional response to Jean Davenport's dancing offers a vivid example of "intimate distance," a term introduced by Elizabeth Maddock Dillon to "describe the way in which colonial culture in the Atlantic world involved bringing communities together and sustaining them—creating intimacy—across great distances."[18] Maintaining close affective ties to the metropole was critical for many white settler-colonists as they sought to affirm their Britishness from afar. In this instance, Jean Davenport's visit to Montreal came shortly after the violent Rebellion of Lower Canada, during which the colony's French-speaking population challenged colonial rule. Although the British successfully squashed the rebellion by the end of 1838, the sight of a young girl singing songs about "home" must have been reassuring to English-speaking settlers looking to reaffirm their cultural superiority. Here, the colonists' reaction to Davenport recalls the audience in Quebec City who wept at Clara Fisher's performance of Little Pickle (see Chapter 2).

Of course, experiences and expressions of intimate distance varied from one colonial context to another. Whereas the Montreal critic relished Jean Davenport's performance because it imaginatively transported him to an *elsewhere*, white settler audiences in Bridgetown, Barbados, clung to the girl because she helped them envision themselves within a larger imperial community despite intense feelings of physical and emotional isolation. Writing in late April 1840, the critic for the *Bridgetown Sun* apologized to Jean Davenport for failing to take note of her previous visit, citing recent colonial negotiations with Britain in the aftermath of emancipation as the source of his distraction. The Davenports, he explains, visited the island at a time "when the leading native families of this island, alarmed at the [slave] insurrection of 1816, and the phantom of Emancipation, are, for the most part, absent from the island, or preparing to be so." As a result, he concludes, the stage has been deprived "of much of that support, which it was accustomed to receive in past times."[19]

I want to pause for a moment to think through the critic's apology to the Davenports and scratch at the racism beneath his words. In equating Emancipation with some phantom menace hanging over Bridgetown, the critic depicts the island's "leading native families" as the victims of circumstances beyond their control. It is not the enslaved rebels who deserve pity but the white men and women whose lives were "alarmed" and disrupted by the *threat* of violence. It is their fear of the unknown, their emotional fragility, their dread at the prospect of a future without slavery that has kept them from the theatre. And so it is Emancipation *itself* that is to blame for the critic's failure to observe Jean Davenport's talents on her first visit to the island colony—or so reads the subtext of this critic's apology.

Despite such dour predictions, Bridgetown audiences flocked to the theatre, encouraged (it would seem) by the actions of colonial leaders who extended their patronage to the actress. On May 6, 1840, Jean Davenport appeared under the patronage of "his excellency the Commander-in-Chief of the land forces," ensuring "a full and respectable house" at the Theatre Royal.[20] Three nights later, she performed under the patronage of His Excellency Sir Evan McGregor, the governor of Barbados, who had "induced" the Davenport company to delay their earlier plans to leave the colony, presumably in an effort to boost morale and shake settler-colonists from their depressed state.[21] The following week, Jean Davenport was "called before the curtain, an honor never before conferred by an audience in Barbados," where she announced that on the following Tuesday she would perform *The Merchant of Venice* and *The Manager's Daughter*, this time under the patronage of Commodore Leith. Upon hearing that *The Manager's Daughter* would be repeated, the audience "gave three cheers," which one writer interpreted "as a mark of their approbation of a Dramatic composition which affords such high entertainment, while giving so great scope to the talent of the Performer."[22] What this writer doesn't say, but which the enthusiastic response implies, is that for the people of Bridgetown, Jean Davenport's virtuosic performance of fixing in *The Manager's Daughter* offered an attractive counter-narrative to their day-to-day experiences, one that allowed them to temporarily forget their fears and revel in a larger imperial community. In other words, a young girl's emotional labor boosted the feelings of downtrodden white men and women, helping them reconnect with their privilege and their place within the grand narrative of British imperial conquest. Indeed, Jean Davenport's popularity among the British military and political elite strongly suggests that these leaders saw her as an icon of British culture, respectability, and ambition: a daughter of the empire, a stabilizing symbol of British civilization, and a valuable asset during a period of considerable uncertainty.

Although *The Manager's Daughter* was Davenport's signature role, she also aligned herself with broader imperial aims in plays like *Old and Young* (sometimes called *The Four Mowbrays*), which presented opportunities for her to display her knowledge and experience of military training routines. For example, in her scenes as the battle-obsessed Hector, she performed the "British Manual Exercise," a military drill designed to remake average men into mechanized killers.[23] A full description of the exercise itself appears on a back page in one of Davenport's tour scrapbooks (c. 1838–1839):

Secure—Arms
Shoulder—Arms
Present—Arms

Post—Arms
Charge—Bayonet
Shoulder—Arms
Order—Arms
Advance—Arms
Shoulder—Arms
Support—Arms
Stand at Ease
Attention
Carry—Arms
Slope—Arms
Stand at Ease
Attention
Carry—Arms
Ready
Present[24]

The exercise's presence in the scrapbook, an object updated on a regular basis, may indicate that it was a new addition to Jean Davenport's repertoire, perhaps introduced to appeal to the soldiers in the audience. Brought into the theatre, the drill remade Jean Davenport like the soldiers she emulated, once again marking her value as a daughter of empire.[25]

The Problem with Kean: Trouble in Jamaica and Newfoundland

Jean Davenport benefited from her role in the performance and promotion of British values, ideals, and ideologies. Colonial audiences applauded her portrayal of Shakespeare's tragic characters from a repertoire increasingly marked as "English" and accepted her posthumous pairing with Edmund Kean.[26] In 1840, a critic in Kingston, Jamaica, claimed that, with the exception of Kean, the young girl's Shylock "far surpassed those who have made it the study of their lives to excel in this great creation of the Poet." For this writer, her depiction of Shylock's "utter prostration, both mentally and bodily" in the trial scene and his despair upon realizing his ruin were "altogether astonishing in so young a person, and so inexperienced in those violent passions and emotions which rack so terribly the human mind."[27] Critics were equally impressed with Davenport's Richard III, especially her enactment of Richard's death and the wooing scene with Lady Anne, once again drawing comparisons to Kean.[28] In 1839, a writer for the *Montreal Royal Gazette* remarked that "It was, in truth, a surprising spectacle to behold a young girl, scarcely twelve years old, perform with credit and judgment, a character which has demanded the powers of the greatest genius that has ever attempted to depicture and realize the conception of Richard III."[29] Another writer, insisting that he was not writing "in slavish subserviency" (i.e., as a paid puffer), described how she "looked and spoke like a Kean in miniature and displayed from her first appearance to her death by the sword of Richmond, a perfect and familiar conception of the crooked back tyrant."[30] Such enthusiastic comparisons of the girl actress and the Romantic actor point to Thomas Davenport's success in shaping critical discourse during the family's tour of British North America and the West Indies.

But not everyone was amused. In Kingston, Jamaica, a vocal group of theatregoers responded unfavorably to the girl, whom they considered something of a humbug.[31] Their responses are best understood within the context of settler anxiety in the post-Emancipation period, when the theatre became a touchstone for Kingston cultural identity.

Slavery in Jamaica officially ended in 1834, as it did throughout the British Empire. What followed was a four-year "apprenticeship" period, a concession offered to the Jamaica planters by the British government as one of a series of compensations for loss of income. During this time, formerly enslaved men and women continued to labor as apprentices for their former masters with the promise that they would "be guided along the paths of social and economic improvement" until they received "complete freedom" in 1838.[32] Most planters saw the transition period as an opportunity to continue exploiting their "apprentices" and "squeeze the last juice out of compulsory labour before the great ruin of freedom set in."[33] Not surprisingly, the apprenticeship system failed: planters struggled to maintain the same rate of production as they had under slavery; other settlers began leaving the island, sensing that the colony was entering a period of rapid economic decline; and apprentices continued to endure many of the same brutal punishments they had experienced as slaves.[34] In the words of historian Richardson Wright, "These were bitter years."[35]

Such bitterness contributed to the deterioration of theatre buildings and the decline of theatrical entertainment more broadly. If, as Kathleen Wilson and others have argued, the audiences who gathered at the theatre in eighteenth-century Kingston enacted "a microcosm of the plantocracy's vision of society,"[36] the shattering of that vision disrupted all that surrounded it. What resulted was a ruinous feedback loop: as the Kingston Theatre fell into disrepair, professional touring companies avoided the island, which in turn limited the financial resources available for the theatre's maintenance and repair, making it even less appealing to traveling players. Although several amateur theatre groups persisted in their efforts to entertain, occasionally joining forces with amateurs in Spanish Town and local regiment offers to produce plays like Thomas Otway's tragedy *Venice Preserved*, the vitality that had once defined colonial theatre in Jamaica all but disappeared.[37]

Jamaica's performance culture continued to thrive nonetheless, thanks in no small part to the innovations of enslaved performers who appropriated Shakespeare and other forms of dominant white culture for their own ends.[38] Annual celebrations like the Jonkonnu performances held at Christmas featured dancing, singing, and elaborate costumes, topped off by pastiche performances of scenes from popular Anglo-American plays. Throughout the year, enslaved children known as "actor boys" transformed the streets of Kingston and Spanish Town into their own stages, performing scenes from Shakespeare, which they had "learned either by rote or by sneaking into the playhouse."[39] *Richard III* was a particular favorite for these actor boys, especially Richard's pathetic, last-gasp plea for a horse.[40] Such performances "delighted and confused white spectators," especially when reenactments of death scenes and duels between white characters concluded with jubilant victory dances. "The theatre of transatlanticism was a dangerous place," Wilson surmises, "where mimesis and citation could exalt and transgress as well as debase—a volatile social space indeed."[41]

In recognition of this volatility, and in an effort to restore and reaffirm their position within the empire's cultural sphere, a group of white citizens led by the dentist John T. Dias submitted a petition to the city council in May 1838, three months before Emancipation. Signed by two-thirds of the Kingston white settler community, the petition called on the council to approve the construction of a new theatre.[42] Although the scheme was approved, building a new theatre proved much more difficult than Dias and his colleagues had originally imagined. Lengthy delays, which compelled the Davenports to open in Spanish Town rather than Kingston as initially planned, sprinkled more salt on wounded egos.

Frustration over the new theatre, not to mention the Davenports' warm reception in Spanish Town, offer some explanation for the fierce attack that greeted Jean Davenport and her family when they finally appeared at the new Kingston Theatre in September. An additional factor seems to have been the Davenports' repertoire, most notably *Richard III*. Although I have found no evidence that the Davenports interacted with (or even knew about) actor boys, I imagine that Kingston audiences may well have had such performers in mind when they attended the theatre and watched Jean Davenport's interpretation of the tyrant king.[43] The day of her Kingston debut, during which she performed both *Richard III* and *The Manager's Daughter*, an anonymous group calling themselves "Trio Voces in Uno" published a letter in the *Kingston Morning Journal* accusing Thomas Davenport of deliberately deceiving the public: "lead not the community to expect that a 'Theatrical Star' has visited our shores when the talent brought forward is of a medium description; rather overrate than overdraw."[44] The Trio took particular offense to comparisons between the young girl's portrayal of Richard III and that of the Romantic actor Edmund Kean: "To us who have seen Kean [and] many of the first Actors of the stage per[sonify] Richard, the consequence attached to the character was entirely lost."[45]

Thomas Davenport responded swiftly, reproaching his unidentified critics for their ungentlemanly behavior and challenging them to make themselves known. When the company's subsequent performance of *The Silent Lady* was interrupted by "a respectable portion of the audience" hissing at the young actress, he insisted that the reaction "emanated in male violence" and demanded that the "originators" stand forth. Recalling the event in a subsequent letter to the *Journal*, a writer using the pseudonym "Censor" (likely a member of the Trio) described Davenport as "assum[ing] the look with which tragedy heroes terrify tyrants" to "frow[n] down the unlucky victim."[46] The Trio and their supporters not only refused to heed Davenport's warning but also insisted that they were fully within their rights to hiss at a performance that displeased them.[47] Disgusted with this behavior, Davenport wrote to the *Morning Journal* representing himself as a "humble servant" dedicated to protecting the public from insult. "If riotous persons are not aware," he warned, "I will tell them, that any one *'hissing causelessly, and creating thereby a nuisance in a Theatre,'* is liable by the Law of England to be punished." He concluded by informing the editor that in England and America, editors of esteemed journals refused to publish "ANONYMOUS attacks on Managers of Theatres." The message was clear: the absence of such civil customs in Jamaica rendered it an uncivil colony.[48]

Words flew wildly in the days that followed, from the stage, the auditorium, and the pages of Kingston's newspapers, as different members of the community voiced their opinions of the actress, her family, and the controversy surrounding them. Here intimate distance enacted at the local level became a problem rather than a solution to strengthening colonial ties. Ultimately, calmer voices prevailed, as a writer calling himself Civis reminded readers of the *Jamaica Despatch, Chronicle, and Gazette* that "The stage may be said, to be as yet, in its very infancy here, and will require the fostering care of a generous and enlightened public, and an absence from invidious criticisms, ere it can be expected to attain that degree of excellence to be wished."[49] Civis's peacemaking comments focus on the importance of civility as a symbol of cultural progress and social maturity.

In *White Civility*, his study of white masculinity in nineteenth- and early twentieth-century Canada, Daniel Coleman argues that for many settlers, demonstrations of "cultivated, polite behavior (most commonly modelled on the figure of the bourgeois gentleman)" were key to individual and collective performances of self.[50] Derived largely from British models, civility was a critical component in the "production and education of the individual citizen," yet was not something that an individual or culture could inherently claim; rather, civility was "something that [a] person or culture *did*." In other words, civility arose through performative acts and constituted a kind of "(White) cultural practice," functioning simultaneously as "a mode of internal management and self-definition" that allowed individuals to monitor their own behavior and as a "mode of external management" that equipped settlers with a rubric or "mandate" for assessing "those perceived as uncivil."[51] Policing the borders of civility was particularly important for settlers who feared that geographic and social distance from the metropole would negatively influence their own social performances. "Caught in the time-space delay between the metropolitan place where civility is made and legislated and the colonial place where it is enacted and enforced," settlers felt the need to perform their civility and police their peers.[52]

Coleman's observations about civility in colonial Canada offer a useful framework for analyzing the newspaper debates that waged in Kingston, Jamaica, despite obvious differences in context. In his calming letter, Civis implies that the men of Kingston have acted childishly and, like their "infant" theatre, need to overcome "invidious criticisms" (or the temptation to make them) in order to reach maturity. That the debate should center so directly on a girl's ability to convincingly portray masculine behavior indicates that the citizens of Kingston were anxious about their own performances of masculinity, particularly as they reflected Jamaica's place within the empire so soon after Emancipation. This "anxiety of belatedness," to use Coleman's phrase, was likely compounded by the actual belatedness of the new theatre's opening and by Jean Davenport's impressive mimetic talents.[53] Civis urged his fellow Kingstonians to adopt a more open, supportive, and generous outlook toward itinerant players. Rather than attack the newcomers with harsh words and unkind actions, they should welcome them as friends.

Trio Voces in Uno were not the only settlers to reject Thomas Davenport's puffery. Elsewhere journalists and other audiences challenged the manager's claims. I turn now to the Newfoundland controversy to further explore how reactions to Jean Davenport's performances of tragic male characters provoked lengthy discussions about the limits of civility, acceptable repertoire for girls, and definitions of gentlemanly behavior.

On August 2, 1841, a "brilliant assemblage" gathered in St. John's, Newfoundland, for Jean Davenport's opening night performances of *Richard III* and *The Manager's Daughter*. Tickets to see the juvenile actress had sold out within an hour of the announcement of her impending arrival and "not a *box* ticket [was] to be had for 'love or money.'"[54] Primed by advance publicity and the festivities of such a unique event, the audience "testified their feelings by loud and lengthened applause."[55] Jean Davenport's visit marked the first time an actress of such stature had appeared in St. John's, and for many colonists it signaled the city's elevation from cultural backwater to attractive cultural center. Historian Patrick O'Flaherty argues that "we can date Newfoundland's entry into the modern world from the 1840s" when the first steamships arrived in the colony.[56] Yet for many citizens of St. John's, it was the 1841 appearance of Jean Davenport that secured its membership alongside other culturally mature settler colonies. This is not to suggest that St. John's audiences were strangers to theatrical entertainment. As Eugene Benson and L. W. Conolly observe, "formal theatrical activity" in the structure of the community concert, which featured a diverse bill of entertainment consisting mainly of songs, recitations, and playlets, was "widespread and produced in all communities throughout the island."[57] Amateur companies also staged melodramas and other popular plays for charity purposes.[58] Before 1841, however, very few professional players had traveled to the colony, certainly none as young or as celebrated as Jean Davenport.[59]

Most St. John's newspapers were unequivocal in their praise of Davenport, calling her "highly accomplished and astonishingly gifted," "extraordinary," and "inimitable in the extreme."[60] "Her elocution was distinct and clear, and her expression of the different passions, even in repose, highly finished," the *Newfoundland Ledger* enthused after her second performance of Shylock.[61] But the *Newfoundland Patriot* was not impressed. In a lengthy editorial published two weeks after Davenport's arrival, *Patriot* editor Robert J. Parsons expressed serious doubts about her abilities, questioning whether it was possible to compare such a young girl to the likes of Kean. "The press have given by far two [*sic*] high an estimate of the dramatic talents of this young lady," Parsons insisted, "and have led people into the erroneous conclusion that hers is the *ne plus ultra* of tragic acting! ... The *masculine* acting of a *Kean* in Richard the Third at *Drury-lane*, London, has been excelled in the little Amateur Theatre of St. John's!" Parsons refused to believe that a girl of thirteen or fourteen could possess the same talent as Kean and was clearly frustrated by the eagerness with which his fellow citizens accepted the comparison. In fact, what appears to have bothered Parsons most about Davenport's reception was that the citizens of St. John's had "no notion of having their senses *puffed* away by the most outrageous descriptions of things in themselves very ordinary and common place."[62] Echoing centuries of antitheatrical writers, he implied that the charming young girl in her masculine impersonations was turning grown men into love-struck boys devoid of reason and decorum. In other words, through their association with the girl and her vain attempts to capture masculine behavior, these men were themselves becoming young, immature, and effeminate.

Thomas Davenport's response to Parsons's attack was immediate and public. In an open letter published in the *Newfoundland Public Ledger*, he declared that as the "Father of Miss Davenport," it was his "duty to repel the unmanly and insidious attack" upon his daughter: "It is the first time during Miss Davenport's public career that she has been assailed by the Editor of a Paper ... therefore you stand 'honourably' alone. To fair criticism I have no objection, even if it condemns; but I must mark as the strongest instance of moral turpitude that has ever come within my notice, an attack by you—a *man*—no!—a *person* who never even saw Miss Davenport." [63] Accusing Parsons of cowardice and behavior unfitting not only a gentleman but *any* man, Davenport questioned the editor's intelligence and education, pointing out that he had misspelled the name of actress Sarah Siddons. In his estimation, Parsons was an illiterate boor who owed his daughter an apology.

The rest of the Newfoundland press—six journals in total led by the *Ledger* and its powerful editor Henry Winton—rallied in support of Jean Davenport and her father. Winton explained that while he generally preferred to keep any correspondence to do with the *Patriot* out of his own publication, he had agreed to publish Davenport's letter "for the vindication of needless and unfounded aspersions." [64] In the 1830s and 1840s the *Ledger* was the leading journal in Newfoundland, the "standard bearer" for many of the colony's English, Protestant conservatives and an "outspoken opponent of the Irish-dominated reform (or liberal) party." [65] Given his political perspective, then, Winton's support of the British Davenports is hardly surprising. In his editorial, he explained to his readers that although Thomas Davenport was a stranger to the citizens of St. John's, he wore "the outward appearance of a gentleman, and ... the internal deportment of one." [66] Compared with Parsons's "defiance of every principle of public and private decorum" in the *Patriot*, Davenport struck Winton as an upstanding gentleman fully deserving the respect and support of the St. John's community.

Winton's willingness to attest to Davenport's gentlemanliness on the basis of his appearance is curious given the actor's brief time in St. John's and the nature of his profession. Like many contemporaries, Winton appears to have ascribed to the belief that an individual's external appearance corresponded with his internal demeanor and that one could therefore judge a man by how he looked. As dissemblers by trade, actors notoriously challenged this view by assuming multiple guises and perfecting a wide repertoire; behind many of the virulent attacks against actors in the eighteenth and nineteenth centuries lay deep anxieties about the nature of human character.[67] Therefore, in light of the debate between Davenport and Parsons, the conservative Winton's insistence that Thomas Davenport was what he appeared is ironic (although surprisingly consistent with Davenport's own claims in *The Manager's Daughter*). Nevertheless, in declaring his support for the Davenports and his disgust with Parsons, Winton found a convenient opportunity to show up one of his most bitter rivals.

But the debate over Jean Davenport was about more than personal rivalries. Implicit in the war of words was an acute awareness of the performativity of masculinity itself, accompanied by anxiety that the male citizens of St. John's were being uncivilized. At a time when the masculinity or manliness exhibited by male citizens was considered an index of a culture's civilization, the ungentlemanly men of St. John's threatened Newfoundland's position within the empire by confirming stereotypes of the uncouth, savage, or effeminate colonialist. Yet the competing definitions of gentlemanly behavior suggest that masculinity itself was in flux. Robert J. Parsons accused his fellow journalists of displaying unmanly behavior in their overwrought declarations of love for the juvenile star. He, in turn, was rebuked by Winton and Davenport for his ungentlemanly critique of the young girl, for his lack of education, and for failing to show the Davenports the courtesy and respect they deserved as strangers in St. John's. Winton judged Thomas Davenport an appropriate recipient for public sympathy because his performance of masculinity—presumably his appearance, education, and manners—adhered to codes of gentlemanly behavior. Rejecting the long-standing critique of actors as immoral dissemblers, Winton reassured his readers that Davenport was an honorable and trustworthy gentleman.

In his subsequent response to Davenport's letter, Parsons poked fun at Winton's testimonial to the actor's character, cheekily suggesting that Davenport must have left his gentlemanly "outward appearance" and "internal deportment" in the "wardrobe! for certainly they are neither discoverable in the sentiment nor in the language of the letter signed 'Thomas Davenport.'"[68] Pursuing the *Patriot*'s mandate to "be a terror to evil doers," Parsons went on to characterize Davenport as a charlatan deceiving the people of St. John's with his puffery. "It is *new* to us in Newfoundland to be '*dared*' by actors and mountebanks," Parsons observed, before concluding: "Mr. Davenport is mistaken if he fancies that he can *bully* us. He shall not do that, nor shall he GULL the public while we are cognizant of the fact."[69] He went on to point out that, contrary to the Davenports' glowing press, the people of Halifax had been less than impressed with the juvenile actress's talents. If Davenport thought that he could count on Newfoundland's geographic isolation to fool its people, he was simply wrong. Firm in his belief that the citizens of St. John's were being duped, Parsons countered Davenport's accusations of ungentlemanly behavior by presenting himself as a guardian of the community, a rational gentleman unwilling to be puffed.[70]

This strand of Parsons's argument echoes the concerns articulated by the Trio Voces in Uno, namely that the Davenports saw colonial audiences as culturally inferior, uncivilized rubes who could be easily fooled by girlish imitations of Edmund Kean. Ironically, in the process of condemning Thomas Davenport and his daughter as cultural imperialists, both Parsons and the Trio affirmed London's importance as the imperial capital — the center of culture, masculinity, and civilization — and revealed their dependency on that capital for their own performances of masculinity.[71] Already anxious about their place within the empire, these men were understandably outraged by their fellow colonists' acceptance of Jean Davenport's portrayals of Shakespeare's tragic men, for it implied that they were everything she was: juvenile, feminine dissemblers.

Controversy and public debate continued to dog the Davenports during their time in Newfoundland and elsewhere throughout their travels. Some newspapers whispered that the sympathetic manager Thomas Davenport played in *The Manager's Daughter* was a fabrication and that the real manager had previously mistreated the actors in his company.[72] Though later accounts proved otherwise, rumors of impropriety continued to hang over the Davenport family.[73] The popularity of Charles Dickens's serial novel *Nicholas Nickleby* did little to dispel such gossip.

Fixed by Dickens

In 1899, Jean Margaret Lander (née Davenport) wrote a letter to the managing editor of *Shakespeareana*, objecting to the recent publication of "an article on what purports to be on Dicken's [*sic*] 'original Vincent

Crummles.'" Her primary objection was the journal's decision to republish excerpts from William Pleater Davidge's 1888 memoirs *Footlight Flashes*, which in her view contained numerous inaccuracies about her career as a girl actress. As noted, Davidge's text includes lively descriptions of the Davenport family and the promotional tactics deployed by Thomas Davenport. Most worrisome for Lander was Davidge's insistence that Charles Dickens had modeled the despicable character Vincent Crummles after her father and that she had been the inspiration for the pathetic Ninetta Crummles, the "infant phenomenon." Such concerns are understandable given the heavy hints Davidge drops in his memoirs. Although he refrains from naming either Dickens or the Davenports, he titles the section of his memoirs "The Phenomenon" and describes his time as "a member of a company in Kent, presided over by a gentleman who, with his daughter, has been photographed by a great writer, presenting as he never fails to do, a most pleasing and droll portraiture."[74] While Davidge notes of the representation that "in no single instance is this like the originals," because the author had not "avail[ed] himself of the facilities for personal observation," the actor nevertheless identifies the "gentleman" and his "daughter" as the caricatured subjects.[75]

From Lander's perspective, Davidge had it all wrong. The association of the Crummles with the Davenports was an unfortunate error, she insisted, the product of a US manager's decision to take the "Dickens sketch as a burlesque" and apply it to her after its publication: "in England where Boz [had] just published his Nicholas Nickleby my name was never mentioned in connection with the managerial sketch—only in New York was it used as a means for popular burlesque."[76] At first the Davenports had merely laughed at the comparison between Dickens's characters and the real-life family, assuming that since it had "no foundation in fact—it would die with the papers.... Indeed we never supposed the public would take it seriously." But of course the Davenports were wrong: the public took the story *very* seriously. What made the matter even more frustrating, Lander continued, was that her father was nothing like Vincent Crummles: "Those who remember my father will recall his *great* cares in avoiding all personal notoriety the profession—the professional life—with vicissitudes & successes—were public—the home life—with its studies & [careful] thoughtful guardianship was carefully kept apart." Despite the differences, however, the Davenports were unable to stop the rumors from circulating in publications after Thomas Davenport had died and Jean Margaret Lander went on to an illustrious career as a tragic actress.[77] "You will see how impossible [it is] to refuse what was copied in a thousand papers all over the U.S.," Lander concluded, "but [to] a publisher ... whose subscription list comprises ... all readers & students of Shakespeare in America—I offer the correction."[78]

Lander's fierce rejection of the Crummles comparison—a comparison most scholars accept today[79]—is at once fascinating and curious. Did the Crummles family spring fully formed from Dickens's vivid imagination or did the author borrow liberally from the lives of the Davenports and their fictional doppelgangers in *The Manager's Daughter*? In writing to the managing editor of *Shakespeareana* did Lander hope to forever rid herself of Ninetta's haunting presence? As the following details show, despite Jean Lander's fierce insistence to the contrary, it seems *very* likely that Dickens modeled his Crummles after the Davenport family. And it seems just as likely that this representation was purposefully unflattering, *not* because Dickens had any particular issue with the Davenports (although he may well have) but because he wanted the characters to serve a larger political purpose.

To test this theory, let's turn to the source. Readers first meet the infant phenomenon in chapter 23 of Dickens's *Nicholas Nickleby*, "Treats of the Company of Mr. Vincent Crummles, and of his Affairs, Domestic and Theatrical." Intriguingly, this chapter was originally published in serial form in April 1838, five months after Jean Davenport's triumphant debut at the Haymarket Theatre in London and just over a year after the Davenport family had spent several months in Portsmouth, where, as Ben Terry later recalled, the actress had played Shylock, "regaled her public with song," danced the Sailor's Hornpipe, and presented "six characters, male and female" in *The Manager's Daughter*.[80] In the opening pages of the chapter, Nicholas Nickleby and Vincent Crummles travel by carriage to Portsmouth, where the Crummles family is performing at the local theatre. As they walk down High Street, Nicholas notices "a great many bills, pasted against the walls and displayed in windows, wherein the names of Mr Vincent Crummles, Mrs Vincent Crummles, Master Crummles, Master P. Crummles, and Miss Crummles, were printed in very large letters, and everything else in very small ones."[81] Tellingly, Crummles's use of playbills resembles the promotional style favored by Thomas Davenport. In fact, as several scholars have speculated, Dickens may well have seen the remnants of Davenports' many playbills on his journey to the Isle of Wight in the fall of 1837. Writing in 1951, literary scholar James Ollé observed that "The sight of a weather-worn playbill, clinging to the theatre's walls, may be the simple explanation of the relationship between T. D. Davenport and his daughter, Jean, and Vincent Crummles and his daughter, 'The Infant Phenomenon.'"[82]

Further evidence of the Crummles–Davenport connection arises from Dickens's descriptions of the Crummles family. Arriving at the theatre, Crummles introduces Nicholas to his wife, "a stout, portly female, apparently between forty and fifty," seated at the side of the stage "at a small mahogany table with rickety legs and of an oblong shape."[83] This scene closely resembles the opening of *The Manager's Daughter*, where audiences meet Mrs. Davenport seated at a table. Was this a deliberate nod to the play or merely a coincidence? Perhaps the strongest, albeit most troubling, connection between the two families comes in the representation of Ninetta Crummles herself. After Mrs. Crummles's brief exchange with Nicholas, whom she deems an "admirable" addition to the Crummles company, her daughter makes a dramatic entrance: "There bounded on to the stage from some mysterious inlet, a little girl in a dirty white frock with tucks up to the knees, short trousers, sandaled shoes, white spencer, pink gauze bonnet, green veil and curl papers; who turned a pirouette, cut twice in the air, turned another pirouette, then, looking off at the opposite wing, shrieked, bounded forward to within six inches of the footlights, and fell into a beautiful attitude of terror, as a shabby gentleman in an old pair of buff slippers came in at one powerful slide, and chattering his teeth, fiercely brandished a walking-stick."[84] Dickens's reference to Ninetta's "dirty white frock," "short trousers," and "sandaled shoes" recalls Davidge's statement that Jean Davenport "was always dressed in short dresses and pantalettes and neat slippers," a comparison borne out by the central image of Davenport in Figure 17. There too the actress appears in a dress, pantaloons, and slippers. Such comparisons are admittedly circumstantial, but they do little to support Lander's claim.

And what of Ninetta's repertoire? Mrs. Crummles explains that the "little girl" and "shabby gentleman" are rehearsing the ballet interlude "The Indian Savage and the Maiden," presumably in preparation for the evening's performance.[85] Nicholas watches with wonder as the two performers mime the progression of the characters' intense relationship, which, he observes, left "the spectators in a state of pleasing uncertainty, whether she would ultimately marry the savage, or return to her friends."[86] Although the Indian savage scenario seems to have been Dickens's own invention, one in keeping with white Anglo-American fascination with Indigenous subjects, we might ask whether news of the Davenport's plans to travel to North America had reached Dickens. Or perhaps it's a mere coincidence that the family boarded the *Sirius* one month after this chapter appeared in print.[87]

It is in his representation of Ninetta's age that Dickens delivers the deepest wounds to his supposed model family. When the rehearsal concludes, Crummles introduces Nicholas to Ninetta and informs him that she is "ten years of age." Nicholas is astounded by this revelation: "for the infant phenomenon, though of short stature, had a comparatively aged countenance, and had moreover been precisely the same age—not perhaps to the full extent of the memory of the oldest inhabitant, but certainly for five good years. But she had been kept up late every night, and put upon an unlimited allowance of gin-and-water from infancy, to prevent her growing tall, and perhaps this system of training had produced in the infant phenomenon these additional phenomena."[88] Later, Nicholas's dawning suspicion about the infant phenomenon's artificially delayed age is confirmed by the disgruntled actor Mr. Folair, who refers to the child as an "Infant humbug." "She may thank her stars she was born a *manager's daughter*," the actor bitterly surmises (my italics). I read this last, seemingly offhand, sentence as an explicit nod to the Davenports and to the play that defined them.

Of course, the Davenports represented in *The Manager's Daughter* are nothing like the Crummles. Unlike the loving, hardworking, and long-suffering Davenports of *The Manager's Daughter*, the Crummles are charlatans and drunks. The family's celebrated infant phenomenon possesses no real acting ability and is nowhere near her advertised age; her growth has been purposefully stunted by the frequent consumption of alcohol. As Caitlin R. Hansen observes in her study of the novel, "Even her name seems to play upon the imbalance of her status as a graceful (if stagey) feminine juvenile phenomenon (Ninetta), and her reality (Crummles)."[89] Unlike the economically innocent Jean Margaret who asserts agency and performs for her father out of a sense of love and obligation, Ninetta Crummles is almost entirely voiceless and performs because she has been raised to do so. Compared with the joyful Jean Margaret in *The Manager's Daughter* who fixes her father's business crisis, Ninetta is a pathetic child, a "machine of monotonous shrieks and twirls"[90] forcefully juvenated by alcohol, curl papers, and "a dirty white frock, with tucks up to the knees."[91]

Yet if we understand Ninetta's juvenation as driven by "the adult desire to freeze the child in place as the personification of youthful innocence,"[92] then the fictional actress begins to resemble the real-life Jean Davenport. As I argued in Chapter 4, Thomas Davenport took great pains to emphasize his daughter's age through advertising, costuming, and the on- and offstage orchestration of her movements. Although he presumably stopped short of prescribing a daily dose of gin and water to halt her physical development, he was unquestionably invested in her juvenation and tested the limits of public intimacy with carefully choreographed appearances at windows. Simply put, Jean Lander's 1899 statement that her father "avoid[ed] all personal notoriety" and ensured that her professional life was "carefully kept apart" from her "home life" rings untrue. Playbills, newspaper clippings, and the very script of *The Manager's Daughter* all point to Thomas Davenport's calculated efforts to collapse public and private in order to promote himself and his family as ideal representatives of the British middle class.

The question, then, is why did Dickens opt to pop the Davenports' bourgeois bubble? One theory is that he was responding out of spite or a general dislike of the family, or more particularly, Thomas Davenport. Robert Simpson Maclean asserts that Dickens likely met Davenport in 1832 while the latter was manager of the theatre in Westminster and may have joined his company for a short time.[93] If the two men had a falling-out, it is possible that Dickens turned to his pen to seek revenge. Another theory, not incompatible with the first, is that Dickens created the Crummles out of a growing sense of concern for the stage child and a desire to fix what he considered wrong with the theatre industry. *Nicholas Nickleby* disrupts the image of bourgeois harmony that the Davenports had labored to perfect and offers in its place the image of the vulnerable, damaged, exploited Ninetta. As Marah Gubar contends, "Dickens warped his source material significantly in his drive to portray child performers as incompetent, voiceless victims" and to equate "precocity with child abuse."[94] And in this he was largely successful: "it can be argued that [Ninetta Crummles] has had more impact on critical accounts of the theatrical cult of the child than any actual performer," Gubar concludes, "since commentators frequently echo many aspects of Dickens's characterization in their efforts to explain the appeal of child actors to the nineteenth-century public."[95] It has only been within the last decade, thanks in large part to Gubar's own work, that historians have questioned the myths surrounding the nineteenth-century stage child—including the long-held belief that most child performers lacked real talent and appealed to audiences primarily on the basis of their charming innocence.

Ninetta Crummles would haunt Jean Lander for the rest of her life, despite the actress's many efforts to shake her fictional surrogate. The great irony is that Ninetta's existence as a fictional character, her perpetual place between the pages of *Nicholas Nickleby* and in later stage and film adaptations, is also a testament to Thomas Davenport's skill as a theatre manager. As the last two chapters have detailed, Davenport's primary aim was to elevate his daughter above Clara Fisher and any other theatrical competition. This he did. But in the process he also brought himself and his family into Dickens's satirical line of fire. It was Dickens who ultimately transformed the dutiful "manager's daughter" into the immortal "infant phenomenon," destabilizing Davenport's carefully constructed vision of the ideal bourgeois family to leave in its place an image of an exploited child and her ridiculous father. And so, in what is undoubtedly one of theatre history's more peculiar moments of dramatic irony, Thomas Davenport's greatest managerial success was also his greatest failure.[96] The figure of Ninetta Crummles still hangs over the life and career of Jean Margaret Davenport.

EPILOGUE

There is no easy way to tie off the many threads I have pulled in the preceding pages—no object or archival find that will permit a tidy bow. Like the nineteenth-century theatregoer, I hope you, dear reader, will be content with a few parting words that resist grand conclusions. If time and space allowed, I might try to identify the many ways that later generations of Anglo-American girl actresses embraced the roles that Clara Fisher and Jean Margaret Davenport had so skillfully occupied for a time. I might say more about Fisher's early mentorship of Charlotte Cushman (1816–1876), one of the most successful and recognizable breeches performers of the mid- to late nineteenth century. Like many of her peers, Cushman first became acquainted with Fisher as a theatregoer, admiring her dynamic performances of jaunty male characters and her ability to transport audiences through song. Later, at the Tremont Theatre in Boston, Cushman worked closely with the actress and her husband, James Maeder, an accomplished musician and vocal coach, who helped Cushman prepare for her professional debut.[1] But it is in Cushman's celebrated yet controversial portrayal of Shakespeare's Romeo, alongside her sister's Juliet, where the link between the two actresses is most apparent. In recent years Cushman has become something of an icon for queer performance history, yet some of that queerness might also be traced through Clara Fisher.[2]

Of course, Cushman was a woman by the time she adopted breeches, and so in considering the legacy of Fisher and Davenport we might instead turn to Caroline (Caddy) Fox, who also got her start in Boston in the late 1830s as a member of the Little Foxes troupe of child actors.[3] Like many of her girl peers, Fox embraced hoydenish Little Pickle and the heroic Young Norval and showed proficiency in protean farces like *Winning a Husband; Or, Seven's the Main*.[4] In 1844, at the age of fifteen, she married fellow actor George Howard, with whom she continued to perform a wide-ranging repertoire. Today, though, she is almost exclusively remembered as the originator of the rambunctious enslaved girl Topsy in George Aiken's 1852 adaptation of *Uncle Tom's Cabin*, which she performed alongside her daughter Cordelia in the role of Little Eva.

Uncle Tom's Cabin represents a peculiar transition point in the history of Anglo-American theatrical girlhood, seen clearly in the dynamic between the black, unloved Topsy and the white, beloved Little Eva. Unlike Topsy, who delights in her wickedness, Little Eva sees good in everyone and floats through life trailing metaphorical clouds of glory, naturalizing the triumvirate of whiteness, innocence, and childhood.[5] With her premature death, she ascends to heaven in a state of delicate girlhood, forever pure and beautiful.[6] Readers can nevertheless discern something of the freedom, defiance, and pathos that typified early nineteenth-century theatrical girlhood in the character of Topsy—at least in Aiken's version, where she has plenty of opportunities to sing, dance, crack jokes, and play tricks.[7] A future research project might consider the extent to which Caroline Howard drew upon her earlier repertoire to portray the free-spirited girl. For while Topsy enjoys none of Little Pickle's class or race privilege, she is strangely akin to the naughty boy and his theatrical sibling, Priscilla Tomboy. Might the relationship between the white supremacy of the tomboy and the racist legacy of Topsy be more closely entangled than historians have imagined?

What would happen if historians followed the crooked line between Priscilla Tomboy, a creole character who threatens her slave with violence, and Topsy, the mischievous, resilient black girl? Might that line provide valuable context for critiquing the racialization of "naughty" behavior in school classrooms today; for rethinking the way punishment is disproportionately meted out on black girls, whose very "girl" status is called into question by authorities who view their behavior as "boyish" and "unfeminine"?[8] Might that line allow historians to ask why naughtiness in white girls is often represented as charming or sexy, as part of a "bad girl" phase, as a necessary rite of passage? Might it yield further evidence of how white supremacy wends its way through daily life disguised as cuteness and innocence in theatres, schools, and homes? As this book has aimed to show, the history of bloody tyrants and little pickles is also the history of whiteness and its privilege.

The limits of this project prevent me from pursuing this line of inquiry further, but I urge other scholars to continue unpacking theatre's participation in the production, circulation, and stabilization of white supremacist worldviews. I will end by noting once again how white girls' expressions of freedom, rebellion, and self-fulfillment have for centuries been enmeshed with the diminishment, rejection, and mistreatment of black girls. Indeed, as much as this book has been an effort to reclaim the lives and repertoire of two of the nineteenth century's most important girl actresses, and to rethink their potential for challenging gender norms, it has also been an attempt to acknowledge the political investments of the audiences who cheered them on and to ask how historical investments in cuteness and precocity have supported white supremacist structures and aesthetics.

NOTES

The following archival and library abbreviations appear in the notes.
BL: British Library
FSL: Folger Shakespeare Library
HRC: Harry Ransom Center, University of Texas at Austin
HTC: Harvard Theatre Collection at Houghton Library, Harvard University
LC: Library of Congress

PROLOGUE

1. Ellen MacKay, "*RE*: Sources / The Wrong Stuff: Staffordshire Figures at the Folger Shakespeare Library," *Theatre Survey* 56, no. 3 (Sept. 2015): 389–401, at 391. My use of "social life" nods to Arjun Appadurai, *The Social Life of Things: Commodities in Cultural Perspective* (Cambridge, MA: Cambridge University Press, 1986).

2. MacKay, "*RE*: Sources," 391.

3. Rohan McWilliam, "The Theatricality of the Staffordshire Figurine," *Journal of Victorian Culture* 10, no. 1 (2005): 107–14, at 108. See also Belinda Beaton, "Materializing the Duke," *Journal of Victorian Culture* 10, no. 1 (2005): 100–107; Simon Morgan, "Material Culture and the Politics of Personality in Early Victorian England," *Journal of Victorian Culture* 17, no. 2 (2012): 127–46.

4. Maclean's name is spelled differently across multiple publications, appearing as McLean, MacLean, or Maclean. From what I can tell, the correct name is Maclean. I cite the name as it appears in published form but have included "Maclean" in brackets. Thanks to Thea Fitz-James for catching this inconsistency.

5. Robert Simpson McLean [Maclean], "The Case of the Silent Figure: A Phenomenal Mystery Revealed," *Dickensian* 91, no. 436 (Summer 1995): 94–98, at 97–98.

6. Robin Bernstein, *Racial Innocence: Performing American Childhood from Slavery to Civil Rights* (New York: New York University Press, 2011), 12.

7. Bernstein, *Racial Innocence*, 13.

8. McWilliam, "Theatricality," 109.

9. Joseph Roach, "Public Intimacy: The Prior History of It," *Theatre and Celebrity in Britain, 1660–2000*, ed. Mary Luckhurst and Jane Moody (Basingstoke: Palgrave Macmillan, 2005), 15–30, at 16. As Bernstein writes, in the mid-nineteenth century "material culture continued to circulate practices of desire between the theater and the home." *Racial Innocence*, 128.

10. Roach, "Public Intimacy," 16; Mary Luckhurst and Jane Moody, "Intro-

duction: The Singularity of Theatrical Celebrity," in *Theatre and Celebrity in Britain*, 4–5, 8.

11. Sarah Bay-Cheng, "Theatre History and Digital Historiography," in *Critical Interventions in Theatre Historiography*, ed. Henry Bial and Scott Magelssen (Ann Arbor: University of Michigan Press, 2010), 125–36.

12. Joseph Roach, *It* (Ann Arbor: University of Michigan Press, 2007), 8.

13. Given that the V&A figurines have been dated to 1837, long after Betty's retirement, it seems likely that both figurines are of the child actress. "Figurine, probably Master Betty." Glazed earthenware, Staffordshire, ca. 1840, Victoria & Albert Collections, http://collections.vam.ac.uk/item/0120239/figurine-unkn own/; "Figurine." Glazed earthenware, Staffordshire, ca. 1840, Victoria & Albert Collections, http://collections.vam.ac.uk/item/0120241/figurine-unknown/.

INTRODUCTION

1. Key studies include Bernstein, *Racial Innocence*; Marah Gubar, *Artful Dodgers: Reconceiving the Golden Age of Children's Literature* (Oxford: Oxford University Press, 2009); Marah Gubar, "The Drama of Precocity: Child Performers on the Victorian Stage," in *The Nineteenth-Century Child and Consumer Culture*. ed. Dennis Denisoff (Burlington, VT: Ashgate, 2008), 64–78; Gillian Arrighi and Victor Emeljanow, eds., *Entertaining Children: The Participation of Youth in the Entertainment Industry* (Basingstoke: Palgrave Macmillan, 2015); Jeanne Klein, "Without Distinction of Age: The Pivotal Roles of Child Actors and Their Spectators in Nineteenth-Century Theatre," *The Lion and the Unicorn* 36, no. 2 (April 2012): 117–35; Jeanne Klein, "Reclaiming Four Child Actors through Seven Plays in US Theatre, 1794–1800," *Journal of American Drama and Theatre* 30, no. 1 (Fall 2017): 1–23; Nan Mulleneaux, "Our Genius, Goodness, and Gumption: Child Actresses and National Identity in Mid-Nineteenth Century America," *Journal of the History of Childhood and Youth* 5, no. 2 (2012): 283–308; Elizabeth Reitz Mullenix, *Wearing the Breeches: Gender on the Antebellum Stage* (New York: St. Martin's Press, 2000); Carolyn Steedman, *Strange Dislocations: Childhood and the Idea of Human Interiority, 1780–1930* (Cambridge, MA: Harvard University Press, 1995); Anne Varty, *Children and Theatre in Victorian Britain: "All Work, No Play"* (Basingstoke: Palgrave Macmillan, 2008); Shauna Vey, *Childhood and Nineteenth-Century American Theatre: The Work of the Marsh Troupe of Juvenile Actors* (Carbondale: Southern Illinois University Press, 2015).

2. Jeanne Klein and Elizabeth Reitz Mullenix are two important exceptions.

3. The field of actress studies is vast. For an excellent overview of recent scholarship see Laura Engel, "Stage Beauties: Actresses and Celebrity Culture in the Long Eighteenth Century," *Literature Compass* 13, no. 12 (2016): 749–61.

4. Klein, "Without Distinction," 118.

5. Though most studies of nineteenth-century girl performers refer to them as "child actresses," I have opted to use the term "girl actress" to foreground the performers' gender and their negotiation of gender norms in performance. In this, I follow Deanne Williams and Roberta Barker, both of whom complicate the easy equation of girl to actress and boy to actor in their studies of the early modern stage. Barker, "'Not One Thing Exactly': Gender, Performance and Critical Debates over the Early Modern Boy-Actress," *Literature Compass* 6, no. 2 (2009): 460–81; Williams, "Introduction: 'Look on't Again,'" in *Childhood, Education and the Stage in Early Modern England*, ed. Richard Preiss and Deanne Williams, 1–13 (Cambridge: Cambridge University Press, 2017), 8, 11.

6. Tracy C. Davis, "Nineteenth-Century Repertoire," *Nineteenth Century Theatre and Film* 36, no. 2 (2009): 6–28, at 6.

7. Davis, "Nineteenth-Century," 10. Davis's "working hypothesis" (7) shares many features of Diana Taylor's important definition of repertoire, specifically Taylor's focus on the centrality of embodied practices such as dance, song, and language to the transmission of knowledge within cultures and over time. Unlike Taylor, however, Davis privileges audience reception as critical to the recognition, development, and subsequent transmission of repertoire. Diana Taylor, *The Archive and the Repertoire: Performing Cultural Memory in the Americas* (Durham, NC: Duke University Press, 2003).

8. Davis, "Nineteenth-Century," 8.

9. Davis, "Nineteenth-Century," 8.

10. Richard Schechner, *Between Theatre and Anthropology* (Philadelphia: University of Pennsylvania Press, 1985), 36.

11. These characteristics distinguish Fisher and Davenport from fellow actress Fanny Kemble, whose 1878 memoirs, *Records of a Girlhood*, acknowledge her professional identification with girlhood. Kemble's 1829 debut as Juliet at the age of twenty came during a moment of family crisis. See Frances Ann Kemble, *Records of a Girlhood*, 2nd ed. (New York: Henry Holt and Company, 1883), accessed December 30, 2018, https://archive.org/details/records ofgirlhoooookembuoft/page/n7; Deirdre David, *Fanny Kemble: A Performed Life* (Philadelphia: University of Pennsylvania Press, 2003); Catherine Clifton, *Fanny Kemble's Civil Wars* (Oxford: Oxford University Press, 2001).

12. On the importance of averageness, see Derek Miller, "Average Broadway," *Theatre Journal* 68, no. 4 (December 2016): 529–33, at 546.

13. Klein, "Without Distinction," 189.

14. Davis, "Nineteenth-Century," 8.

15. See Drury Lane playbills, British Library. Davis, "Nineteenth-Century," 8, 14. Elsewhere, an evening's entertainment could include burlesques of popular plays, comic dances, juggling, and other acrobatic performances.

16. On the challenges of the actress's life, see Felicity Nussbaum, *Rival Queens: Actresses, Performance, and Eighteenth-Century British Theater* (Philadelphia: University of Pennsylvania Press, 2010); Chelsea Phillips, "Bodies in Play: Maternity, Repertory, and the Rival *Romeo and Juliets, 1748–51*," *Theatre Survey* 60, no. 2 (May 2019): 207–36; Laura Engel and Elaine M. McGirr, eds., *Stage Mothers: Women, Work, and the Theater, 1660–1830* (Lewisburg, PA: Bucknell University Press, 2014); Laura Engel, *Fashioning Celebrity: Eighteenth-Century British Actresses and Strategies for Image Making* (Columbus: Ohio State University Press, 2011); Gilli Bush-Bailey, *Performing Herself: Autobiography and Fanny Kelly's Dramatic Recollections* (Manchester: Manchester University Press, 2017).

17. Aparna Gollapudi, "Recovering Miss Rose: Acting as a Girl on the Eighteenth-Century Stage," *Theatre Survey* 60, no. 1 (January 2019): 6–34, at 9.

18. Katrina Straub, "Performing Variety, Packaging Difference," in *The Oxford Handbook of the Georgian Theatre 1737–1832*, ed. Julia Swindells and David Francis Taylor (Oxford: Oxford University Press, 2014), 229–46, at 242–43. See also Gollapudi, "Recovering Miss Rose," 6–34. John Rich produced a version of the *Beggar's Opera* with only child actors at Lincoln's Inn Fields in 1729, although it's unclear if girls appeared in the company. And in 1756, David Garrick wrote *Lilliput*, an adaptation of *Gulliver's Travels*, for a company of boy actors. Frederick Burwick, "Georgian Theories of the Actor," in *The Oxford Handbook of the Georgian Theatre, 1737–1832* (Oxford: Oxford University Press, 2014), 177–91, at 188.

19. Straub, "Performing Variety," 243.

20. Straub, "Performing Variety," 244.

21. Straub, "Performing Variety," 244.

22. Katie Knowles, *Shakespeare's Boys: A Cultural History* (Basingstoke: Palgrave Macmillan, 2014), 136–42.

23. Jennifer Helgren and Colleen A. Vasconcellos, *Girlhood: A Global History* (New Brunswick, NJ: Rutgers University Press, 2010), 4.

24. On girlhood studies see Catherine Driscoll, *Girls: Feminine Adolescence in Popular Culture and Cultural Theory* (New York: Columbia University Press, 2002); Helgren and Vasconcellos, *Girlhood*; Tammy C. Owens et al., "Towards an Interdisciplinary Field of Black Girlhood Studies," *Departures in Critical Qualitative Research* 6, no. 3 (2017): 116–32; Aimee Meredith Cox, *Shapeshifters: Black Girls and the Choreography of Citizenship* (Durham, NC: Duke University Press, 2015). On girlhood and performance see Kristen Hatch, *Shirley Temple: The Performance of Girlhood* (New Brunswick, NJ: Rutgers University Press, 2015); Gaylyn Studlar, *Precocious Charms: Stars Performing Girlhood in Classical Hollywood Cinema* (Berkeley: University of California Press, 2013); Heather Warren-Crow, *Girlhood and the Plastic Image* (Hanover,

NH: Dartmouth College Press, 2014); "Performing Girlhoods," Special issue, *Theatre Survey* 60, no. 1 (January 2019); Deanne Williams, *Shakespeare and the Performance of Girlhood* (Basingstoke: Palgrave Macmillan, 2014).

25. Williams, *Shakespeare*, 2.

26. Helgren and Vasconcellos, *Girlhood*, 3. See also Catherine Robson, *Men in Wonderland: The Lost Girlhood of the Victorian Gentleman* (Princeton, NJ: Princeton University Press, 2001); Ruby Lal, *Coming of Age in Nineteenth-Century India: The Girl-Child and the Art of Playfulness* (Cambridge: Cambridge University Press, 2013); Kyra D. Gaunt, *The Games Black Girls Play: Learning the Ropes from Double-Dutch to Hip-Hop* (New York: New York University Press, 2006); Nazera Sadiq Wright, *Black Girlhood in the Nineteenth Century* (Champaign: University of Illinois Press, 2016).

27. Driscoll, *Girls*, 2.

28. Driscoll, *Girls*, 2–3; Helgren and Vasconcellos, *Girlhood*, 3.

29. Judith Butler, "Performative Acts and Gender Constitution: An Essay in Phenomenology and Feminist Theory," *Theatre Journal* 40, no. 4 (Dec. 1988): 519–31, at 519.

30. Driscoll, *Girls*, 47.

31. Warren-Crow, *Girlhood*, 2.

32. Catherine Malabou, *What Should We Do with Our Brain?* trans. Sebastian Rand (New York: Fordham University Press, 2008), 12.

33. Malabou, *What Should We Do?* 12.

34. Malabou, *What Should We Do?* 5.

35. Malabou, *What Should We Do?* 12.

36. Boys can be plastic too, but as Warren-Crow asserts, plasticity is generally associated with girls in a negative or derogatory way: Warren-Crow, *Girlhood and the Plastic Image*, 11.

37. Although this book is not a history of theatrical queerness per se, many of its central arguments are indebted to histories of queer and LGBTQ2 performances. Key studies include Robert A. Schanke and Kim Marra, eds., *Passing Performances: Queer Readings of Leading Players in American Theater History* (Ann Arbor: University of Michigan Press, 1998); Kim Marra, *Strange Duets: Impresarios and Actresses in the American Theatre* (Iowa City: University of Iowa Press, 2006); Sharon Marcus, *Between Women: Friendship, Desire, and Marriage in Victorian England* (Princeton, NJ: Princeton University Press, 2007); Steven Bruhm and Natasha Hurley, eds., *Curiouser: On the Queerness of Children* (Minneapolis: University of Minnesota Press, 2004).

38. Karen Sánchez-Eppler, *Dependent States: The Child's Part in Nineteenth-Century American Culture* (Chicago: University of Chicago Press, 2005), xxv.

39. Bernstein, *Racial Innocence*, 71. See also Tavia Nyong'o, "Racial Kitsch and Black Performance," *Yale Journal of Criticism* 15, no. 2 (Fall 2002): 371–91.

40. Kristen J. Warner, "In the Time of Plastic Representation," *Film Quarterly* 71, no. 2 (Winter 2017), https://filmquarterly.org/2017/12/04/in-the-time-of-plastic-representation/, accessed January 17, 2020.

41. Judith Plotz, *Romanticism and the Vocation of Childhood* (New York: Palgrave, 2000), xv, 13.

42. Robson, *Men in Wonderland*.

43. Bernstein, *Racial Innocence*, 36.

44. Sara Ahmed, "Willful Parts; Problem Characters or the Problem of Character," *New Literary History* 42, no. 2 (Spring 2011): 231–53, at 236. Rousseau's primary focus was on the education of boys; when he wrote of the education of girls or women, it was in the context of their future roles as wives and mothers. Heather E. Wallace, "Women's Education According to Rousseau and Wollstonecraft," *Feminism and Women's Studies, Feminism- eserver.org*. January 1, 2005, accessed Aug. 8, 2016. http://feminism.eserver.org/theory/papers/womens-education.txt. See also Philippe Ariès, *Centuries of Childhood: A Social History of Family Life*, trans. Robert Baldick (New York: Vintage Books, 1962 [1960]).

45. Locke, qtd. in Ahmed, "Willful Parts," 236.

46. Ahmed, "Willful Parts," 237.

47. Teresa Michals, "Experiments before Breakfast: Toys, Education, and Middle-Class Childhood," in *The Nineteenth-Century Child and Consumer Culture*, ed. Dennis Denisoff (Aldershot: Ashgate, 2008), 29–42.

48. William Wordsworth, "Ode 536: Intimations of Immortality from Recollections of Early Childhood," line 65, *Bartleby.com*, 1999, accessed July 30, 2016, http://www.bartleby.com/101/536.html.

49. See James R. Kincaid, *Child-Loving: The Erotic Child and Victorian Culture* (New York: Routledge, 1994).

50. Historical conceptions of childhood were often contradictory, as recent studies have shown. Gubar, *Artful Dodgers*; Plotz, *Romanticism*; Vey, *Childhood*.

51. Plotz, *Romanticism*, 39–40. Plotz argues that scholarly interest in the Romantic poets has obscured the influence of contemporary female children's writers, many of whom disagreed with the Romantics' idealized view of the sacred child and saw less of a chronological, spiritual, and developmental divide between children and adults (xv). Marah Gubar has similarly shown that previous claims about the hegemonic hold of the "cult of the child" have oversimplified the complex relationships that existed between adults and children. Gubar, *Artful Dodgers*, 4, 5.

52. Viviana Zelizer, *Pricing the Priceless Child: The Changing Social Value of Children* (Princeton, NJ: Princeton University Press, 1994).

53. Dennis Denisoff, "Introduction," in *The Nineteenth-Century Child and Consumer Culture*, 1–25, at 6.

54. David Hamlin, "The Structures of Toy Consumption: Bourgeois Domesticity and Demand for Toys in Nineteenth-Century Germany," *Journal of Social History* (Summer 2003): 857–69, at 857.

55. On the immaterial labor of consumption see Maurya Wickstrom, *Performing Consumers: Global Capital and Its Theatrical Seductions* (New York: Routledge, 2006).

56. Marah Gubar, "Entertaining Children of All Ages: Nineteenth-Century Theater as Children's Theater," *American Quarterly* 66, no. 1 (March 2014): 1–34.

57. Jeanne Klein, "An Epoch of Child Spectators in Early US Theatre," *Journal of the History of Childhood and Youth* 10, no. 1 (Winter 2017): 21–39, at 23.

58. Playbill, National Theatre, April 12, 1838. George C. Howard and Family Collection. Subseries A. Fox Company, 1833–1846, Playbills, 1833–1846. HRC.

59. Klein, "An Epoch," 30.

60. Playbill for November 23, 1836, Jean Margaret Davenport, Playbills, HTC.

61. Bernstein, *Racial Innocence*; Galia Benziman, *Narratives of Child Neglect in Romantic and Victorian Culture* (Basingstoke: Palgrave Macmillan, 2012); Plotz, *Romanticism*.

62. Megan A. Norcia, "Playing Empire: Children's Parlor Games, Home Theatricals, and Improvisational Play," *Children's Literature Association Quarterly* 29, no. 4 (Winter 2004): 294–314; M. Daphne Kutzer, *Empire's Children: Empire and Imperialism in Classic British Children's Books* (New York: Garland, 2000); Roderick McGillis, *A Little Princess: Gender and Empire* (New York: Twayne, 1996); Michelle J. Smith, *Empire in British Girls' Literature and Culture: Imperial Girls, 1880–1915* (London: Palgrave Macmillan, 2011).

63. Kathleen Wilson, "Introduction: Three Theses on Performance and History," *Eighteenth-Century Studies*, spec. issue on Performance, 48, no. 4 (Summer 2015): 375–90.

64. On performance and empire see Nicole Anae, "Infant Phenomenon in Colonial Australia—The Case of Anna Maria Quinn, 1854–1858," *Historian* 70, no. 1 (2009): 55–78; J. S. Bratton, Richard Allan Cave et al., *Acts of Supremacy: The British Empire and the Stage, 1790–1930* (Manchester: Manchester University Press, 1991); Lauren R. Clay, *Stagestruck: The Business of Theater in Eighteenth-Century France and Its Colonies* (Ithaca, NY: Cornell University Press, 2013); Elizabeth Maddock Dillon, *New World Drama: The Performative Commons in the Atlantic World, 1649–1849* (Durham, NC: Duke University Press, 2014); Edward Ziter, *The Orient on the Victorian Stage* (Cambridge: Cambridge University Press, 2003).

65. Steedman, *Strange Dislocations*, 68.

66. Steedman, *Strange Dislocations*, 20.

67. This is contrary to Steedman's claim that early Victorian theatregoers didn't care about the specific chronological age of a child performer as long as the child seemed convincingly young. Steedman, *Strange Dislocations*, 138–39.

68. Judith Burdan, "Girls *Must* Be Seen *and* Heard: Domestic Surveillance in Sarah Fielding's *The Governess*," *Children's Literature Association Quarterly* 19, no. 1 (1994): 8–14, at 9; Judith Pascoe, "Tales for Young Housekeepers: T. S. Arthur and the American Girl," *The Girl's Own: Cultural Histories of the Anglo-American Girl, 1830–1915* (Athens: University of Georgia Press, 2010), 34–51; Robson, *Men in Wonderland*; Sánchez-Eppler, *Dependent States*.

69. Ellis, qtd. in Robson, *Men in Wonderland*, 55.

70. Robson, *Men in Wonderland*, 55; Sánchez-Eppler, *Dependent States*.

71. Burdan, "Girls," 10.

72. Sánchez-Eppler, *Dependent States*, 69–100; Pascoe, "Tales," 34–51.

73. Robson, *Men in Wonderland*, 7.

74. On this debate see Kincaid, *Child-Loving*; Gubar, "The Drama of Precocity," 63–78; Jim Davis, "Freaks, Prodigies, and Marvelous Mimicry: Child Actors of Shakespeare on the Nineteenth-Century Stage," *Shakespeare* 2, no. 2 (December 2006): 179–93; Varty, *Children and Theatre*.

75. Steedman, *Strange Dislocations*, 134. Gubar has persuasively challenged this view of performing children. *Artful Dodgers*, 164.

76. Kincaid, *Child-Loving*.

77. Kincaid, *Child-Loving*, 198.

78. Gubar, *Artful Dodgers*, 164.

79. Mullenix, *Wearing*, 155.

80. Mullenix, *Wearing*, 159–60.

81. Sánchez-Eppler, *Dependent States*, xvi–xvii.

82. Engel, "Stage Beauties," 753.

83. Innovative examples include Saidya V. Hartman, *Wayward Lives, Beautiful Experiments: Intimate Histories of Social Upheaval* (New York: Norton, 2019); Bush-Bailey, *Performing Herself*; Judith Pascoe, *The Sarah Siddons Audio Files: Romanticism and the Lost Voice* (Ann Arbor: University of Michigan Press, 2013).

84. Odai Johnson's *Ruins: Classical Theater and Broken Memory* (Ann Arbor: University of Michigan Press, 2018) offers a master class for theatre historians in this regard.

85. Important studies of this phenomenon include Lawrence Levine, *Highbrow/Lowbrow: The Emergence of Cultural Hierarchy in America* (Cambridge, MA: Harvard University Press, 1999); David Savran, *Highbrow/Lowdown: Theater, Jazz, and the Making of the New Middle Class* (Ann Arbor: University of Michigan Press, 2009).

86. See, for example, Jacky Bratton, *The Making of the West End Stage* (Cambridge: Cambridge University Press, 2011); Tracy C. Davis and Peter Holland, eds., *The Performing Century: Nineteenth-Century Theatre's History* (Basingstoke: Palgrave Macmillan, 2007); Tracy C. Davis, ed., *The Broadview Anthology of Nineteenth-Century British Performance* (Peterborough, ON: Broadview Press, 2011).

87. Christopher Grobe's *The Art of Confession: The Performance of Self from Robert Lowell to Reality TV* (New York: New York University Press, 2017) also makes effective use of interludes between chapters.

INTERLUDE 1

1. "Young Albert, the Roscius," PN2598 B65 Y7 Ex ill. FSL. See also Georgianna Ziegler, "Introducing Shakespeare: The Earliest Versions for Children," *Shakespeare* 2, no. 2 (2006): 132–51, at 139–40; Hannah Field, "'A Story, Exemplified in a Series of Figures': Paper Doll versus Moral Tale in the Nineteenth Century," *Girlhood Studies* 5, no. 1 (Summer 2012): 37–56.

2. Qtd. in Selena Couture, "Siddons's Ghost: Celebrity and Gender in Sheridan's *Pizarro*," *Theatre Journal* 65, no. 2 (May 2013): 183–96, at 185, 186.

3. George Davies Harley, *An Authentic Biographical Sketch of the Life, Education, and Personal Character of William Henry West Betty, the Celebrated Young Roscius* (London: Richard Phillips, 1804), 12.

4. Harley, *An Authentic*, 12. On Siddons as Elvira see Couture, "Siddons's Ghost."

5. Harley, *An Authentic*, 12.

6. See Richard Brinsley Sheridan, *Pizarro; A Tragedy*, ed. Alexander Dick and Selena Couture (Peterborough, ON: Broadview Press, 2017). For an account of orientalist tropes later in the century, see Ziter, *The Orient*.

7. Harley, *An Authentic*, 15.

8. For details of Betty's earliest performances see Jeffrey Kahan, *Bettymania and the Birth of Celebrity Culture* (Bethlehem: Lehigh University Press, 2010); William L. Slout and Sue Rudisill, "The Enigma of the Master Betty Mania," *Journal of Popular Culture* 8, no. 1 (Summer 1974): 81–90.

9. Theatre, Birmingham, Aug. 20, 1805, p. 70 in *Collectanea, Or, A Collection of Advertisements and Paragraphs from the Newspapers, Relating to various Subjects*, vol. 1. Printed at Strawberry-Hill by Thomas Kirgate, For the Collector, Daniel Lysons, n.d. FLS.

10. "Roscius," *Encyclopedia Britannica*, https://www.britannica.com/biography/Roscius, accessed March 27, 2020.

11. "Critical Morceau," May 12, 1805, *Collectanea*, p. 83.

12. Betty's occupation of adult male roles hints at the eighteenth-century be-

lief that children were "little adults" who had yet to reach full maturity. On this idea see Ariès, *Centuries of Childhood*; Laurence Senelick, *The Age and Stage of George L. Fox, 1825–1877* (Iowa City: University of Iowa Press, 1999), ch. 1.

13. "Young Roscius," clipping, Dec. 10, 1804, *Collectanea*, p. 73. In February 1805, Betty visited the House of Commons with his father, where he chatted with several representatives and dined with the Duke of Clarence. "Master Betty Accompanied . . . ," *Morning Herald* clipping, Feb. 7, 1805, *Collectanea*, p. 77.

14. Slout and Rudisill, "Enigma," 83.

15. See, for example, Davis, "Freaks," and Hazel Waters, "'That Astonishing Clever Child': Performers and Prodigies in the Early and Mid-Victorian Theatre," *Theatre Notebook* 50, no. 2 (1996): 78–94.

16. Davis, "Freaks," 183.

17. Kahan, *Bettymania*, 55–56.

18. Taylor, in Kahan, *Bettymania*, 56.

19. Kahan, *Bettymania*, 56.

20. Kahan, *Bettymania*, 58.

21. Kahan, *Bettymania*. For more on celebrity and performance, see Roach, *It*; Sharon Marcus, *The Drama of Celebrity* (Princeton, NJ: Princeton University Press, 2019).

22. For more on this, see Schweitzer, "Consuming Celebrity: Commodities and Cuteness in the Circulation of Master William Henry West Betty," in *The Retro-Futurism of Cuteness*, ed. Jen E. Boyle and Wan-Chuan Kao (Santa Barbara: Punctum Books, 2017), 111–35.

23. "The Attraction of the Young *Roscius* . . ." *Morning Herald*, Dec. 13, 1804, *Collectanea*, p. 75.

24. "Some People Affect to be Angry . . ." *Morning Herald*, Dec. 15, 1804, *Collectanea*, p. 75.

25. Roach, *It*, 8.

26. "The Young Roscius," *Morning Herald*, Dec. 19, 1804, *Collectanea*, p. 76.

27. "The Young Roscius," *Morning Herald*, Dec. 22, 1804, *Collectanea*, p. 76.

28. Here, I reference Sianne Ngai's *Our Aesthetic Categories: Zany, Cute, Interesting* (Cambridge, MA: Harvard University Press, 2012).

29. Lori Merish, "Cuteness and Commodity Aesthetics: Tom Thumb and Shirley Temple," in *Freakery: Cultural Spectacles of the Extraordinary Body*, ed. Rosemarie Garland-Thomson (New York: NYU Press, 1996), 187.

30. Ngai, *Our Aesthetic*, 53–109.

31. "Covent Garden," clipping, Feb. 11, 1805, *Collectanea*, p. 70.

32. Qtd. in Kahan, *Bettymania*, 61. Also "Drury Lane Theatre," clipping, March 15, 1805, *Collectanea*, p. 81. Against such criticism, Betty's friends and fans sprang to his defense, protecting the boy from attacks they considered

unwarranted and unjust. A Sincere Friend of the Young Roscius, "The Young Roscius," *Morning Herald*, March 25, 1805, *Collectanea*, p. 82; J. Bisset, *Critical Essays on the Dramatic Excellencies of the YOUNG ROSCIUS, By Gentlemen of Distinguished Literary Talents and Theatrical Amateurs Opposed to the Hypercriticisms of Anonymous Writers, Who assume the Signatures of Justus, Ennius, & Critus* (Birmingham: Knott and Lloyd; London: J. Johnson, Cardell and Davies et al., 1804), 50–63.

33. Peter Pangloss, *The Young Rosciad, An Admonitory Poem. Well-Seasoned with Attic Salt* (London: J. Roach, Russell Court, 1805), 26.

34. Pangloss, *Rosciad*, 14.

35. Slout and Rudisill, "Enigma," 86.

36. Qtd. in Waters, "'That Astonishing,'" at 79.

37. Holland, "A Cart Load of Young Players on their Journey to London," Caricatures, HTC. See also S. W. Forbes's February 1805 caricature, "John Bull in Lilliput or Theatricals for the Nineteenth Century," HTC.

38. "Infantine acting," *Morning Herald*, Dec. 18 [?], 1804, *Collectanea*, p. 52.

39. "New Theatre-Royal," n.d. 1805, *Collectanea*, p. 116. Kahan, *Bettymania*, 99 [for Wigley]. Kahan also identifies the following boy wonders: Master Saunders, "the Infant Clown," age 14; "the ORMSKIRE (or Ormskirk?) Roscius," age 13; Master MORI, the "Young Orpheus," age 8; Master Byrne, the "Infant Vestris," age 8; Master Romney Robinson, age 12. Girl wonders included Miss Freron, "the Infant Billington," age 8; Miss Lee Sugg, "the Infant Billington and Roscius," age 7; Miss Saunders, "the Infant Columbine"; Miss Quantrell, age 11; Miss Swindells, age 11. Listed in Kahan, *Bettymania*, 98–99. In addition to this list, the *Collectanea* collection at the Folger includes references to Master Watt; Master Tokeley; Master Wallack; Master Schirmer; Miss Lettile. See *Collecteana* clippings, 89–91. And Dunlap includes the "Young Orpheus, Infant Vestris, Infant Clown, Comic Roscius, Infant Degvill, Infant Hercules, and Infant Candlesnuffer" (Dunlop, qtd. in Waters, "'That Astonishing,'" 80).

40. Kahan, *Bettymania*, 98–99.

41. Marcus, *Drama*, 202–4. Marcus also discusses "mirror repertory," which involves actors performing the same role simultaneously at different theatres (205–8).

42. *Collecteana* clippings, 71. According to Burwick, Charles Dibdin maintained a school at the Royal Circus, Henry Francis Greville ran one at Sans Souci, and Robert Elliston operated a school at the Surrey. Burwick, "Georgian Theories," 189. Elliston's interest in training young actors is worth noting as he would later influence Clara Fisher's repertoire (see Chapter 3). For later discussions of children and acting, see Thomas Rede, *The Road to the Stage* (1827), and George Grant, *Essays on the Science of Acting* (1828).

43. In fact, Payne had attempted to follow Betty's lead as early as 1805 but his father directed his attention toward publishing theatrical reviews instead. Willis T. Hanson, *The Early Life of John Howard Payne* (Boston: Printed for members of the Bibliophile Society, 1913), 18–20. On Payne's negotiation of his Jewishness, see Heather Nathans, *Hideous Characters and Beautiful Pagans: Performing Jewish Identity on the Antebellum American Stage* (Ann Arbor: University of Michigan Press, 2017), 97–98. Unlike Betty, whose career petered out before he left his teens, Payne enjoyed a healthy career as an actor and playwright before turning to other forms of writing.

44. Qtd. in Davis, "Freaks," 185–86. See also Gubar, *Artful Dodgers*, 159.

45. David Erskine Baker, *Biographica Dramatica, Or, a Companion to the Playhouse* (London, 1812), lxi–lxiii.

46. Baker, *Biographica Dramatica*, lxiv.

47. Davis, "Freaks," 185–86.

CHAPTER 1

1. *British Press*, Dec. 31, 1817, qtd. in M. Burton, *A Sketch of the Life of Miss Clara Fisher, the Lilliputian Actress, of the Theatres-Royal Drury-Lane and Covent Garden* (London: W. J. Collier, 1819), 31.

2. "The British Stage," Jan. 1818, qtd. in Burton, *A Sketch*, 10.

3. *Morning Chronicle*, Dec. 11, 1817, qtd. in Burton, *A Sketch*, 13.

4. Ibid.; *British Press*, Dec. 11, 1817, qtd. in Burton, *A Sketch*, 18–19; original emphasis.

5. "The British Stage," 10.

6. *British Press*, Dec. 11, 1817, qtd. in Burton, *A Sketch*, 18–19.

7. For an overview of the attacks on Master Betty, see Bisset, *Critical Essays*.

8. See Gubar, *Artful Dodgers*, 159–61; and Waters, "'That Astonishing,'" 78–94.

9. Clara Fisher Maeder, *Autobiography of Clara Fisher Maeder*, ed. Douglas Taylor (New York: Burt Franklin, 1897 [1979]), 7.

10. "The Drama," *Universal Magazine* 4 (Sept. [?] 1805): 249.

11. Celestine Woo, "Sarah Siddons's Performances as Hamlet: Breaching the Breeches Part," *European Romantic Review* 18, no. 2 (Dec. 2007): 573–95, at 576.

12. Woo, "Sarah Siddons's," 576.

13. Helen E. M. Brooks, *Actresses, Gender, and the Eighteenth-Century Stage: Playing Women* (Basingstoke: Palgrave Macmillan, 2015), 64.

14. Woo, "Sarah Siddons's," 574–75.

15. Brooks, *Actresses*, 65–76.

16. "Eventful Careers: A Record of Over Seventy Years Upon the Stage, Mrs.

Clara Fisher-Maeder's Remarkable Experience. A Chat with Mr. Actor, Mr. George C. Boniface," n.d., Clippings – Clara Fisher, HTC.

17. One important exception is a Mrs. Thompson who in 1844 played the Duke of "Gloster" in the first act of *Richard III* as part of a benefit performance in Auckland, New Zealand. This performance marks one of the earliest known performances of Shakespeare in New Zealand. Anthony Tedeschi, "Vale Shakespeare: Highlights from the Turnbull Collection," National Library of New Zealand, https://natlib.govt.nz/blog/posts/vale-shakespeare-highlights-from-the-turnbull-collections, accessed Feb. 19, 2019.

18. "Memoir of Master Burke," *Dramatic Magazine*, June 1, 1830, 130; Anthony Sansonetti, "Master Joseph Burke," *Ambassadors of Empire: Child Performers and Anglo-American Audiences, 1800s–1880*, http://childperformers.ca/master-joseph-burke/1.

19. Marah Gubar, "Who Watched *The Children's Pinafore*? Age Transvestism on the Nineteenth-Century Stage," *Victorian Studies* 54, no. 3 (Spring 2012): 410–26, at 411.

20. Marjorie Garber acknowledges that "The nineteenth century's penchant for both child actors and male impersonators makes their Shylocks less anomalous than they might seem at first" (230), but doesn't investigate *Richard III* at any length. Key texts on the history of cross-dressed performance include Marjorie Garber, *Vested Interests: Cross-Dressing and Cultural Anxiety* (New York: Routledge, 1992); Lisa Merrill, *When Romeo Was a Woman: Charlotte Cushman and Her Circle of Female Spectators* (Ann Arbor: University of Michigan Press, 1999); Mullenix, *Wearing*; Laurence Senelick, *Sex, Drag, and Theatre* (New York: Taylor & Francis, 2003); Woo, "Sarah Siddons's." See Denise A. Walen, "Such a Romeo as We Had Never Ventured to Hope For," in Schanke and Marra, *Passing Performances* for a similar question about Cushman's decision to play Romeo. Anne Russell suggests that female Romeos didn't begin appearing until 1830s. Anne Russell, "Tragedy, Gender, Performance: Women as Tragic Heroes on the Nineteenth-Century Stage," *Comparative Drama* 30, no. 2 (Summer 1996): 135–57, at 138. Curiously, Charlotte Cushman, one of the most famous Romeos of the nineteenth century, was trained by the Maeders.

21. Davis, "Freaks," 179.

22. William Winter states that she died June 4, 1869, in her seventy-seventh year. Winter, *Brief Chronicles* (New York: Dunlap Society, 1889), 291. According to a clipping from 1805, she was born in October.

23. The Fishers had six children: John, Jane, Amelia, Caroline, Charles, and Clara.

24. W. Longman, *Tokens of the Eighteenth Century Connected with Booksellers and Bookmakers* (London: Longmans, Green and Co., 1916), 25. Fisher

also ran the local post office in Brighton and seems to have been an important purveyor of knowledge and information (67). On libraries as sites of sociality in the eighteenth and early nineteenth centuries, see James Raven, "Libraries for Sociability: The Advance of the Subscription Library," in *The Cambridge History of Libraries in Britain and Ireland*, ed. Peter Hoare (Cambridge: Cambridge University Press, 2008), 241–63.

25. Maeder, *Autobiography*, 12. I have found very few direct references to *Mrs.* Fisher, although I expect she was present as well during these sessions.

26. Henry Pitt Phelps, *Players of a Century: A Record of the Albany Stage* (Albany: Joseph McDonough, 1880), 113.

27. Caroline Gonda, *Reading Daughters' Fictions, 1709–1834: Novels and Society from Manley to Edgeworth* (Cambridge: Cambridge University Press, 1996), 30. See also Ruth Perry, *Novel Relations: The Transformation of Kinship in English Literature and Culture, 1748–1818* (Cambridge: Cambridge University Press, 2006).

28. Jean I. Marsden, "Shakespeare for Girls: Mary Lamb and *Tales from Shakespeare*," *Children's Literature* 17, no. 1 (1989): 47–63, at 47.

29. Avery, qtd. in Darlene Ciraulo and Daniel Schierenbeck, "Shakespeare and Education in the Lambs' *Poetry for Children* and *Tales from Shakespeare*," spec. issue on "Shakespeare for Children," *Borrowers and Lenders: The Journal of Shakespeare and Appropriation*, 2, no. 1 (Spring/Summer 2004): 1–16, at 4. See also Janet Bottoms, "The Battle of the (Children's) Books," *Romanticism* 12, no. 3 (2006): 212–22; Felicity James, "Wild 'Tales' from Shakespeare: Readings of Charles and Mary Lamb," *Shakespeare* 2, no. 2 (December 2006): 152–67; Mitzi Myers, "'A Taste for Truth and Realities': Early Advice to Mothers on Books for Girls," *Children's Literature Association Quarterly* 12, no. 3 (Fall 1987): 118–24.

30. Marsden, "Shakespeare," 47.

31. Bowdler and Bowdler, viii, qtd. in Ciraulo and Schierenbeck, "Shakespeare," 2. See also Bottoms, "The Battle," 216; Ziegler, "Introducing Shakespeare."

32. Godwin, qtd. in James, "'Wild Tales,'" 156.

33. See Pamela Clemit, "Mary Shelley and William Godwin: A Literary-Political Partnership, 1823–36," *Women's Writing* 6, no. 3 (October 1999): 285–95.

34. See National Archives, 179 East Sussex Record Office. Archive of the Davies-Gilbert Family of Eastbourne, East Sussex and Trelissick, Cornwall. See also "Monthly List of Bankruptcies from the London Gazette," *Monthly Visitor, and New Family Magazine* 5, no. 20 (Dec. 1805): 424–27, at 427, British Periodicals. Here Fisher's profession is listed as a "bookseller." The 1804 edition of Fisher's *Brighton Guide* includes a reference to Fisher setting up an

auction house in Brighton, which may have been an attempt to recoup some of the losses from 1803. Frederick George Fisher, *Fisher's New Brighton Guide* (London: Printed, for the Editor, and Sold by F. G. Fisher, Styne, Brighthelmston, 1804), 22–24.

35. Laurence Hutton claims that Jane Fisher was ten years old when she made her stage debut. Laurence Hutton, "Infant Phenomena," *Frank Leslie's Popular Monthly* 21, no. 4 (April 1886): 439 (and following), at 439, American Periodicals. This may have been possible, although the earliest records I have seen c. 1804 refer to her as a twelve-year-old. Other biographical accounts suggest that Jane Fisher made her stage debut in 1817 alongside her sister Clara. This seems unlikely given Frederick George Fisher's investment in his daughters' careers, and may instead be evidence of the family's revisionist attempts to detract from Jane's earlier career, possibly out of shame or frustration with Bettymania.

36. Theatre Glocester playbill, July 24, 1805, *Collectanea*, p. 95. Unfortunately, I have not been able to corroborate this claim as I have found no references to Jane Fisher in the Drury Lane playbill collections at the British Library.

37. "The Royal Saloon of Arts," G.H., Oct. 5, 1805, *Collectanea*, p. 88.

38. Clipping, "New Theatre Royal—Cheltenham," July 8, 1805, *Collectanea*, p. 86.

39. Clipping, "New Theatre Royal—Cheltenham."

40. Clipping, "New Theatre Royal—Cheltenham." According to a playbill for Jane Fisher's July 24, 1805 performance at Theatre Glocester, she played Little Pickle for "seven successive nights" in the winter "with great Applause." Playbill, *Collectanea*, p. 85.

41. The first Folio contains 3,470 lines, while Cibber's condensed version ranges between 2,050 and 2,380 lines. See Joe Falocco, "'So Much for Shakespeare': Cibber, Barrymore, Barton and the History of *Richard III* in Performance," *Upstart: A Journal of English Renaissance Studies* (August 2013), https://upstart.sites.clemson.edu/Essays/so-much/so-much.xhtml.

42. Clipping, July 8, 1805, *Collectanea*, p. 86.

43. Clipping, July 8, 1805, *Collectanea*, p. 86.

44. Clipping, July 8, 1805, *Collectanea*, p. 86.

45. Clipping, July 8, 1805, *Collectanea*, p. 86. It is unclear whether such praise represents more than an individual assessment of Fisher's talents—or if the enthusiasm was in some way impelled by Fisher's father.

46. Clipping, July 20, 1805, *Collectanea*, p. 86.

47. Clipping, July 20, 1805, *Collectanea*, p. 86.

48. *Some Account of the English Stage from the Restoration in 1660 to 1830, vol. 8—Bath* (Bath: H. E. Carrington, 1832), 59–114. See also 27, 31, 111, 157.

49. Kahan, *Bettymania*, 126.

50. Davis, "Freaks"; Kahan, *Bettymania*, 107–56.

51. Knowles, *Shakespeare's Boys*, 25.

52. Unlike other eighteenth-century adaptations, Cibber refrained from introducing new characters, calling for spectacular scenic effects, or altering the ending. Nicoletta Caputo, "Looking for Richard III in Romantic Times: Thomas Bridgman's and William Charles Macready's Abortive Stage Adaptations," *Theatre Survey* 52, no. 2 (Nov. 2011): 275–300, at 276–77.

53. London Green, "Edmund Kean's Richard III," *Theatre Journal* 36, no. 4 (Dec. 1984): 505–34, at 506.

54. Caputo, "Looking," 277.

55. Caputo, "Looking," 277; Shaw, qtd. in Caputo, "Looking," 277. See also Green, "Edmund Kean's," 506.

56. Cibber's version of the play dominated the stage for two centuries, taking precedence over Shakespeare's original. Caputo, "Looking," at 276.

57. Julia H. Fawcett, *Spectacular Disappearances: Celebrity and Privacy, 1696–1801* (Ann Arbor: University of Michigan Press, 2016), 23.

58. Fawcett, *Spectacular*, 25.

59. Fawcett, *Spectacular*, 3. Overexpression is akin to the phenomenon identified by Felicity Nussbaum as "interiority effects," a strategy used with particular skill by eighteenth-century actresses to give audiences the impression that they were peering into the actresses' inner lives (Nussbaum, *Rival Queens*, 18–22). With overexpression, however, there is no illusion of access; the audience is invited to admire the actor's creation while recognizing that the self beneath is out of reach.

60. Fawcett, *Spectacular*, 33–34.

61. William Shakespeare, *Henry VI*, act 5, sc. 6. Cibber moved this late scene from *Henry VI* into his *Richard*. See Fawcett, *Spectacular*, 39.

62. Fawcett, *Spectacular*, 39.

63. Maeder, *Autobiography*, 12.

64. Straub, "Performing Variety," 243.

65. According to Charles Beecher Hogan's *Shakespeare in the Theatre, 1701–1800: A Record of Performances in London 1751–1800* (Oxford: Clarendon Press, 1957), between 1751 and 1800, the following thirty-seven girls played the princes at Drury Lane, Covent Garden, and Haymarket: Miss Yates, Miss Mullart, Miss Hallam, Miss Morrison, Miss Minors, Miss Simson, Miss Valois, Miss Rogers, Miss Read, Miss Collett, Miss Besford, Miss Rose, Miss Cokayne, Miss Hopkins, Miss Besford, Miss Linds, Miss [S] Smith, Miss P. Hopkins, Miss Russell, Miss [C] Morris, Miss Field, Miss [S] Francis, Miss Painter, Miss Langrish, Miss Thomas, Miss Meyhboyrn, Miss Heard, Miss Stageldoir, Miss Beaufield, Miss Gaudry, Miss DeCamp, Miss Standen, Miss [M] Menage, Miss Granger, Miss Sims, Miss Gilbert, Miss Jackson.

66. Knowles, *Shakespeare's Boys*, 137.

67. Knowles, *Shakespeare's Boys*, 25.

68. Knowles, *Shakespeare's Boys*, 137. See also Klein, "Without Distinction," 120–21; Gemma Miller, "Many a Time and Oft Had I Broken My Neck for Amusement': The Corpse, the Child, and the Aestheticization of Death in Shakespeare's *Richard III* and *King John*," *Comparative Drama* 50, nos. 2–3 (Summer/Fall 2016): 209–32.

69. Knowles, *Shakespeare's Boys*, 137.

70. Klein, "Without Distinction," 120–21. See also Charlotte Scott, "Incapable and Shallow Innocents," in *Childhood, Education and the Stage in Early Modern England*, ed. Richard Preiss and Deanne Williams (Cambridge: Cambridge University Press, 2017), 58–78, at 69.

71. Fawcett, *Spectacular*, 24.

72. Fawcett, *Spectacular*, 25.

73. Gemma Miller interprets recent practices of cross-gender casting for early modern plays as "a bold feminist activism." See Miller, "Cross-Gender Casting as Feminist Activism in the Staging of Early Modern Plays," *Journal of International Women's Studies* 16, no. 1 (2014): 4–17.

74. Susan Stewart, *On Longing: Narratives of the Miniature, the Gigantic, the Souvenir, the Collection* (Durham, NC: Duke University Press, 1992), 44. See also Melanie Dawson, "The Miniaturization of Girlhood: Nineteenth-Century Playtime and Gendered Theories of Development," in *The American Child: A Cultural Studies Reader*, ed. Caroline F. Levander and Carol J. Singley (New Brunswick: Rutgers University Press, 2003), 63–84.

75. Tracy C. Davis, "'Reading Shakespeare by Flashes of Lightning': Challenging the Foundations of Romantic Acting Theory," *ELH* 62, no. 4 (Winter 1995): 933–54, at 934–36.

76. Frederick Burwick, "The Ideal Shatters," in *The Oxford Handbook of the Georgian Theatre, 1737–1832*, ed. Julia Swindells and David Francis Taylor (Oxford: Oxford University Press, 2014), 129–49.

77. Caputo, "Looking," 276. See also Nicoletta Caputo, "Performing the Passions," *Assaph: Studies in the Theatre* 24 (2010): 75–108.

78. Qtd. in Ionna Papageorgiou, "Enchanting Evil: English Romantic Criticism on Edmund Kean's Interpretation of *Richard III* and Schiller's Theory on the Immortal Characters in Art," *Restoration and Eighteenth-Century Theatre Research* 23, no. 1 (2008): 19–33, at 22. See also John I. Ades, "Charles Lamb, Shakespeare, and Early Nineteenth-Century Theater," *PMLA* 85, no. 3 (May 1970): 514–26, at 523–24; Davis, "'Reading Shakespeare,'" 933–54.

79. Qtd. in Papageorgiou, "Enchanting Evil," 23.

80. Detail mentioned in Burton, *A Sketch*, 5, HTC.

81. Burton, *A Sketch of the Life of Miss Clara Fisher*, 2nd ed., 4, BL. This

entry is from the expanded second edition of this volume, which included additional reviews of Fisher's performances. It is worth noting the similarities between this description of Fisher's introduction to the theatre and the description of Betty's first encounter. Both child performers were transformed by the experience and attempted to reenact the scenes they had witnessed. On *Jane Shore*, see Brooks, *Actresses*, 42–62.

82. Anon. [Burton], *A Sketch*, HTC.

83. Corri was a former theatre manager in Edinburgh, as well as a manager of Vauxhall Pleasure Gardens, and therefore clearly experienced in meeting the needs of the public.

84. *British Stage*, Dec. 10 [1817], reprinted in Burton, *A Sketch*, 13.

85. Burton, *A Sketch*, 6–7, BL. This information about Fisher's involvement in the preparation of *Lilliput* is absent from the first edition of *A Sketch of the Life of Miss Clara Fisher*. However, Fisher is credited with writing "additional Songs and a Masque" on the cover of the *Lilliput* sheet music published shortly after the production's 1817 opening. See Domenico Corri (with additional Songs and a Masque written by F.G. Fisher), *Lilliput: A Dramatic Romance* (London: Goulding, D'Almaine, Potter & Co., c. 1818).

86. Fisher may have had his own business interests in mind when inserting a substantial Shakespeare scene into *Lilliput*. According to a February 1818 article in the *World*, Fisher was planning to "complete a museum, in which he intends to furnish accurate models of every subject that can elucidate the history or perpetuate the memory of the most remarkable events in the life of Shakespeare." Several of Fisher's finished models, including one of the Globe Theatre, were already on display in the "Great Room at the Shakespeare Tavern, Great Russell-Street, Covent Garden" (*World*, Feb. 1, 1818; reprinted in *A Sketch*, 51, BL). Fisher later published sketches and detailed descriptions of these models in a volume entitled *A Catalogue of the Various Articles Contained in Clara Fisher's Shaksperian* [*sic*] *Cabinet* (1830). Many of these models exist today and are on display in the Rosenbach Museum in Philadelphia.

87. Maeder, *Autobiography*, 5.

88. Davis, "'Reading Shakespeare,'" 933.

89. Green, "Edmund Kean's," 512.

90. Green, "Edmund Kean's," 523.

91. "The British Stage," Jan. 1818, qtd. in Burton, *A Sketch*, 10; *Morning Chronicle*, Dec. 11, 1817, qtd. in Burton, *A Sketch*, 13.

92. *British Press*, qtd. in Burton, *A Sketch*, 19.

93. Gubar has explored how this tension between seeing child performers as "both artful and natural, both inscribed and original" played out throughout the nineteenth century. *Artful Dodgers*, 158–59.

94. *Morning Herald*, Dec. 11, 1817, qtd. in Burton, *A Sketch*, 1st ed., 17.

95. *Birmingham Commercial Herald*, March 21, 1818, qtd. in Burton, *A Sketch*, 41, British Library.

96. *British Press*, Dec. 31, 1817.

97. *Day and New Times*, Dec. 13, 1817, qtd. in Burton, *A Sketch*, 36, HTC; *Courier*, 15 Jan. 1818, qtd. in Burton, *A Sketch*, 33, HTC.

98. Theatre Royal, Drury-Lane playbill, Dec. 10, 1817, Drury Lane Playbills, Box 6, HRC.

99. Maeder, *Autobiography*, 17.

100. Maeder, *Autobiography*, 17.

101. "Eventful Careers."

102. Maeder, *Autobiography*, 9.

103. Combe, in Maeder, *Autobiography*, 113; "Eventful Careers."

104. Maeder, *Autobiography*, 5–6.

105. Playbill for Theatre Royal, Edinburgh, June 9, 1819, Victorian Popular Culture database, Adam Matthew, http://www.victorianpopularculture.am digital.co.uk/; Playbill for Theatre Royal, Newcastle, "For Three Nights Only," May 17, 1819, "Shakespeare at the old Theatre Royal," April 26, 2016, https://blogs.ncl.ac.uk/speccoll/tag/king-richard-the-third/.

106. "Memoirs of Miss Clara Fisher," in Maeder, *Autobiography*, 128.

107. "Eventful Careers"; Playbill for Theatre Royal, Edinburgh, June 9, 1819.

108. Maeder, *Autobiography*, 7.

109. Maeder, *Autobiography*, 7.

110. "Miss Clara Fisher: To the Editor," *Kaleidoscope: or, Literary and Scientific Mirror*, June 11, 1822, 392, Google Books.

111. The Edinburgh Phrenological Society was established on February 22, 1820.

112. The Library of Congress includes several playbills from Fisher's 1820 appearance at the Theatre Royal Edinburgh, where she performed in *The Merchant of Venice, Richard III, The Spoiled Child*, and *Lilliput*. See Thr. A3, Box 2, Folder 1, and Thr. A4, Box 2, Folder 1, LC.

113. Combe, "Report Upon the Cast of Miss Clara Fisher [1820]," in Maeder, *Autobiography*, 107.

114. Combe, *Elements of Phrenology* (Edinburgh: John Anderson Jun., 1824), 15–16.

115. Combe, *Elements*, 35.

116. For a full discussion of all thirty-three organs, see Combe, *Elements*. On the history of phrenology, see John B. Davies, *Phrenology: Fad and Science, A Nineteenth-Century American Crusade* (New Haven: Yale University Press, 1955 [1971]); Charles Colbert, *A Measure of Perfection: Phrenology and the Fine*

Arts in America (Chapel Hill: University of North Carolina Press, 1997); and John van Wyhe, *Phrenology and the Origins of Victorian Scientific Naturalism* (Aldershot: Ashgate, 2004).

117. Combe, *A System of Phrenology*, 3rd ed. (Edinburgh: John Anderson, Jr., 1830), 90–91.

118. Phrenological Society, *Transactions of the Phrenological Society*, vol. 1. (Edinburgh: John Anderson Jr., 1824), xv–xvi.

119. "Notices Relating to the Fine Arts in Edinburgh," *Scots Magazine and Edinburgh Literary Miscellany*, vol. 78, part 1 (Edinburgh: Archibald Constable and Co., 1816), 207.

120. See "Wars of Independence: Robert (1) the Bruce," *future museum.co .uk*, http://www.futuremuseum.co.uk/collections/people/lives-in-key-periods /the-medieval-period-(1100ad-1499ad)/wars-of-independence/robert-(i)-the -bruce/robert-the-bruce,-cast-of-his-skull.aspx, accessed Dec. 28, 2015.

121. In April 1821 Scoular was commissioned to create a commemorative sculpture of Princess Elizabeth of Clarence, who died at age three months. This sculpture is on display in the Entrance Hall and Main Stairway of Frogmore House. "Princess Elizabeth of Clarence (1820–21) c. 1821," Royal Collection Trust, https://www.rct.uk/collection/53354/princess-elizabeth-of-clarence-1820 -21, accessed April 1, 2020.

122. Maeder, *Autobiography*, 13.

123. Maeder, *Autobiography*, 13.

124. Maeder, *Autobiography*, 13.

125. Ute Kornmeier, "Almost Alive: The Spectacle of Verisimilitude in Madame Tussaud's Waxworks," in *Ephemeral Bodies: Wax Sculpture and the Human Figure*, ed. Roberta Panzanelli and Julius Ritter von Schlosser, 67–82 (Los Angeles: Getty Research Institute, 2008), 76.

126. Combe, *Elements*, 24.

127. Combe, "Report," 107.

128. Clara Fisher was the first of a number of child performers to undergo phrenological analysis. Others include Ellen and Kate Bateman, Louisa Vinning, and Cordelia Howard. "Little Cordelia Howard," *American Phrenological Journal* 23, no. 5 (May 1865): 107; "Mr. Cull on a Case of Musical Talent [Monday, 21st September]," *Phrenological Journal and Magazine of Moral Science* 14, no. 66 (1841): 25–31.

129. Combe, "Report," 108.

130. Combe, "Report," 109.

131. Mrs. Henry Siddons was Harriet Murray, proprietor of the Theatre Royal Edinburgh and the widow of Sarah Siddons's son Henry.

132. Combe, "Report," 109.

133. Combe, "Report," 109.

134. See Combe, "Report," 113.

135. Combe, "Report," 110.

136. Combe, "Report," 111 (emphasis in original).

137. Combe, "Report," 111.

138. Schechner, *Between Theatre*, 110.

139. "Although not strictly phrenological," he writes, "I may, perhaps, be excused, for adding a few additional remarks on her conception of this character." Combe, "Report," 111.

140. Combe, "Report," 108, 112.

141. Combe, "Report," 112.

142. Combe, "Report," 112.

143. Combe met Fisher not long after becoming friends with Mrs. Henry Siddons. David Stack, *Queen Victoria's Skull* (London: Hambledon Continuum, 2008), 104. Combe was undoubtedly familiar with her late husband's treatise *Practical Illustrations of Rhetorical Gesture and Action* (1807), a revised translation of Johann Jakob Engel's *Ideen zu Einer Mimik*, which applies biological principles to the study of human gesture and includes a lengthy analysis of his mother Sarah's meticulously crafted death scenes. Combe shared Henry's belief in the importance of collecting and classifying "different physiognomies" in order to understand human behavior. Henry Siddons, *Practical Illustrations of Rhetorical Gesture and Action: Adapted to the English Drama from a Work on the Subject by M. Engel*, 2nd ed. (London: Sherwood, Neely, and Jones, 1822 [1807]), 25.

144. For example, for her May 13, 1820, benefit performance, Fisher played *An Actress of All Work* after *Richard III*. Thr. A3, box 2, folder 2, (King) Richard III, 15 March 1819–6 September 1824, Playbills Collection, LC.

145. In this respect, the statue, the life cast, and the protean farce resemble theatre history's most infamous human remain—the skull. See Aoife Monks, "Human Remains: Acting, Objects, and Belief in Performance," *Theatre Journal* 64, no. 3 (Oct. 2012): 355–71.

146. Fawcett, *Spectacular*, 39.

147. Phrenological Society, *Transactions*, 299.

148. Featured types included (names as they appeared in the text): Brazil Indian, Ceylonese, New Zealander, New Hollande, Sandwich Islander, North American Indian, and Peruvian. Celebrated individuals included Shakespeare, Pope Alexander VI, Raphael, and Sheridan. Combe, *System*, 6.

149. Combe, *System*, 6.

150. Combe, *System*, 197.

151. Other phrenologists seized the opportunity to use Clara Fisher's head in their own writing. In his 1836 book *Practical Phrenology*, US phrenologist Silas Jones devotes an entire chapter to "Mrs. Maeder—Better Known as Miss

Clara Fisher—An Actress." Jones admits that he has never seen Fisher or had the opportunity to view her cast and instead bases his assessment of her abilities on "a print published by Bourne of New York." Silas Jones, *Practical Phrenology* (Boston: Russell, Shattuck, & Williams, 1836), 321–22.

152. Combe, *Lectures on Phrenology* (New York: Samuel Colman, 1839), 224.

153. The cast of Clara Fisher's head might exist still. Its last known location, according to Fisher, was the Canadian province of British Columbia, where a man named Louis F. Post encountered it in the mid-1890s (Maeder, *The Autobiography*, 14).

INTERLUDE 2

1. Qtd. in Michelle Ann Abate, *Tomboys: A Literary and Cultural History* (Philadelphia: Temple University Press, 2008), xiii. See also "Tomboy" and "Hoyden" in the *Oxford English Dictionary*.

2. Qtd. in Abate, *Tomboys*, xiv.

3. Abate, *Tomboys*, xiv.

4. Abate, *Tomboys*, 2.

5. Abate, *Tomboys*, 4. In her article on tomboys, Elizabeth Segel defines the term "pickle" as "an amusing little rascal presented purely for the readers' entertainment," but doesn't consider the source of the nickname. Segel, "The Gypsy Breynton Series: Setting the Pattern for American Tomboy Heroines," *Children's Literature Association Quarterly* 14, no. 2 (Summer 1989): 67–71, at 70. See also Jane H. Hunter, *How Young Ladies Became Girls: The Victorian Origins of American Girlhood* (New Haven: Yale University Press, 2002), 140; Renée M. Sentilles, *American Tomboys 1850–1915* (Amherst: University of Massachusetts Press, 2018), 3; Sarah Burns, "Making Mischief," in *Angels and Tomboys: Girlhood in Nineteenth-Century American Art*, ed. Holly Pyne Connor (Newark Museum: San Francisco: Pomegranate, 2012), 86.

6. Abate, *Tomboys*, 6; also Burns, "Making Mischief," 87.

7. Sentilles, *American Tomboys*, 10.

8. Sentilles, *American Tomboys*, 10.

9. Abate, *Tomboys*, xxvi.

10. Peter A. Tasch, *The Dramatic Cobbler: The Life and Works of Isaac Bickerstaff* (Lewisburg, PA: Bucknell University Press, 1971), 258.

11. Tasch, *Dramatic Cobbler*, 119; reviews, see 105–29.

12. For a plot synopsis of *Love in the City* and links to other resources on the play, see *Collection No. 4: Love in the City, By Isaac Bickerstaff*, http://projects.chass.utoronto.ca/prescrip/18thcComedy/plays/04_bick_lovecity.html, viewed June 28, 2017.

13. Tasch, *Dramatic Cobbler*, 120.

14. Tasch, *Dramatic Cobbler*, 121.

15. In one of his stage directions, Bickerstaff calls for Priscilla to enter "in a Hoydening manner." Isaac Bickerstaff, *The Romp, A Musical Entertainment in Two Acts* (London: W. Lowndes and J. Barker, 1789), 15.

16. Bickerstaff, *The Romp*, 10.

17. Bickerstaff, *The Romp*, 22.

18. Bickerstaff, *The Romp*, 6.

19. Bickerstaff, *The Romp*, 6.

20. This is confirmed by Mme. La Blond when she refers to the "West Indian fortune in the house." Bickerstaff, *The Romp*, 15.

21. Clay, *Stagestruck*, 214; also Maddock Dillon, *New World Drama*, 172.

22. Long, qtd. in Maddock Dillon, *New World Drama*, 172.

23. Maddock Dillon, *New World Drama*, 172–73.

24. I nod to Sara Ahmed's important feminist analysis of willfulness in *Willful Subjects* (Durham, NC: Duke University Press, 2014).

25. Bickerstaff, *The Romp*, 8.

26. Bickerstaff, *The Romp*, 8–9.

27. Bickerstaff, *The Romp*, 8.

28. Saidya V. Hartman, *Scenes of Subjection: Terror, Slavery, and Self-Making in Nineteenth-Century America* (New York: Oxford University Press, 1997), 17–48. Ann Huang also writes about this scene in "Alongside Slavery's Asides: Reverberations of Edward Young's Revenge" (draft essay).

29. This is one of Maddock Dillon's most salient arguments.

30. In this respect, the play anticipates a similar process that occurs with white and black children in the nineteenth century. Bernstein, *Racial Innocence*, 30–68.

31. Maddock Dillon, *New World Drama*, 54.

32. Maddock Dillon, *New World Drama*, 55.

33. Tasch refers to the work of Wylie Sypher here (*Dramatic Cobbler*, 121).

34. Sentilles, *American Tomboys*, 6.

35. Qtd. in Tasch, *Dramatic Cobbler*, 120.

36. Burney, qtd. in Claire Tomalin, *Mrs. Jordan's Profession: The Actress and the Prince* (New York: Alfred A. Knopf, 1995), 83.

37. *Child of Nature* was itself a translation of the French play *Zélie* by Mme. de Genlis. Patricia Clancy, "Mme de Genlis, Elizabeth Inchbald, and *The Child of Nature*," *Australian Journal of French Studies* 30, no. 3 (Sept. 1993): 324–40, at 325. Clancy demonstrates the influence of Rousseau's *Émile* on Mme. de Genlis's play. One of the most important sources on Jordan's offstage life is Claire Tomalin's biography, *Mrs. Jordan's Profession*. On Jordan's hair and curls, see Gill Perry, "Staging Gender and 'Hairy Signs': Representing Dorothy Jordan," *Eighteenth-Century Studies* 38, no. 1 (2004): 145–63; on Jordan more broadly, see Jean I. Marsden, "Modesty Unshackled: Dorothy Jordan and the

Dangers of Cross-dressing," *Studies in Eighteenth-Century Culture* 22 (1993): 21–35; Jocelyn Margaret Harris, "Jane Austen and Celebrity Culture: Shakespeare, Dorothy Jordan and Elizabeth Bennet," *Shakespeare* 6, no. 4 (Dec. 2010): 410–30; Brooks, *Actresses*, 93–116.

38. Perry, "Staging Gender," 146.

39. Hazlitt, qtd. in Perry, "Staging Gender," 146.

40. Perry, "Staging Gender," 146.

CHAPTER 2

1. The *New Monthly Magazine* was less impressed with other aspects of the painting, noting that it was "sadly deficient in the merits of portraiture." *New Monthly Magazine* 9 (June 1, 1823), 254. For more on Clint, see Jim Davis, *Comic Acting and Portraiture in Late-Georgian and Regency England* (Cambridge: Cambridge University Press, 2015).

2. For this chapter, I consulted four versions of *The Spoiled Child* in physical and virtual archives, including the 1790 copy submitted to the Lord Chamberlain, the 1805 "authentic edition . . . strictly conformable to the prompter's book," an 1822 publication associated with W. Oxberry's production of the play, and a much later (c. 1851) one-act version published by Thomas Hailes Lacy. The existence of these many versions attests to the popularity and fluidity of the play. For the most part, I refer to the 1805 edition in my analysis of the play, but also draw on additional materials (e.g., prefatory remarks) from the other publications. Spelling of the word "spoiled" varies in these publications with "spoil'd" and "spoil't" also used. Unless quoting directly, I use "spoiled" in this chapter, while acknowledging the original spelling in notes. See *The Spoilt Child: A Farce in Two Acts*, March 15, 1790, mssLA 1–2503, John Larpent papers, 1737–1824, Huntington Library; *The Spoil'd Child, A Farce, In Two Acts* (London: Barker and Son, 1805), Google Books; *The Spoiled Child, A Farce. With Preparatory Notes* (London: W. Simpkin, and R. Marshall, 1822), Google Books; *The Spoiled Child, a Farce in One Act* (London: Thomas Hailes Lacy, c. 1851), BL.

3. D——G, "Remarks," *The Spoiled Child* (c. 1851), 10.

4. "Bristol Theatre, Miss Clara Fisher," clipping, HTC.

5. Mrs. John Drew (Louisa Lane), *Autobiography of Mrs. John Drew* (New York: Charles Scribner's Sons, 1899), 29.

6. Varty, *Children and Theatre*, 110, 273, 393n; T. Allston Brown, *A History of the New York Stage from the First Performance in 1732 to 1901* (New York: Dodd, Mead and Company, 1903), 34–37, 192–93, 210, 287, 322, 360, 363, 396. See, for example, Drew, *Autobiography*, 28–29. Jane Austen's family may also have staged a parlor version of *The Spoilt Child*. See Harris, "Jane Austen," 412.

7. Ellen Malenas Ledoux, "Working Mothers on the Romantic Stage: Sarah Siddons and Mary Robinson," in *Stage Mothers: Women, Work, and the Theater, 1600–1830*, ed. Laura Engel and Elaine M. McGirr, 79–104 (Lewisburg, PA: Bucknell University Press, 2014); Brooks, *Actresses*, 117–41; Gollapudi, "Recovering Miss Rose," 6–34.

8. Leigh Hunt, *Critical Essays &c &c.* (London: John Hunt, 1807), 163.

9. Mullenix, *Wearing*, 155.

10. Steven Mintz, *Huck's Raft: A History of American Childhood* (Cambridge, MA: Harvard University Press, 2004), 83–84.

11. Robson, *Men in Wonderland*.

12. Anne Varty reads Little Pickle as the epitome of a monstrous, "savage child," *Children and Theatre*, 214.

13. The otherwise anonymous P.P. states matter-of-factly in the preface that "The name of its author is unknown: for all inquiries upon the subject have hitherto failed to unravel the important mystery." "Remarks," *The Spoiled Child* (1822), ii.

14. James Boaden, *The Biography of Mrs. Dorothy Jordan* (New York: Athenaeum Press, 1830), 166.

15. Tasch, *Dramatic Cobbler*, 222–23.

16. D——G, "Remarks," *The Spoiled Child* (c. 1851), 11.

17. *The Spoiled Child* (c. 1851), iii.

18. See, for example, Dror Wahrman, "*Percy's* Prologue: From Gender Play to Gender Panic in Eighteenth-Century England," *Past & Present* 159, no. 1 (May 1998): 113–60.

19. Bickerstaff and Jordan's biographers generally agree that the play is Bickerstaff's. Tasch cites a note from John Kemble's Memoranda books identifying *The Spoiled Child* as "written by Mr. Bickerstaffe," as well as a short article in *The World* stating that Bickerstaff had sent the play to Jordan from Italy, although Tasch questions the accuracy of the latter claim (*Dramatic Cobbler*, 250). Claire Tomalin briefly entertains the prospect that the actress wrote the play "when she was home with [her newborn] during the winter, to amuse herself, and as a vehicle for a range of stage effects she knew she could pull off" (*Mrs. Jordan's Profession*, 109). Tomalin points out that Jordan was a capable writer later credited for assisting fellow actress Mary Robinson with her play *Nobody* but she ultimately dismisses Jordan's contribution to the play in favor of crediting Bickerstaff (145n, *Mrs. Jordan's Profession*). Neither discusses the prologue, however, which offers evidence of *some* involvement on Jordan's part.

20. Brooks, *Actresses*, 89–90.

21. Prologue, *The Spoiled Child* (1805), iv.

22. The anonymous editor P.P. claimed that *The Spoiled Child* was "'The Romp,' with another title; and we may be assured that, but for Mrs. Jordan's excellence as *Priscilla Tomboy, Little Pickle* would never have been heard of." "Remarks," *The Spoiled Child* (1822), i.

23. In his memoranda books, John Kemble notes that the play "was hissed, but I think it will do yet.—Mrs. Jordan played well in the Farce." Qtd. in Tasch, *Dramatic Cobbler*, 250.

24. P.P., "Remarks," *The Spoiled Child* (1822), i–ii.

25. *The Spoiled Child* (1805), 7.

26. I first came across Miller's work in Ahmed, *Willful Subjects*, 2. For more, see Alice Miller, *For Your Own Good: Hidden Cruelty in Child-Rearing and the Roots of Violence* (New York: Farrar, Straus and Giroux, 1983), 3–102.

27. Bernstein, *Racial Innocence*, 36. Also Ahmed, *Willful Subjects*.

28. John Wesley, *The Works of the Rev. John Wesley*, vol. 6 (New York: J. & J. Harper, 1826), 172, Google Books.

29. Wesley, *The Works of the Rev. John Wesley*, 173. See also Bernstein, *Racial Innocence*, 37.

30. "Spoil," *Oxford English Dictionary*. Wycherley, *The Double-Dealer*, 188 (act 4, sc. 11).

31. Ahmed, "Willful Parts," 238.

32. Qtd. in Ahmed, "Willful Parts," 239.

33. Ahmed, "Willful Parts," 248.

34. D——G, "Remarks," 5.

35. *The Spoiled Child* (1805), 8.

36. *The Spoiled Child* (1805), 9.

37. Locke, qtd. in Ahmed, *Willful Subjects*, 69.

38. Wordsworth, "Ode 536: Intimations of Immortality from Recollections of Early Childhood." Varty suggests that Little Pickle's naughtiness supports Calvinist understandings of children as savage beasts in need of training (214). Although Miss Pickle seems to hold this view of child-rearing, Mr. Pickle does not share this perspective.

39. Ahmed, *Willful Subjects*, 73.

40. Ahmed, *Willful Subjects*, 74.

41. Qtd. Ahmed, *Willful Subjects*, 74.

42. Ahmed, *Willful Subjects*, 75.

43. See Burdan, "Girls," 9.

44. Clancy, "Mme de Genlis," 328. Clancy dismisses earlier scholars who denied the influence of Rousseau or Voltaire on *Zélie*. For her part, Inchbald drew on aspects of Rousseau when writing *Such Things Are* (1788) and in 1790 briefly entertained plans to translate the philosopher's *Confessions*.

45. Miss Pickle's poor choice in suitors threatens the stability of the Pickle

family home. Little Pickle's disruption of his aunt's tryst with Tagg is thus more than a practical joke; it secures the family's financial future.

46. See, for example, playbills for May 27, June 9, Dec. 1, Dec. 8, 1795. *The London Stage*, 1759, 1761, 1810, 1812.

47. *The Spoiled Child* (1805), 9.

48. *The Spoiled Child* (1805), 9.

49. Varty reports that at least six versions of the song were sold between 1790 and 1806. *Children and Theatre*, 112. The British Library holds copies of at least three versions of these songs, according to its online catalogue. See also "Since then I'm doomed," Notated Music, Library of Congress, https://www.loc.gov/resource/musm1a1.10362.0?st=gallery.

50. The literal sidelining of Maria as a character is intriguing when considering representations of nineteenth-century girlhood.

51. The 1822 version offers a different take on the father-son reconciliation. When Pickle reprimands his son for playing such cruel tricks on him, Little Pickle has the final word, reminding his father that he has already forgiven his sins: "Trick! Oh, sir, recollect you have pardoned them already; and, if these our kind and generous spectators will but own they have been amused by my efforts, I shall be tempted once more to transgress" (1822, p. 22). This ending implies that unlike Rousseau's *Émile*, Little Pickle has not discovered through gentle instruction the dangers of leading a willful life but rather has learned that parents will forgive all transgressions and can therefore be disobeyed without consequence. In sum, he has spoiled their lesson and bent *them* to his will.

52. *The Spoiled Child* (1805), 33.

53. *The Spoiled Child* (1805), 34.

54. D——G, "Remarks," (c. 1851), 5.

55. Plotz, *Romanticism*, xii.

56. Plotz, *Romanticism*, xv.

57. Plotz, *Romanticism*, xv.

58. Plotz, *Romanticism*, xv.

59. Gubar, *Artful Dodgers*, 4. See also Straub, "Performing Variety," 229–46; 243.

60. *The Spoiled Child* (1822), 22.

61. Gubar's term "age transvestism" applies here as well. Gubar, "Who Watched *The Children's Pinafore*?" 411.

62. Mullenix, *Wearing*, 42. *The Spoiled Child* anticipates the popularity of protean farces whereby actors and actresses played upward of seven roles in a single performance. See Chapters 3 and 4.

63. Straub, *Sexual Suspects*, 129. See also Marjean D. Purinton, "Cross-Dressing and the Performance of Gender in Romantic-Period Comic Plays by Women," in *Spheres of Action: Speech and Performance in Romantic Culture,*

ed. Alexander Dick and Angela Esterhammer, 178–93 (Toronto: University of Toronto Press, 2009).

64. Brooks, *Actresses*, 6.

65. Straub, *Sexual Subjects*, 131.

66. Boaden, *Biography*, 43–44.

67. Hunt, *Critical Essays*, 163. Emphasis in original.

68. Here I invoke Marvin Carlson's important concept of "ghosting," as explored in *The Haunted Stage: The Theatre as Memory Machine* (Ann Arbor: University of Michigan Press, 2001).

69. Hunt, *Critical Essays*, 166–67.

70. Ahmed, *Queer Phenomenology: Orientations, Objects, Others* (Durham, NC: Duke University Press, 2006), 66.

71. Ironically, it is Jordan's adherence to a particular "line of business," i.e. breeches roles, and her apparent reluctance to step "out of line" that Hunt finds so troubling. On "lines of business," see Lisa A. Freeman, *Character's Theater: Genre and Identity on the Eighteenth-Century Stage* (Philadelphia: University of Pennsylvania Press, 2002), 30; Michael Booth, *Theatre in the Victorian Age* (Cambridge: Cambridge University Press, 1991), 125–30.

72. Hunt's writing about Jordan's body transformed by years of masculine action anticipates Judith Butler's writing on the performativity of gender. Butler, "Performative Acts." Also Marsden, "Modesty," 23.

73. Ahmed, *Willful Subjects*, 71.

74. Ahmed's work on willfulness resonates powerfully with Saidya Hartman's writing about waywardness as it shaped the lives of young black women in the early twentieth century: "The acts of the wayward—the wild thoughts, reckless dreams, interminable protests, spontaneous strikes, riotous behavior, nonparticipation, willfulness, and bold-faced refusal—redistributed the balance of need and want and sought a line of escape from debt and duty in the attempt to create a path elsewhere." Saidya Hartman, *Wayward Lives, Beautiful Experiments: Intimate Histories of Social Upheaval* (New York: W. W. Norton, 2019), 237.

75. Marsden, "Modesty," 31.

76. Marsden, "Modesty," 32.

77. Straub, *Sexual Subjects*, 128. See also Brooks, *Actresses*, 6–7.

78. According to the *London Stage*, *The Spoilt Child* played at Covent Garden on the following dates: Oct. 3, Oct. 10, Oct. 12, Oct. 19, Oct. 24, Oct. 26, Nov. 2, Dec. 8, 1798, Jan. 9, Jan. 18, Apr. 24, May 30, 1799. *London Stage*, 2114, 2115, 2116, 2118, 2119, 2120, 2129, 2137, 2139, 2166, 2180. The records of the *London Stage* show that by the late 1790s Jordan was slowly ceding the role to other performers, including Mrs. Mills at Covent Garden and Mrs. Litchfield at the Haymarket.

79. Gill Perry, *Spectacular Flirtations: Viewing the British Actress in Art and Theatre* (New Haven: Yale University Press, 2007), at 98.

80. See, for example, Thomas Gainsborough's c. 1781 painting of Mary Robinson (Perdita), and especially Joshua Reynolds's 1771 portrait of Frances Abington as Miss Prue. For more on the eroticism of Jordan's portraits, see Perry, "Ambiguity and Desire."

81. On cuteness and children see Merish, "Cuteness," 185–203; Ngai, *Our Aesthetic*; Daniel Harris, *Cute, Quaint, Hungry and Romantic: The Aesthetics of Consumerism* (Cambridge, MA: Da Capo Press, 2001). On Master Betty and cuteness, see Chapter 1 and Schweitzer, "Consuming Celebrity."

82. This transition was far from instantaneous or complete, however, as adult actresses continued to play Little Pickle throughout the nineteenth century. Clipping, Clara Fisher, Bristol Theatre, HTC.

83. See engraved image of Mme Vestris as Little Pickle, c. 1830, Harry Beard Collection, Victoria & Albert Museum.

84. Klein, "Reclaiming," 11.

85. Klein, "Reclaiming," 11–12.

86. Arthur Hobson Quinn, "Chapter 1: The Heritage," in *Edgar Allan Poe: A Critical Biography* (1941): 1–50, https://www.eapoe.org/PAPERS/misc1921/quinnc01.htm#fn01011. Arnold, who was Poe's mother, is recorded in the part of Little Pickle at Newport, April 12, 1797. See p. 7n11. This was not the first appearance of Little Pickle in North America. In January 1796, Mrs. J. Brown Williamson made her debut at the Haymarket Theatre in Boston as Little Pickle. See Brown, *A History*, 396.

87. Qtd. in Quinn, *Edgar Allan Poe*, 6. See also Geddeth Smith, *The Brief Career of Eliza Poe* (Teaneck, NJ: Fairleigh Dickinson University Press, 1988).

88. Heather S. Nathans references the early career of Miss Solomon, who in 1794 inspired an admirer to publish a poem in the *Philadelphia Minerva* dedicated to her talents. Nathans, *Hideous Characters*, 148.

89. Quinn, *Edgar Allan Poe*, 11n22.

90. Klein, "Reclaiming," 11–12.

91. "The Drama," *Universal Magazine*, vol. 4, Sept. [?] 1805, 248–50, Google Books.

92. "The Drama," *Literary Chronicle and Weekly Review*, Nov. 3, 1821, 701, Google Books.

93. "Bristol Theatre, Clara Fisher," clipping, HTC.

94. Similar praise can be found in subsequent reviews, which record the "thunders of applause" that greeted her Little Pickle in Drury Lane. "Drury-Lane, Clara Fisher," clipping.

95. This rhetorical strategy, implying that the child is merely playing and not working—would become a standard justification for the employment of child

actors, especially in the late nineteenth century when labor activists began to challenge the theatre profession. I discuss this further in Chapter 4. See Zelizer, *Pricing*; Hatch, *Shirley Temple*, 132.

96. The costuming was firmly prescribed by 1826 with the publication of the play. Varty, *Children and Theatre*, 110.

97. Later in the nineteenth century the boy actors Charles Frederick Hall and Master Julian Reed also played Little Pickle. See "Amusements. Memphis Theater," *Public Ledger* (Memphis, TN), February 14, 1871, *Chronicling America: Historic American Newspapers, Library of Congress*, http://chroniclingamerica.loc.gov/lccn/sn85033673/1871-02-14/ed-1/seq-3/; George Dubourg, *The Violin: Being an Account of that Leading Instrument and Its Most Eminent Professors* (London: Robert Cocks and Co., 1878), 227.

98. *New-York Mirror, and Ladies' Literary Gazette*, clipping, HTC.

99. Mullenix, *Wearing*, 155.

100. Clara Fisher's popularity with US audiences suggests that she appealed to quite a range of ages. Since most afterpieces came at the end of an evening's performance, they may have appealed especially to male audiences, although not necessarily for sexual reasons. Mullenix notes that evidence of the sexual objectification of breeches performers is "extremely rare." Mullenix, *Wearing*, 43.

101. D. C. Johnston, *The Aurora Borealis or Flashes of Wit Calculated to Drown Dull Care and Eradicate the Blue Devils* (Boston: Editor of the Galaxy of Wit, 1831), 17, Google Books.

102. The British Library holds a number of copies of these songs. See, for example, "Since then I'm doom'd" (1800), BL.

103. Varty, *Children and Theatre*, 112.

104. A.L.E., *A Diary of Two Years and Two Days* (Wexford, Ireland: John Greene, 1834), 38, Google Books.

INTERLUDE 3

1. Drew is celebrated for her lengthy stage career and her role as matriarch of one of the United States' oldest surviving theatrical families. Her legacy continues today with her great-great-granddaughter, the film star and producer Drew Barrymore. For more on Drew, see Rivka Kelly, "*The Duchess: An Analysis of the Life and Legacy of Louisa Lane Drew*," Paper 23, senior dissertation, University of Vermont, 2014; James Kotsilibas-Davis, *Great Times, Good Times: The Odyssey of Maurice Barrymore* (New York: Doubleday, 1977).

2. Drew, *Autobiography*, 69.

3. Drew, *Autobiography*, 69.

4. Terry Eagleton, *Literary Theory: An Introduction* (Hoboken: Blackwell, 1983), 133.

5. Alex D. Boutilier, "The Citadel on Stage: The Rise and Decline of Garrison Theatre in Halifax," M.A. thesis, Saint Mary's University, Halifax, 2005, 47.

6. On shipboard theatricals see Patrick O'Neill, "Theatre in the North: Staging Practices of the British Navy in the Canadian Arctic," *Dalhousie Review* 74, no. 3 (1994): 356–84; Mary Isbell, "P(l)aying off Old Ironsides and the Old Wagon: Melville's Depiction of Shipboard Theatricals in *White-Jacket*," *Leviathan: A Journal of Melville Studies* 15, no. 1 (2013): 6–39; and Heather Davis-Fisch, *Loss and Cultural Remains in Performance: The Ghosts of the Franklin Expedition* (Basingstoke: Palgrave Macmillan, 2012), 29–60.

7. I nod toward Alan Filewod's use of Benedict Anderson's concept of "imagined community" to discuss the role of theatre in pre-Confederation Canada. See Alan Filewod, *Performing Canada: The Nation Enacted in the Imagined Theatre* (Kamloops: Textual Studies in Canada, 2002), 11–33.

8. Boutilier, "The Citadel," 46, 47.

9. Boutilier, "The Citadel," 54. For other work on Halifax theatre in the early nineteenth century, see Yashdip S. Bains, *English Canadian Theatre, 1765–1825* (Frankfurt am Main: Peter Lang, 1998).

10. "Theatre," *Acadian Recorder*, June 1, 1833, 3.

11. Patrick O'Neill, "Nova Scotia, The Theatre of," in *The Oxford Companion to Canadian Theatre*, ed. Eugene Benson and L. W. Conolly (Toronto: Oxford University Press, 1989), 388–94, at 389.

12. Patrick O'Neill, "Blake, William Rufus," in *The Oxford Companion to Canadian Theatre*, 54.

13. O'Neill, "Blake," 54.

14. Although O'Neill's entry on Blake doesn't include a reference to the Warren Theatre, his career, like that of his contemporaries, was highly mobile.

15. Drew, *Autobiography*, 67.

16. Benjamin MacArthur, *Actors and American Culture, 1880–1920* (Iowa City: University of Iowa Press, 2000), 85–122; also Robin C. Whittaker, "*Un/Disciplined Performance: Nonprofessionalized Theatre in Canada's Professional Era*," Ph.D. dissertation, University of Toronto, 2010, 45.

17. "Great Novelty," *Novascotian*, May 9, 1833, 139.

18. Drew, *Autobiography*, 5.

19. Drew, *Autobiography*, 5.

20. Drew, *Autobiography*, 17.

21. Drew, *Autobiography*, 18.

22. Drew, *Autobiography*, 21–26.

23. Drew, *Autobiography*, 26.

24. Drew, *Autobiography*, 28–29.

25. Drew, *Autobiography*, 29.

26. Drew, *Autobiography*, 32.

27. Drew, *Autobiography*, 34.

28. Drew, *Autobiography*, 36.

29. Drew, *Autobiography*, 38.

30. Gad Heuman, "A Tale of Two Jamaica Rebellions," *Jamaican Historical Review* 19 (Jan. 1996): 1–8.

31. Drew, *Autobiography*, 69.

32. Halifax is notably absent from many studies of transatlantic and/or hemispheric theatre culture. See, for example, Joseph Roach, *Cities of the Dead: Circum-Atlantic Performance* (Ann Arbor: University of Michigan Press, 1996); Maddock Dillon, *New World Drama*; and Wilson, "Introduction," 375–90.

33. Maddock Dillon, *New World Drama*, 57–58.

34. I discuss these gaps more fully in Schweitzer, "Three Sentences: A Child Actress in Halifax," in *Canadian Performance Histories and Historiographies*, ed. Heather Davis-Fisch (Toronto: Playwrights Canada Press, 2017), 280–98.

35. Maddock Dillon, *New World Drama*, 58.

36. The now-defunct Atlantic Canada Theatre Site (ACTS) was an incredibly valuable source. One of its features was a Theatre Playbill Archive, which extended back to the eighteenth century.

37. Maintaining a professional company in Halifax was difficult in the 1830s, not least because the city's population was insufficient to support a permanent company longer than a season or two; by the 1840s Halifax regularly hosted touring companies. Denis Salter, "William Rufus Blake and the Gentlemanly Art of Comic Acting," in *The Proceedings of the Theatre in Atlantic Canada Symposium*, ed. Ric Knowles, Anchorage Series 4 (Sackville, New Brunswick: Centre for Canadian Studies, 1988), 68–99. Intriguingly, the 1833 issue of the *Novascotian* that references the Blake company's production of *Romeo and Juliet* also alludes to a much-anticipated visit of the British actors Charles Kemble and his daughter Fanny. *Novascotian*, May 9, 1833, 138. These hopes did not materialize, although the Kembles did stop in Montreal and Quebec City in July and August 1833. See Yashdip S. Bains and Norma Jenckes, "Fanny Kemble and Charles Kemble: As Canadians Saw Them in 1833," *Theatre Research in Canada* 5, no. 2 (1984): 115–31.

38. Salter, "William Rufus Blake," 64.

39. Writing about colonial Jamaica, Kathleen Wilson observes how "strolling players ... hailed from diverse locations, all around the British isles and indeed the world" (Wilson, "Introduction," 383). This was also true for the soldiers temporarily garrisoned in Halifax. See also Kathleen Wilson, *The Island Race: Englishness, Empire and Gender in the Eighteenth Century* (London: Routledge, 2003).

40. Davenport does warrant a mention in Errol Hill, *The Jamaican Stage, 1655–1900: Profile of a Colonial Theatre* (Ann Arbor: University of Michigan Press, 1992), 85.

CHAPTER 3

Epigraph: "Impromptu on Miss Fisher," *Mirror of Literature, Amusement, and Instruction, Nov. 1822–June 1847*, 2, no. 54 (Nov. 1, 1823): 383.

1. "Eventful Careers."

2. "English Opera House," *Theatrical Examiner*, Aug. 4, 1822, 761. For other critics' takes on the actress and her repertoire at the English Opera House, see "English Opera House," *Literary Gazette*, Aug. 3, 1822; "The Drama," *London Magazine* 8 (July–Dec. 1823): 549; "The Drama, and Public Amusements [English Opera House]," *Literary Chronicle and Weekly Review*, May 22, 1819–Dec. 28, 1822; London 164 (July 6, 1822): 430.

3. "Miss Clara Fisher," *The Drama; Or, Theatrical Pocket Magazine* 4, no. 3 (Sept. 1822): 158.

4. "Miss Clara Fisher," 157, 158.

5. "English Opera House," *Theatrical Examiner*, 761.

6. "English Opera House," *Theatrical Examiner*, 761.

7. Anne Higonnet, *Pictures of Innocence: The History and Crisis of Ideal Childhood* (London: Thames and Hudson, 1998); Sara Holdsworth and Joan Crossley, *Innocence and Experience: Images of Children in British Art from 1600 to the Present* (Manchester: Manchester City Art Galleries, 1992); Erika Langmuir, *Imagining Childhood* (New Haven: Yale University Press, 2006); Claire Perry, *Young America: Childhood in Nineteenth-Century Art and Culture* (New Haven: Yale University Press, 2006).

8. My thinking on what it meant to perform "as a girl" is indebted to Aparna Gollapudi's "Recovering Miss Rose," 6–34.

9. Valerie Barnes Lipscomb and Leni Marshall, eds., *Staging Age: The Performance of Age in Theatre, Dance, and Film* (Basingstoke: Palgrave Macmillan, 2010), 2. See also Anne Davis Basting, *The Stages of Age: Performing Age in Contemporary American Culture* (Ann Arbor: University of Michigan Press, 1998); Margaret Morganroth Gullette, *Aged by Culture* (Chicago: University of Chicago Press, 2004).

10. Sam Sam's-Son, "Provincial Drama," *British Stage and Literary Cabinet* 5, no. 57 (Sept. 1821): 298–303.

11. These rumors persisted. In an 1825 review, the *Edinburgh Dramatic Review* referred to Fisher as "a girl—or rather a woman—of seventeen years of age." *Edinburgh Dramatic Review* 1, no. 23 (Dec. 13, 1825): 87–88. In fact, this assessment was incorrect and Fisher was only thirteen and a half at the time of

her 1824 visit. "Notice to Correspondents," *Edinburgh Dramatic Review* 1, no. 29 (Dec. 20, 1824): 113. Critics seem to have been divided over the matter of Fisher's age. In 1823, a writer for *London Magazine* insisted that Fisher "cannot possibly be so *old* as she is represented by some." "The Drama," *London Magazine* 7 (July–Dec. 1823): 549.

12. "English Opera House," *Theatrical Examiner.*

13. Shauna Vey discusses changes in child performers' repertoire as part of a process of "aging up." Vey, *Childhood.*

14. Ahmed, *Queer Phenomenology*, 66.

15. "Clara Fisher," 158.

16. "Clara Fisher," 159.

17. "Clara Fisher," 159.

18. "Clara Fisher," 159.

19. Denisoff, "Introduction," 4.

20. Anne Higonnet, "Picturing Childhood in the Modern West," in *The Routledge History of Childhood in the Western World*, ed. Paula S. Fass (Abingdon: Routledge, 2013), 296–312, at 298.

21. Higonnet, *Pictures*, 46.

22. Higonnet, *Pictures*, 47.

23. Mary Wollstonecraft, *A Vindication of the Rights of Woman*, in Corinne Field, "'Made Women of When They Are Mere Children': Mary Wollstonecraft's Critique of Eighteenth-Century Girlhood," *Journal of the History of Childhood and Youth* 4, no. 2 (Spring 2011): 197–222, at 201.

24. Higonnet, "Picturing," 298.

25. Holdsworth and Crossley, *Innocence and Experience*, 34.

26. Perry, *Young America*, 41.

27. Perry, *Young America*, 41. As Steven Mintz observes, "Boys and girls were assumed to differ in their constitution, stature, temperament, and behavior. Femininity was defined in terms of self-sacrifice and service; masculinity, in terms of aggressiveness and daring." Mintz, *Huck's Raft*, 82–83.

28. "The Drama," 1822, reprinted in "Appendix" in Maeder, *Autobiography*, 116.

29. Plotz, *Romanticism*, 31.

30. Plotz, *Romanticism*, 33.

31. "English Opera House," *Literary Gazette*, 492.

32. John Finlay, "Clara Fisher 1823," in *Miscellanies. The Foreign Relations of the British Empire: The Internal Resources of Ireland: Sketches of Character: Dramatic Criticism: Etc. Etc. Etc.* (Dublin: John Cumming, 1835), 272.

33. Maeder, *Autobiography*, 8.

34. *Kaleidoscope: or Literary and Scientific Mirror*; Liverpool 3, no. 115 (Sept. 10, 1822): 80.

35. Drury Lane Playbills, Nov. 22, 1822, Image 52, BL.

36. The playbill's parenthetical notes support Jacky Bratton's contention that playbills are valuable, and often underutilized, sources that can offer surprising insights into extratheatrical developments and cultural preoccupations. Jacky Bratton, *New Readings in Theatre History* (Cambridge: Cambridge University Press, 2003), 39.

37. Prior to becoming actor-manager at Drury Lane, Elliston had run an acting school for children at the Surrey Theatre and therefore had considerable experience working with child actors. Burwick, "Georgian Theories," 189.

38. On the emergence or "discovery" of childhood as a distinct life stage in the eighteenth century (a thesis now contested), see Ariès, *Centuries of Childhood*.

39. Maeder, *Autobiography*, 14.

40. Sánchez-Eppler, *Dependent States*, xxi. While Sánchez-Eppler's focus is on American culture, many of her conclusions apply to the British context as well.

41. "The Drama, and Public Amusements," *Literary Chronicle and Weekly Review* (London) 164 (July 1822): 429–30, British Periodicals.

42. Robert William Elliston, *Memoirs of Robert William Elliston, Comedian* (London: John Mortimer, 1845), 352–53.

43. His play *Stella and Leatherlungs* debuted the following year. See *Oxberry's Dramatic Biography and Histrionic Anecdotes, volume 4; The Literary Gazette and Journal of Belles Lettres, Arts, Sciences, Part 2*, no. 307, December 7, 1822, 105–6, Google Books.

44. George Colman, *Stella and Leatherlungs* manuscript, John Larpent papers, 1737–1824, Huntington Library, 6.

45. Colman, *Stella and Leatherlungs*, 10–11.

46. "The Drama," *New Monthly*, Nov. 1, 1823, 490.

47. "The Drama," 490.

48. Elliston, *Memoirs*, 353.

49. I have found no evidence to suggest that Fisher played *Stella and Leatherlungs* elsewhere.

50. "Letter from a Contributor in Love," *Blackwood's Edinburgh Magazine*, 14, Oct. 1823, 472, Google Books.

51. "English Theatricals," *Belle Assemblee: Or, Court and Fashionable Magazine* (Jan. 1823), 232, Google Books.

52. S. Poole, *The Popular Farce Called Old and Young* [From the French of Eugène Scribe and Germond Delivne] (London: J. Tabby, Mr. Miller, 1822). The title page indicates that Fisher was still performing the play ("with unbounded Applause") at the Theatre Royal, Drury Lane, which suggests that it is the most accurate version of the performance text. For this reason, I use it as the primary text for most of the analysis that follows. I did, however, consult the manuscript

of the play originally submitted to the Lord Chamberlain for licensing (now in the John Larpent Plays collection at the Huntington Library) as well as a later c.1831 publication available in the British Library.

53. *Old and Young* may be the first British play written explicitly for a girl actress. I have yet to come across evidence to suggest otherwise. Plays like *Lilliput* were adapted for girls—and girls' dancing companies performed fairytales like *Cinderella*—but these were adaptations rather than original works.

54. Gollapudi, "Recovering Miss Rose," 6–34.

55. Jane Goodall, *Performance and Evolution in the Age of Darwin: Out of the Natural Order* (London: Routledge, 2002), 124.

56. "The Olympic Theatre," *Literary Gazette: A Weekly Journal of Literature, Science, and the Fine Arts* 102 (Jan. 2, 1819): 142.

57. See, for example, the farces *Twelve O'Clock Precisely* (1821) and *Winning a Husband; Or Seven's the Main* (1830).

58. "Miss Lane," Playbills, female stars, HTC.

59. "Lowell Museum/Splendid Attraction!! The Foxes!" George C. Howard and Family Collection. Series II, Acting Companies, 1833–1928, Subseries A. Fox Company, 1833–1846, HRC.

60. Michael R. Booth, "Lines of Business," in *The Oxford Encyclopedia of Theatre and Performance*, ed. Dennis Kennedy, 125–30 (Oxford: Oxford University Press, 2003); Booth, *Theatre in the Victorian Age*, 125–30.

61. Goodall, *Performance and Evolution*, 126.

62. Goodall, *Performance and Evolution*, 126.

63. "Lowell Museum/Splendid Attraction!! The Foxes!" Dec. 1844. George C. Howard and Family Collection 1833–1963, HRC.

64. Goodall, *Performance and Evolution*, 124.

65. "The Drama: English Opera House," *New Monthly Magazine and Historical Register* 6 (1822): 396.

66. "English Opera House," *Literary Chronicle and Weekly Review*, London, 164 (1822): 430.

67. "The Drama," *London Magazine* 8 (July–Dec. 1823): 549.

68. Intriguingly, while Elliston resisted casting Fisher in adult roles, he seems to have had no qualms about her playing boy characters or dressing in male clothing. In 1825, Fisher debuted the role of Albert in *William Tell*. See Drury Lane Playbills, April 20, 1825.

69. "Drury Lane," *Mirror of the Stage; or, New Dramatic Censor*, London (Dec. 16, 1822): 152–53.

70. *Literary Gazette and Journal of Belles Lettres, Arts, Sciences, Part 2*, no. 307 (Dec. 7, 1822): 779.

71. Drury Lane Playbills Collection, 1822–1823, BL. A January 24 playbill noted that Fisher's appearance as the Four Mowbrays had "increased [*sic*] in

attention on each succeeding representation." Those eager to read the play for themselves could also purchase a copy of the script from J. Tabby Printer at the theatre.

72. Maeder, *Autobiography*, 10.

73. Maeder, *Autobiography*, 8.

74. Fisher continued to play "men's characters" when she toured the provinces and even at her own Drury Lane benefit, which suggests that she did not abandon these roles entirely. It's also possible she overstated her dislike for playing male characters out of a feeling of shame or regret. By the 1890s when she was writing her memoirs, actresses rarely appeared in cross-dressed roles (important exceptions include Sarah Bernhardt and Maude Adams) and so Fisher may well have wanted to distance herself from this practice.

75. Brian Eugenio Herrera, *Latin Numbers: Playing Latino in Twentieth-Century U.S. Popular Performance* (Ann Arbor: University of Michigan Press, 2015), 141. For Herrera, the concept offers a way to tease out the many layers at work in the performances of twentieth-century Latinx actresses like Rita Moreno and Charo who embraced the stereotype of the "red hot" Latina.

76. Malabou, *What Should We Do?* 5.

77. Denisoff, "Introduction," 4.

78. D——G [George Daniel], "Remarks," *Old and Young: Or, The Four Mowbrays. A Farce, in One Act* (London: Thomas Hailes Lacy, c. 1831), 6, British Library.

79. Roy Porter and G. S. Rousseau, *Gout: The Patrician Malady* (New Haven: Yale University Press, 2000), 143.

80. Davis, *The Stages of Age*, 9. The term "decline narrative" was first coined by Gullette, *Aged by Culture*.

81. Andrea Charise, "Spots of Future Time: Tableaux, Masculinity, and the Enactment of Aging," *Modern Drama* 59, no. 2 (Summer 2016): 155–76, at 159.

82. This relationship between old and young is a feature of later Victorian literature. As Claudia Nelson argues, some texts "showed youth and age as interdependent allies against a more powerful mainstream." Qtd. in Vanessa Joosen, "Second Childhood and Intergenerational Dialogues: How Children's Literature and Age Studies Can Supplement Each Other," *Children's Literature Association Quarterly* 40, no. 2 (Summer 2015): 126–40. See also Vanessa Joosen, ed., *Connecting Childhood and Old Age in Popular Media* (Jackson: University Press of Mississippi, 2018), 128.

83. Poole, *Old and Young* [1822], 8.

84. D——G, "Remarks," 8.

85. Poole, *Old and Young* [1822], 12.

86. Poole, *Old and Young* [1822], 19. This scene is comically depicted in the frontispiece of the 1831 edition of the play.

87. Poole, *Old and Young* [1822], 17.

88. Holdsworth and Crossley, *Innocence*, 106.

89. Holdsworth and Crossley, *Innocence*, 106.

90. His name is an obvious reference to Lord Foppington from John Vanbrugh's *The Relapse*.

91. Poole, *Old and Young* [1822], 23.

92. The term "strategic essentialism" was first coined by Gayatri Chakravorty Spivak to acknowledge the value of working with essentialist notions of identity in pursuit of greater political goals. See Rashka Pande, "Strategic Essentialism," *Wiley Online Library*, 2017, https://doi.org/10.1002/9781118786352.wbieg1170, accessed August 22, 2019.

93. The Larpent manuscript offers a slight variation, wherein Wilton declares that he will teach Matilda "Every day—this is an Occupation I have Long Desired." *Old and Young* by John Poole, John Larpent Plays, 1737–1824, Huntington Library, 15.

94. Poole, *Old and Young* [1822], 28. The Larpent manuscript offers a slight variation: "What I have done Uncle was to convince you that you [had] a better chance of happiness with one Little Girl that Loved you than with ten or a Dozen Boys who would turn your house Topsy Turvy." *Old and Young* by John Poole, 17.

95. *Old and Young* by John Poole, 17.

96. *Old and Young* by John Poole, 17.

97. Plotz, *Romanticism*, xv.

98. In this respect, *Old and Young* anticipates later nineteenth-century novels and plays, which, as Marah Gubar has shown, emphasized the collaborative aspect of identity formation, "blurring rather than policing the subject positions of child and adult." *Artful Dodgers*, 7–8.

99. Poole, *Old and Young* [1822], 29.

100. Later versions of the play stress the ease with which Matilda transitions from one masculine character to another by overlaying a series of earlier lines from each of the boys, concluding with Hector's rousing "Huzza! Huzza!" Poole, *Old and Young* [1831], 30.

101. Celestine Woo, *Romantic Actors and Bardolatry: Performing Shakespeare from Garrick to Kean* (New York: Peter Lang, 2008), 118.

102. Nussbaum, *Rival Queens*, 195.

103. To date, most scholarship on breeching in the eighteenth and nineteenth centuries has focused on women's adoption of male dress. See, for example, Mullenix, *Wearing*; Merrill, *When Romeo*; Straub, *Sexual Suspects*; Woo, *Romantic Actors*; Patricia Fara, *Pandora's Breeches: Women, Science and Power in the Enlightenment* (London: Pimlico, 2004); Brooks, *Actresses*.

104. Chantel Lavoie, *"Tristram Shandy* and Breeching," *Eighteenth-Century Fiction* 28, no. 1 (Fall 2015): 85–107, at 88.

105. Lavoie, *"Tristram Shandy,"* 88.

106. Lavoie, *"Tristram Shandy,"* 95.

107. Lavoie, *"Tristram Shandy,"* 91. The specific timing of a boy's breeching varied according to class, individual family dynamics, and school expectations. Although some boys were breeched as early as the age of three, wealthier families tended to delay breeching to as late as seven (88–89).

108. Lavoie, *"Tristram Shandy,"* 89.

109. Nussbaum, *Rival Queens*, 210.

110. See Drury Lane playbills, BL.

111. Playbill, Dec. 7, 1822. Drury Lane playbills, BL.

112. Playbills for Fisher's appearance at the Boston Theater in November 1827 list *Old and Young*. Sixteen at the time, she was still considered a girl due to her unmarried status but was no longer a prepubescent child. Fisher playbills, HTC.

113. *Quarterly Oriental Magazine Review and Register* 6 (Nov. 25, 1826): cxxxxv.

114. Frank W. Boyd, *Records of the Dundee Stage, from the Earliest Times to the Present* (Dundee: W. and D. C. Thompson, 1886), 46.

115. For Drew, see Drew, *Autobiography*, 26–30. For Heron, see Noah M. Ludlow, *Dramatic Life as I Found It* (St. Louis: G. I. Jones and Company, 1880), 682. For the Batemans, see Guy Herbert Keeton, "The Theatre in Mississippi from 1840 to 1870," Ph.D. dissertation, Louisiana State University, 1979; and Ludlow, *Dramatic Life*, 709; For Jean Margaret Davenport, see "Miss Davenport's Juliet," *Kingston Dispatch*, Sept. 24, 1840, in Jean Davenport Lander Scrapbook, Library of Congress. See also Miss Meadows in Ludlow, *Dramatic Life*, 458, 483.

116. By the mid-1820s, the appearance of talented boy actors like Master Joseph Burke (the "Irish Roscius"), whose repertoire included Richard III, Romeo, Shylock, Hamlet, and Young Norval, provoked fresh questions about whether it was appropriate for girls like Clara Fisher to play roles typically associated with adult men. Brown, *History*, 57; "Memoir of Master Burke," *Dramatic Magazine* (June 1, 1830): 130; Anthony Sansonetti, "Master Joseph Burke," *Ambassadors of Empire: Child Performers and Anglo-American Audiences, 1800s–1880*, http://childperformers.ca/master-joseph-burke/.

INTERLUDE 4

1. See playbills collection for Fisher at the Boston Theatre, HTC.

2. Eugene H. Jones, "Fisher, Clara," in *Notable Women in the American The-*

atre: A Biographical Dictionary, ed. Alice M. Robinson, Vera Mowry Roberts, and Milly S. Barranger (New York: Greenwood Press, 1989), 278–79.

3. Boston Theatre playbill, Dec. 5, 1827, HTC.

4. Walter M. Leman, *Reminiscences of an Old Actor* (San Francisco: A. Roman Co., 1886), 73.

5. Congdon, qtd. in Brander Matthews and Laurence Hutton, eds., *Kean and Booth and Their Contemporaries: Actors and Actresses of Great Britain and the United States* (Boston: L. C. Page, 1900), 272.

6. "Wilt Thou Meet Me There, Love?" and "The Merry Mountain Horn" (M1 62, nos. 19 and 30, respectively) in the New-York Historical Society's sheet music collection.

7. Joe Cowell, *Thirty Years Passed among the Players in England and America* (New York: Harper & Brothers, 1844), 82. Other sources indicate that Fisher's name was also "given to steamboats, and to brands of cigars, and to bonnets, and to neck-ties"; see Laurence Hutton, *Talks in a Library with Laurence Hutton*, recorded by Isabel Moore (New York: G. P. Putnam's Sons, 1905), 117. An entry in the *American Turf Register and Sporting Magazine* 1 (April 1830): 412, includes a reference to the horse Clara Fisher. And in 1834, Mrs. Charles Mathews observed "Clara Fisher" pass by "in the form of an omnibus." Qtd. in Mrs. Mathews (Anne Jackson), *Memoirs of Charles Mathews, Comedian*, vol. 4 (London: Richard Bentley, 1838), 293.

8. "The Olympian Gods and Goddesses," *New York Clipper* May 20, 1868, in William L. Slout, ed., *Old Gotham Theatricals: Selections from a Series "Reminiscences About Town,"* by Col. Tom Picton (San Bernadino, CA: Borgo Press, 1995), 95–97.

9. Marcus, *Drama*, 127.

10. Rebecca Schneider, *Performing Remains: Art and War in Times of Theatrical Reenactment* (New York: Routledge, 2011), 135 (emphasis in original).

11. Joseph P. Reed and William S. Walsh, "Beauties of the American Stage," *Cosmopolitan* 14 (1893): 294–304, esp. 297.

12. "From Joseph Norton Ireland's Records of the New York Stage, Part Theatre, 1827," in Maeder, *Autobiography*, 135–36.

13. Susan Honeyman, "Trans(cending) Gender Through Childhood," in *The Children's Table: Childhood Studies and the Humanities*, ed. Anna Marie Duane (Athens: University of Georgia Press, 2013), 167–82.

14. Jack Halberstam, *Female Masculinity* (Durham, NC: Duke University Press, 1998); Abate, *Tomboys*, xix; Hunter, *How Young Ladies*, 141–43.

15. Taylor, *The Archive and the Repertoire*; Carlson, *The Haunted Stage*.

CHAPTER 4

Epigraph: Playbill, Joseph N. Ireland scrapbook, HTC.

1. *Sunday Times*, May 22, 1836, clipping. Jean Davenport Lander scrapbooks, LC.

2. For a more detailed list of child actors in this period, see Klein, "Without Distinction," 117–35, esp. 122.

3. Ironically, Ben Terry, father of Ellen Terry, modeled his own daughters after Jean Davenport, whom he first saw perform in Portsmouth in 1837. According to Nina Auerbach, Terry was impressed with the young actress's versatility, which he saw as a testament to her "virtuosity"; her wide-ranging performance included Shylock, a series of songs, a hornpipe, and the six [*sic*] characters from *The Manager's Daughter*. Nina Auerbach, "Dickens and Acting Women," in *Dramatic Dickens*, ed. Carol Hanbery MacKay (Basingstoke: Palgrave Macmillan, 1989), 81–86, at 83–84.

4. Joseph Roach, qtd. in Bernstein, *Racial Innocence*, 23–24.

5. E. R. Lancaster, *The Manager's Daughter*, Lord Chamberlain's Plays, ff. 893–903, BL.

6. Throughout the chapter I use the name "Jean Margaret" to denote the fictionalized character in *The Manager's Daughter* and "Jean Davenport" to refer to the "real" actress.

7. Varty, *Children and Theater*, 123.

8. "Fix, v.," *Oxford English Dictionary*, accessed June 2, 2016.

9. "Jean Margaret Davenport Lander," Find a Grave.com, https://www.finda grave.com/memorial/37272951/jean-margaret-lander, accessed June 16, 2018.

10. Lying about a child's age remained a fairly common practice for parents and managers of child performers well into the twentieth century. Consider, for example, Shirley Temple.

11. Robert Simpson McLean [Maclean], "How 'the Infant Phenomenon' Began the World: The Managing of Jean Margaret Davenport (182?–1903)," *Dickensian* 88, no. 3 (1992): 133–52; and McLean [Maclean], "He Played with Crummles: The Life and Career of William Pleater Davidge, Anglo-American Actor, Author and Dickens Enthusiast," *Dickensian* 89, no. 430 (Summer 1993): 103–17; Waters, "'That Astonishing,'" 78.

12. McLean [Maclean], "How" and "He Played"; Waters, "'That Astonishing,'" 78.

13. McLean [Maclean], "How," 143.

14. McLean [Maclean], "How," 144.

15. Marcus, *Drama*, 199–202.

16. *Sunday Times* May 22, 1836, clipping. Jean Davenport Lander scrapbooks, LC.

17. Qtd. in McLean [Maclean], "How," 147.

18. McLean [Maclean], "How," 147.

19. Bernstein, *Racial Innocence*, 24.

20. Bernstein, *Racial Innocence*, 27.

21. Jan. 19, 1838, playbill from Belfast qtd. in McLean [Maclean], "How," 146.

22. McLean [Maclean], "How," 136.

23. Deborah Lutz, *Relics of Death in Victorian Literature and Culture* (Cambridge: Cambridge University Press, 2015), 24.

24. Other records suggest that Davenport remained vague about who presented the hat to his daughter. In an 1837 announcement for a performance in Lynn, Massachusetts, he claimed that the hat had been presented to Jean after her first appearance "before a Richmond Audience after the late Mr. Kean." Qtd. in McLean [Maclean], "How," 136.

25. Jean Margaret Lander (Davenport), Letter to *Shakespeareana*, Y.c.736 (1 a–c), FSL.

26. Lancaster, *Manager's Daughter*, ff. 894.

27. Lancaster, *Manager's Daughter*, ff. 894.

28. Lancaster, *Manager's Daughter*, ff. 894.

29. Lancaster, *Manager's Daughter*, ff. 894.

30. Lancaster, *Manager's Daughter*, ff. 894 verso.

31. Lancaster, *Manager's Daughter*, ff 895.

32. Lancaster, *Manager's Daughter*, ff. 896.

33. Lancaster, *Manager's Daughter*, ff. 897.

34. Lancaster, *Manager's Daughter*, ff. 899, verso.

35. Lancaster, *Manager's Daughter*, ff. 902, verso.

36. Lancaster, *Manager's Daughter*, ff. 902, verso.

37. Lancaster, *Manager's Daughter*, ff. 903.

38. "In propria persona," *Merriam-Webster*, https://www.merriam-webster .com/dictionary/in%20propria%20persona, accessed June 16, 2018.

39. Lancaster, *Manager's Daughter*, ff. 903.

40. The second edition of *The Manager's Daughter* includes the subtitle *Or, The Young Actress of All Work*—a seemingly deliberate reference to the original *Actress of All Work*.

41. Freeman, *Character's Theater*, 57.

42. See Martin, *Theatre of the Real* (Basingstoke: Palgrave Macmillan, 2013); Jenn Stephenson, *Insecurity: Perils and Products of Theatres of the Real* (Toronto: University of Toronto Press, 2019).

43. Freeman, *Character's Theater*, 50. One can also think of Molière as well as the use of prologues/epilogues in which actors spoke in propria personae. On Sarah Siddons and Anne Oldfield's strategic performance of motherhood see J. D. Phillipson, "The Inconvenience of the Female Condition, Anne Oldfield's Pregnancies," in Engel and McGirr, eds., *Stage Mothers*, 43–62; and Ellen Ma-

lenas Ledoux, "Working Mothers on the Romantic Stage: Sarah Siddons and Mary Robinson," 79–104, in Engel and McGirr, eds., *Stage Mothers*.

44. When Boucicault tried to adapt the play for Agnes Robertson under the title *The Young Actress*, critics almost immediately recognized his source material. See Robert Hogan, *Dion Boucicault* (New York: Twayne, 1969), 36–37.

45. Roach, *It*, 44.

46. Roach, "Public Intimacy," 16. See also Fawcett, *Spectacular*; Nussbaum, *Rival Queens*.

47. Steven Horwitz, "How Capitalism and the Bourgeois Virtues Transformed and Humanized the Family," *Journal of Socio-Economics* 41 (2012): 792–95, at 793.

48. Horwitz, "How Capitalism," 795. See also Sánchez-Eppler, *Dependent States*.

49. This practice of caring for fathers was known as "cossetting" or "petting." Studlar, *Precocious Charms*, 57.

50. See Heather Fitzsimmons Frey, "Victorian Girls and At-Home Theatricals: Performing and Playing with Possible Futures," Ph.D. dissertation, University of Toronto, 2015.

51. Gubar, *Artful Dodgers*, 159.

52. Zelizer, *Pricing*, 95.

53. It is perhaps no coincidence that Jean Margaret's performance of "economic innocence" in *The Manager's Daughter* came during a period of economic instability following the Panic of 1837, which affected managerial practices on both sides of the Atlantic. Klein, "Without Distinction," 124; Nicole Berkin, "The Economies of Touring in American Culture, 1835–1861," Ph.D. dissertation, City University of New York, 2015, 22–23, 76.

54. Catherine Burroughs, "The Erotics of Home: Staging Sexual Fantasy in British Women's Drama," in *Women's Romantic Theatre and Drama: History, Agency, and Performativity*, ed. Lilla Maria Crisafulli and Kerin Elam (Cambridge: Cambridge University Press, 2000), 118.

55. Burroughs, "The Erotics of Home," 118.

56. See various entries in Jean Davenport scrapbook, Box 11, F. W. Lander Papers, Manuscripts, Library of Congress. See also *Romeo and Juliet* playbill, Thr. A5 Box 2, Folder 6, *Romeo and Juliet*, Feb. 17, 1845–Feb. 20, 1845, Theatre playbills for Shakespeare's plays, Library of Congress.

57. Michals, "Experiments before Breakfast," 38.

58. Hamlin, "Structures," 859; Miriam Formanek-Brunell, *Made to Play House: Dolls and the Commercialization of American Girlhood, 1830–1930* (New Haven: Yale University Press, 1993).

59. Lancaster, *Manager's Daughter*, ff. 894.

60. Harris, *Cute*, 13.

61. Harris, *Cute*, 14.

62. Eugenia Gonzalez, "'I Sometimes Think She Is a Spy on All My Actions': Dolls, Girls, and Disciplinary Surveillance in the Nineteenth-Century Doll Tale," *Nineteenth Century Literature* 39 (2011): 33–57, at 34; Formanek-Brunell, *Made to Play House*; Dawson, "Miniaturization," 63–84.

63. Gonzalez, paraphrasing Formanek-Brunell, *Made to Play House*, 34 (1).

64. Bernstein, *Racial Innocence*.

65. A fleeting reference to the time she "broke [her] last doll's nose" hints at Jean Margaret's potential for naughty behavior. Lancaster, *Manager's Daughter*, ff. 895.

66. Varty, *Children and Theatre*, 119–21.

67. Varty, *Children and Theatre*, 119–21.

68. Merish, "Cuteness," 188–89.

69. Varty, *Children and Theatre*, 120.

70. Vey, *Childhood*, 102.

71. Hartley, qtd. in Studlar, *Precocious Charms*, 1.

72. Studlar, *Precocious Charms*, 2.

73. For example, Mary Pickford's long curly ringlets, pinafore dresses, and doll-like face were critical to her performance of girlishness in films like *Rebecca of Sunnybrook Farm*, in which the adult actress portrayed the prepubescent Rebecca. Studlar, *Precocious Charms*, 9.

74. William Pleater Davidge, *New York Mirror*, Aug. 11, 1888, qtd. in McLean [Maclean], "How," 133–34. It is important to take Davidge's account with a degree of skepticism, given that he was writing fifty years after his time with the company. Intriguingly, he leaves some of these details out of his earlier collected memoirs; see Davidge, *Footlight Flashes* (New York: American News Company, 1866), 51–54.

75. Bernstein, *Racial Innocence*, 27.

76. Qtd. in McLean [Maclean], "How," 134, and Varty, *Children and Theatre*, 119–20.

77. Qtd. in McLean [Maclean], "How," 134.

INTERLUDE 5

1. Unless otherwise noted, all primary source quotations are from Scrap Book #2, Jean Davenport scrapbook, Box 11, F. W. Lander and J. M. Lander Papers, Manuscripts Collection, LC.

2. Patricia P. Buckler and C. Kay Leeper, "An Antebellum Woman's Scrapbook as Autobiographical Composition," *Journal of American Culture* 14, no. 1 (March 1991): 1.

3. Schneider, *Performing Remains*, 109 (emphasis in original).

4. Ellen Gruber Garvey, *Writing with Scissors: American Scrapbooks from*

the Civil War to the Harlem Renaissance (New York: Oxford University Press, 2012 [online 2013]), 4.

5. Garvey, *Writing*, 15.

6. Buckler and Leeper, "An Antebellum Woman's," 1.

7. Garvey, *Writing*, 116.

8. Garvey, *Writing*, 15.

9. Marcus, "The Theatrical Scrapbook," *Theatre Survey* 54, no. 2 (May 2013): 283–307, at 287. Marcus also references scrapbooks extensively throughout *The Drama of Celebrity*.

10. Garvey, *Writing*, 29.

11. Garvey, *Writing*, 207.

12. Marcus, "Theatrical Scrapbook," 297.

13. Garvey, *Writing*, 10.

14. Garvey, *Writing*, 207.

15. Garvey, *Writing*, 208.

16. Garvey, *Writing*, 208. This is not to suggest that readers cannot read against the grain or refuse to follow the scrapbook's script. As Bernstein points out, the idea of "script" is flexible enough to account for reader agency.

17. Hill, *Jamaican Stage*, 40.

18. Hill, *Jamaican Stage*, 41–42.

19. "We hope the people," *Kingston Dispatch*, June 8, 1840, clipping, Jean Davenport scrapbook.

20. "We feel pleasure," *Kingston Dispatch*, Aug. 31, 1840, clipping, Jean Davenport scrapbook.

21. This is the only drawing I've come across in *any* of the Davenport scrapbooks, which suggests that the scrapbook collector also considered it important.

CHAPTER 5

1. "Under the Patronage of His Honor and the Administrator of the Government." *Newfoundland Public Ledger*, July 31, 1841, np.

2. On this see Gubar, *Artful Dodgers*; and Bernstein, *Racial Innocence*.

3. Wilson, "Introduction," 377.

4. Wilson, "Introduction," 377.

5. Benedict Anderson, *Imagined Communities: Reflections on the Origins and Spread of Nationalism* (New York: Verso, 1991).

6. Marcus, *Drama*, 3–9.

7. Charles Mathews was celebrated for his impersonations of various Scottish, Irish, French, German, and American types, not to mention his more infamous representation of African Americans following his first tour of the United States. Jim Davis, "Representing the Comic Actor at Work: The Harlow Portrait of Charles Mathews," *Theatre and Film* 31, no. 2 (Winter 2004): 3–15.

8. Davidge claims that he first encountered Jim Crow via Jean Margaret's ventriloquized performance. Davidge, *Footlight Flashes*, 51.

9. Varty, *Children and Theatre*, 123.

10. Maddock Dillon, *New World Drama*, 116.

11. Richard Foulkes, *Performing Shakespeare in the Age of Empire* (Cambridge: Cambridge University Press, 2002), 3.

12. Foulkes, *Performing Shakespeare*, 3.

13. See, for example, Alan Hughes, "Charles Kean in Victoria: Touring Actors and Local Politics in 1864," *BC Studies* (1987): 21–32.

14. "The Passing of Mrs. Lander," *Dramatic Mirror*, Aug. 15, 1903, clipping, HTC.

15. The timing of the Davenports' transatlantic crossing coincided with Jean Davenport's arrival at puberty, which suggests that the techniques of juvenation discussed may have been more important as the family traveled. This may also explain the audience frustration that greeted them in several colonial cities.

16. *Montreal Royal Gazette*, Aug. 8, 1839, Jean Davenport scrapbook, Box 11, F. W. Lander and J. M. Lander Papers, Manuscripts, LC (Scrap Book #2).

17. Wilson, "Introduction," 377.

18. Maddock Dillon, *New World Drama*, 56. See also Coleman, *White Civility*.

19. *Bridgetown Sun* [Barbados] April 24, 1840, Jean Davenport scrapbook, Box 11, F. W. Lander Papers, Manuscripts, Library of Congress.

20. *Bridgetown Sun*, May 6, 1840, Jean Davenport scrapbook.

21. *Bridgetown Sun*, May 6, 1840.

22. *Bridgetown Sun*, May 6, 1840.

23. Hill, *Jamaican Stage*, 86.

24. Inside back page, Jean Davenport scrapbook.

25. Curiously, Caroline Fox also introduced the Manual Exercise into her repertoire c. 1840, as part of a "new Dance, entitled the Little Corporal," for which she appeared in "Full Uniform." Whether this additional material was a direct response to Jean Davenport is uncertain, although she may have witnessed the Davenports perform *Old and Young* when they toured Boston in the fall of 1838. "Grand Juvenile Concert," 1840, George C. Howard, and Family, Series II, Acting Companies, 1833–1928, Subseries A, Fox Company, 1833–1846, HRC.

26. Elizabeth Klett, *Cross-Gender Shakespeare and English National Identity: Wearing the Codpiece* (London: Palgrave Macmillan, 2009), 23.

27. "Theatre," *Kingston Dispatch*, Sept.11, 1840, clipping, Jean Davenport scrapbook.

28. "Theatre," *Kingston Dispatch*, Sept. 8, 1840, clipping, Jean Davenport scrapbook.

29. "Last Night Miss Davenport . . . ," *Montreal Royal Gazette*, Aug. 6, 1849, clipping, Jean Davenport scrapbook.

30. "Miss Davenport," Dec. 28, 1839, clipping, Jean Davenport scrapbook.

31. For more on the controversy surrounding Davenport, see Schweitzer, "'Too Much Tragedy in Real Life': Theatre in Post-Emancipation Jamaica," *Nineteenth Century Theatre and Film* 44, no. 1 (May 2017): 8–27.

32. D. G. Hall, "The Apprenticeship Period in Jamaica, 1834–1838," *Caribbean Quarterly* 3, no. 3 (1953): 142–66, at 142.

33. Hall, "Apprenticeship," 142.

34. Hall, "Apprenticeship," 142–66; and Richardson Wright, *Revels in Jamaica, 1682–1838: Plays and Players of a Century Tumblers and Conjurers* (New York: Dodd, Mead, 1937), 315.

35. Wright, *Revels*, 315.

36. Wilson, *Island Race*, 164.

37. Hill, *Jamaican Stage*, 40.

38. Sandra L. Richards, "Horned Ancestral Masks, Shakespearean Actor Boys, and Scotch-Inspired Set Girls: Social Relations in Nineteenth-Century Jamaican Jonkonnu," in *The African Diaspora: African Origins and New World Identities*, ed. Carole Boyce Davies, Ali Mazrui, and Isidore Okpewho (Bloomington: Indiana University Press, 1999), 254–71. See also Maddock Dillon, *New World Drama*, 202–14.

39. Wilson, *Island Race*, 167. Richards suggests that they may also have learned the lines while filling seats for their masters or waiting to drive them home ("Horned," 259).

40. Richards, "Horned," 259.

41. Wilson, *Island Race*, 167.

42. Hill, *Jamaican Stage*, 41.

43. For a lengthier discussion of the controversy surrounding Davenport, see Schweitzer, "An 'Unmanly and Insidious Attack': Child Actress Jean Davenport and the Performance of Masculinity in 1840s Jamaica and Newfoundland," *Theatre Research in Canada*, 35, no. 1 (Winter 2014): 49–68.

44. "Kingston Theatre," *Morning Journal*, n.d., clipping, Jean Davenport scrapbook.

45. "Kingston Theatre," *Morning Journal*, n.d., clipping, Jean Davenport scrapbook.

46. Censor, "Letter to the Editor," *Kingston Morning Journal*, Sept. 21, 1840, clipping, Jean Davenport scrapbook.

47. Redcap, "Letter to the Editor," *Kingston Morning Journal*, Sept. 21, 1840, Jean Davenport scrapbook.

48. Thomas Davenport, "Letter to the Editor," *Kingston Morning Journal*, Sept. 22, 1840, clipping, Jean Davenport scrapbook.

49. Civis, "Letter to the Editor," *Jamaica Despatch, Chronicle, and Gazette*, Sept. 24, 1840, clipping, Jean Davenport scrapbook.

50. Daniel Coleman, *White Civility: The Literary Project of English Canada* (Toronto: University of Toronto Press, 2006), 10.

51. Coleman, *White Civility*, 12.

52. "Under the Patronage."

53. Coleman, *White Civility*, 16.

54. "Theatre," *Newfoundlander*, Aug. 19, 1841, clipping, Jean Davenport scrapbook.

55. "Miss Davenport," *Newfoundland Times*, Aug. 4, 1841, clipping, Jean Davenport scrapbook.

56. Patrick O'Flaherty, *Lost Country: The Rise and Fall of Newfoundland, 1843–1933* (St. John's: Long Beach Press, 2005), 1.

57. Eugene Benson and L. W. Conolly, *English Canadian Theatre* (Toronto: Oxford University Press, 1987), 376.

58. Paul O'Neil, *The Oldest City: The Story of St. John's* (St. John's, Newfoundland: Press Porcepic, 1975), 246.

59. Some historians maintain that Davenport was one of the first female performers to grace any stage in Newfoundland. Rev. Lewis Amadeus Anspach, *Encyclopedia of Newfoundland and Labrador, Vol. III* (St. John's: Newfoundland Book Publishers, 1981), 354.

60. Newfoundland clippings, *Gazette*, Aug. 18, 1841; *Newfoundland Times*, Aug. 11, 18, 1841.

61. "The Theatre," *Newfoundland Ledger*, Aug. 10, 1841, n.p.

62. Editorial, *Newfoundland Patriot*, Aug. 18, 1841, clipping, Jean Davenport scrapbook.

63. Thomas Davenport, "Letter to the Editor," *Newfoundland Public Ledger*, Aug. 20, 1841, clipping, Jean Davenport scrapbook.

64. Winton, "Editorial," *Newfoundland Public Ledger*, Aug. 20, 1841, clipping, Jean Davenport scrapbook.

65. O'Flaherty, *Lost Country*, 3.

66. Winton, "Editorial."

67. See Jonas Barish, *The Anti-theatrical Prejudice* (Berkeley: University of California Press, 1985); Lisa A. Freeman, *Antitheatricality and the Body Public* (Philadelphia: University of Pennsylvania Press, 2017).

68. "Remarks," *Newfoundland Patriot*, Aug. 25, 1841, Jean Davenport scrapbook.

69. "Remarks," *Newfoundland Patriot*, Aug. 25, 1841.

70. Though Jean Davenport was too young to participate in the public debate over her ability to portray adult male roles convincingly, her scrapbook offers some indication that she felt personally attacked by Parsons and the *New-*

foundland Patriot. The handwritten words, "Letters & remarks relative to the attack of the Newfoundland Patriot" appear on a long strip of paper pasted above the first *Patriot* editorial; Jean Davenport scrapbook.

71. Thanks to Roberta Barker for pointing out this connection.

72. "Kingston Theatre," *Morning Journal*, n.d., clipping, Jean Davenport scrapbook.

73. If true, this may explain the Davenports' "impromptu" decision to travel to the United States on board the *Sirius*.

74. Davidge, *Footlight*, 51.

75. Davidge, *Footlight*, 51.

76. Lander, *Shakespeareana*.

77. Here are two examples of the lingering impression of Davenport as Dickens's model: "It is stated, upon good authority, that little Jean Davenport was the original that Dickens caricatured so mercilessly as 'Miss Ninetta Crummels' [*sic*]," Pitt, *Players of a Century*, 214; "Infant Phenomenon Is Now Mrs. Lander, in Philadelphia," *Lincoln Nebraska State Journal*, Jan. 19, 1877.

78. Lander, *Shakespeareana*.

79. McLean [Maclean], "How" and "He Played with Crummles"; Waters, "'That Astonishing,'" 78; Lander, *Shakespeareana*. Malcolm Morley and Maclean outline the numerous connections between the Crummles family and the real-life Davenports. See McLean [Maclean], "How" and "He Played with Crummles," and Malcolm Morley, "Dickens Goes to the Theatre," *Dickensian* 59 (1963): 165–71, and Morley, "More About Crummles," *Dickensian* 59 (1963): 51–56.

80. Qtd. in Nina Auerbach, "Dickens and Acting Women," in *Dramatic Dickens*, ed. Carol Hanbery MacKay, 81–86 (Basingstoke: Palgrave Macmillan, 1989), 83–84.

81. Charles Dickens, *The Life and Adventures of Nicholas Nickleby, vol. 1* (London: Chapman and Hall, 1858), 300.

82. Qtd. in McLean [Maclean], "How," 150.

83. Dickens, *Life and Adventures*, 301.

84. Dickens, *Life and Adventures*, 301.

85. Playbills show that an evening's entertainment with the Davenport company featured a range of songs, dances, and other interludes, all intended to amplify Jean Davenport's abilities. See, for example, playbills in Joseph N. Ireland scrapbook, HRC.

86. Dickens, *Life and Adventures*, 302–3.

87. The "savage" character may also have been a reference to Edmund Kean, who in 1826 visited with four Huron chiefs and was given an honorary Indigenous name. "Edmund Kean Reciting Before the Hurons," c. 1826, http://www.canadianshakespeares.ca/spotlight/s_p_kean.cfm.

88. Dickens, *Life and Adventures*, 302–3.

89. Caitlin R. Hansen, "The Infant Phenomenon: Shakespeare, the Mimetic Child, and Nineteenth-Century British Literature," Ph.D. dissertation, University of Washington, 2013, 224.

90. Auerbach, "Dickens and Acting Women," 83.

91. Dickens, *Life and Adventures*, 301.

92. Gubar, "Drama of Precocity," 63.

93. MacLean, "How," 141.

94. Gubar, *Artful Dodgers*, 161, 172.

95. Gubar, "Drama of Precocity," 63.

96. See Gubar, "Drama of Precocity," 78.

EPILOGUE

1. Merrill, *When Romeo*, 24–27.

2. See Walen, "Such a Romeo," 41–62; Merrill, *When Romeo*.

3. On the Foxes see, Senelick, *Age and Stage of George L. Fox*.

4. Playbills in the George C. Howard and Family Collection, 1833–1963, Series II, Acting Companies, Subseries A, Fox Company, 1833–1846, Playbills. HRC.

5. Bernstein, *Racial Innocence*, 6.

6. Bernstein, *Racial Innocence*, 6.

7. George C. Aiken, *Uncle Tom's Cabin* (1852), in *The Broadview Anthology of Drama*, volume 2 (Peterborough: Broadview Press, 2003).

8. Christina Sharpe, *In the Wake: On Blackness and Being* (Durham: Duke University Press, 2016), 121–22; Calin Rashaud Zimmerman, "The Penalty of Being a Young Black Girl: Kindergarten Teachers' Perceptions of Children's Problem Behaviors and Student-Teacher Conflict by the Intersection of Race and Gender," *Journal of Negro Education* 87, no. 2 (Spring 2018): 154–68; Kimberlé Crenshaw, with Priscilla Ocen and Jyoti Nanda, *Black Girls Matter: Pushed Out, Overpoliced and Underprotected* (New York: African American Policy Forum / Center for Intersectionality and Social Policy Studies, 2015).

BIBLIOGRAPHY

A.L.E. *A Diary of Two Years and Two Days*. Wexford: John Greene, 1834. Google Books.

Abate, Michelle Ann. *Tomboys: A Literary and Cultural History*. Philadelphia: Temple University Press, 2008.

Ades, John I. "Charles Lamb, Shakespeare, and Early Nineteenth-Century Theater." *PMLA* 85, no. 3 (May 1970): 514–26.

Ahmed, Sara. *Queer Phenomenology: Orientations, Objects, Others*. Durham, NC: Duke University Press, 2006.

———. "Willful Parts: Problem Characters or the Problem of Character." *New Literary History* 42, no. 2 (Spring 2011): 231–53.

———. *Willful Subjects*. Raleigh, NC: Duke University Press, 2014.

Aiken, George. *Uncle Tom's Cabin* (1852). In *The Broadview Anthology of Drama*, volume 2. Peterborough: Broadview Press, 2003.

American Turf Register and Sporting Magazine. Vol. 1 (April 1830): 412. Google Books.

"Amusements. Memphis Theater," *Public Ledger* (Memphis, TN), February 14, 1871. Web, November 18, 2015, Chronicling America: Historic American Newspapers, Library of Congress, http://chroniclingamerica.loc.gov/lccn /sn85033673/1871-02-14/ed-1/seq-3/.

Anae, Nicole. "Infant Phenomenon in Colonial Australia—The Case of Anna Maria Quinn, 1854–1858." *The Historian* 71, no. 1 (March 2009): 55–78.

Anderson, Benedict. *Imagined Communities: Reflections on the Origins and Spread of Nationalism*. New York: Verso, 1991.

Anspach, Rev. Lewis Amadeus. *Encyclopedia of Newfoundland and Labrador, Vol. III*. St. John's: Newfoundland Book Publishers, 1981.

Appadurai, Arjun. *The Social Life of Things: Commodities in Cultural Perspective*. Cambridge: Cambridge University Press, 1986.

Ariès, Philippe. *Centuries of Childhood: A Social History of Family Life*. Translated by Robert Baldick. New York: Vintage Books, 1962 [1960].

Arrighi, Gillian, and Victor Emeljanow, eds. *Entertaining Children: The Participation of Youth in the Entertainment Industry*. Basingstoke: Palgrave Macmillan, 2015.

Auerbach, Nina. "Dickens and Acting Women." In *Dramatic Dickens*, edited by Carol Hanbery MacKay, 81–86. Basingstoke: Palgrave Macmillan, 1989.

Bains, Yashdip S. *English Canadian Theatre, 1765-1825*. Frankfurt am Main: Peter Lang, 1998.

Bains, Yashdip S., and Norma Jenckes. "Fanny Kemble and Charles Kemble: As Canadians Saw Them in 1833." *Theatre Research in Canada* 5, no. 2 (1984): 115–31.

Baker, David Erskine. *Biographia Dramatica, Or a Companion to the Playhouse: Containing Historical and Critical Memoirs, Original Anecdotes, of British and Irish Dramatic Writers*. Vol. 1. London: Longman, Hurst, Rees, Orme, and Brown, 1812.

Barish, Jonas. *The Anti-theatrical Prejudice*. Berkeley: University of California Press, 1985.

Barker, Roberta. "'Not One Thing Exactly': Gender, Performance and Critical Debates over the Early Modern Boy-Actress." *Literature Compass* 6, no. 2 (2009): 460–81.

Basting, Anne Davis. *The Stages of Age: Performing Age in Contemporary American Culture*. Ann Arbor: University of Michigan Press, 1998.

Bay-Cheng, Sarah. "Theatre History and Digital Historiography." In *Critical Interventions in Theatre Historiography*, edited by Henry Bial and Scott Magelssen, 125–36. Ann Arbor: University of Michigan Press, 2010.

Beaton, Belinda. "Materializing the Duke." *Journal of Victorian Culture* 10, no. 1 (2005): 100–107.

Benson, Eugene, and L. W. Conolly. *English-Canadian Theatre*. Toronto: Oxford University Press, 1987.

Benziman, Galia. *Narratives of Child Neglect in Romantic and Victorian Culture*. Basingstoke: Palgrave Macmillan, 2012.

Berkin, Nicole. "Economies of Touring in American Culture, 1835–1861." Ph.D. dissertation, City University of New York, 2015.

Bernstein, Robin. *Racial Innocence: Performing American Childhood from Slavery to Civil Rights*. New York: New York University Press, 2011.

Bickerstaff, Isaac. *The Romp: A Musical Entertainment in Two Acts*. London: W. Lowndes and J. Barker, 1789.

———. *The Spoil'd Child, A Farce, In Two Acts*. London: Barker and Son, 1805. Google Books.

———. *The Spoiled Child, A Farce. With Preparatory Notes*. London: W. Simpkin and R. Marshall, 1822. Google Books.

———. *The Spoiled Child, a Farce in One Act*. London: Thomas Hailes Lacy, c. 1851. British Library.

———. *The Spoilt Child: A Farce in Two Acts*. March 15, 1790. mssLA 1-2503, John Larpent Papers, 1737–1824, Huntington Library.

Bisset, J. *Critical Essays on the Dramatic Excellencies of the YOUNG ROSCIUS, By Gentlemen of Distinguished Literary Talents and Theatrical Amateurs Opposed to the Hypercriticisms of Anonymous Writers, Who assume the*

Signatures of Justus, Ennius, & Critus. Birmingham: Knott and Lloyd; London: J. Johnson, Cardell and Davies et al., 1804.

Boaden, James. *The Biography of Mrs. Dorothy Jordan*. New York: Athenaeum Press, 1830.

Booth, Michael. "Lines of Business." In *The Oxford Encyclopedia of Theatre and Performance*, edited by Dennis Kennedy, 125–30. Oxford: Oxford University Press, 2003.

———. *Theatre in the Victorian Age*. Cambridge: Cambridge University Press, 1991.

Bottoms, Janet. "The Battle of the (Children's) Books." *Romanticism* 12, no. 3 (2006): 212–22.

Boutilier, Alex D. "The Citadel on Stage: The Rise and Decline of Garrison Theatre in Halifax." M.A. thesis, Saint Mary's University, Halifax, 2005.

Boyd, Frank W. *Records of the Dundee Stage, from the Earliest Times to the Present*. Dundee, Ireland: W. and D. C. Thompson, 1886.

Bratton, J. S., Richard Allan Cave et al. *Acts of Supremacy: The British Empire and the Stage, 1790–1930*. Manchester: Manchester University Press, 1991.

———. *The Making of the West End Stage*. Cambridge: Cambridge University Press, 2011.

———. *New Readings in Theatre History*. Cambridge: Cambridge University Press, 2003.

Bridgetown Sun [Barbados]. April 24, 1840, Jean Davenport scrapbook, Box 11, F. W. and J. M. Lander Papers, LC.

Bridgetown Sun. May 6, 1840, Jean Davenport scrapbook, Box 11, F. W. and J. M. Lander Papers, LC.

"Bristol Theatre, Miss Clara Fisher." Clipping, HTC.

Brooks, Helen E. M. *Actresses, Gender, and the Eighteenth-Century Stage: Playing Women*. Basingstoke: Palgrave Macmillan, 2015.

Brown, T. Allston. *A History of the New York Stage from the First Performance in 1732 to 1901*. New York: Dodd, Mead and Company, 1903.

Bruhm, Steven, and Natasha Hurley, eds. *Curiouser: On the Queerness of Children*. Minneapolis: University of Minnesota Press, 2004.

Buckler, Patricia P., and C. Kay Leeper. "An Antebellum Woman's Scrapbook as Autobiographical Composition." *Journal of American Culture* 14, no. 1 (March 1991): 1.

Burdan, Judith. "Girls *Must* Be Seen *and* Heard: Domestic Surveillance in Sarah Fielding's *The Governess*." *Children's Literature Association Quarterly* 19, no. 1 (1994): 8–14.

Burns, Sarah. "Making Mischief: Tomboys Acting Up and Out of Bounds."

In *Angels and Tomboys: Girlhood in Nineteenth-Century American Art*, edited by Holly Pyne Connor. Newark Museum. San Francisco: Pomegranate Communications, 2012.

Burroughs, Catherine. "The Erotics of Home: Staging Sexual Fantasy in British Women's Drama." In *Women's Romantic Theatre and Drama: History, Agency, and Performativity*, edited by Lilla Maria Crisafulli and Kerin Elam, 103–21. Cambridge: Cambridge University Press, 2000.

Burton, M. [Anonymous]. *A Sketch of the Life of Miss Clara Fisher, the Lilliputian Actress, of the Theatres-Royal Drury-Lane and Covent Garden*, 1st ed. London: W. J. Collier, 1819, HTC.

Burton, M. *A Sketch of the Life of Miss Clara Fisher, the Lilliputian Actress, of the Theatres-Royal Drury-Lane and Covent Garden*. 2nd ed. London: W. J. Collier, 1819. BL.

Burwick, Frederick. "Georgian Theories of the Actor." In *The Oxford Handbook of the Georgian Theatre, 1737–1832*, edited by Julia Swindells and David Francis Taylor, 177–91. Oxford: Oxford University Press, 2014.

———. "The Ideal Shatters." In *The Oxford Handbook of the Georgian Theatre, 1737–1832*, edited by Julia Swindells and David Francis Taylor, 129–49. Oxford: Oxford University Press, 2014.

Bush–Bailey, Gilli. *Performing Herself: Autobiography and Fanny Kelly's Dramatic Recollections*. Manchester: Manchester University Press, 2017.

Butler, Judith. "Performative Acts and Gender Constitution: An Essay in Phenomenology and Feminist Theory." *Theatre Journal* 40, no. 4 (Dec. 1988): 519–31.

Caputo, Nicoletta. "Looking for Richard III in Romantic Times: Thomas Bridgman's and William Charles Macready's Abortive Stage Adaptations." *Theatre Survey* 52, no. 2 (Nov. 2011): 275–300.

———. "Performing the Passions," *Assaph: Studies in the Theatre* 24 (2010): 75–108.

Carlson, Marvin. *The Haunted Stage: The Theatre as Memory Machine*. Ann Arbor: University of Michigan Press, 2001.

Censor. "Letter to the Editor." *Kingston Morning Journal*, Sept. 21, 1840. Clipping, Jean Davenport scrapbook, Box 11, F. W. Lander and J. M. Lander Papers, LC.

Charise, Andrea. "Spots of Future Time: Tableaux, Masculinity, and the Enactment of Aging." *Modern Drama*, spec. issue, 59, no. 2 (Summer 2016): 155–76.

Ciraulo, Darlene, and Daniel Schierenbeck. "Shakespeare and Education in the Lambs' *Poetry for Children* and *Tales from Shakespeare*." Spec. issue on "Shakespeare for Children," *Borrowers and Lenders: The Journal of Shakespeare and Appropriation* 2, no. 1 (Spring/Summer 2004): 1–16.

Civis. "Letter to the Editor." *Kingston Morning Journal*, Sept. 21, 1840. Jean Davenport scrapbook, Box 11, F. W. Lander and J. M. Lander Papers, LC.

Clancy, Patricia. "Mme de Genlis, Elizabeth Inchbald, and *The Child of Nature*." *Australian Journal of French Studies* 30, no. 3 (Sept. 1993): 324–40.

Clay, Lauren R. *Stagestruck: The Business of Theater in Eighteenth-Century France and Its Colonies*. Ithaca, NY: Cornell University Press, 2013.

Clemit, Pamela. "Mary Shelley and William Godwin: A Literary-Political Partnership, 1823–36." *Women's Writing* 6, no. 3 (October 1999): 285–95.

Clifton, Catherine. *Fanny Kemble's Civil Wars*. Oxford: Oxford University Press, 2001.

Coleman, Daniel. *White Civility: The Literary Project of English Canada*. Toronto: University of Toronto Press, 2006.

Collectanea; Or, A Collection of Advertisements and Paragraphs From the Newspapers, Relating to various Subjects, vol. 1. Printed at Strawberry-Hill By Thomas Kirgate, For the Collector, Daniel Lysons, n.d. FSL.

Collection No. 4: Love in the City, By Isaac Bickerstaff, http://projects.chass .utoronto.ca/prescrip/18thcComedy/plays/04_bick_lovecity.html, viewed June 28, 2017.

Colman, George. *Stella and Leatherlungs*. Manuscript, John Larpent Papers, 1737–1824, Huntington Library.

Combe, George. *Elements of Phrenology*. Edinburgh: John Anderson Jr., 1824.

———. *Lectures on Phrenology*. New York: Samuel Colman, 1839.

———. "Report Upon the Cast of Miss Clara Fisher." In Clara Fisher Maeder, *Autobiography of Clara Fisher Maeder*, edited by Douglas Taylor, 107–13. New York: Burt Franklin, 1897 [1979].

———. *A System of Phrenology*, 3rd ed. Edinburgh: John Anderson, Jr., 1830.

Corri, Domenico. *Lilliput: A Dramatic Romance*. With additional Songs and a Masque written by F. G. Fisher. London: Goulding, D'Almaine, Potter & Co., c. 1818.

Couture, Selena. "Siddons's Ghost: Celebrity and Gender in Sheridan's *Pizarro*." *Theatre Journal* 65, no. 2 (May 2013): 183–96.

Cowell, Joe. *Thirty Years Passed among the Players in England and America*. New York: Harper & Brothers, 1844.

Cox, Aimee Meredith. *Shapeshifters: Black Girls and the Choreography of Citizenship*. Durham, NC: Duke University Press, 2015.

Crenshaw, Kimberlé, with Priscilla Ocen and Jyoti Nanda. *Black Girls Matter: Pushed Out, Overpoliced and Underprotected*. New York: African American Policy Forum / Center for Intersectionality and Social Policy Studies, 2015.

D——G [George Daniel]. "Remarks." In Bickerstaff, *The Spoiled Child, a Farce in One Act*. London: Thomas Hailes Lacy, c. 1851.

Davenport, Thomas. "Letter to the Editor." *Kingston Morning Journal*, Sept. 22, 1840. Clipping, Jean Davenport scrapbook, Box 11, F. W. Lander and J. M. Lander Papers, LC.

———. "Letter to the Editor." *Newfoundland Public Ledger*, Aug. 20, 1841. Clipping, Jean Davenport scrapbook, Box 11, F. W. Lander and J. M. Lander Papers, LC.

David, Deirdre. *Fanny Kemble: A Performed Life*. Philadelphia: University of Pennsylvania Press, 2003.

Davidge, William Pleater. *Footlight Flashes*. New York: American News Company, 1866.

Davies, John B. *Phrenology: Fad and Science, A Nineteenth-Century American Crusade*. New Haven: Yale University Press, 1955 [1971].

Davis, Jim. *Comic Acting and Portraiture in Late-Georgian and Regency England*. Cambridge: Cambridge University Press, 2015.

———. "Freaks, Prodigies, and Marvelous Mimicry: Child Actors of Shakespeare on the Nineteenth-Century Stage." *Shakespeare* 2, no. 2 (December 2006): 179–93.

———. "Representing the Comic Actor at Work: The Harlow Portrait of Charles Mathews." *Nineteenth Century Theatre and Film* 31, no. 2 (Winter 2004): 3–15.

Davis, Tracy C. "Nineteenth-Century Repertoire," *Nineteenth Century Theatre and Film* 36, no. 2 (2009): 6–28.

———. "'Reading Shakespeare by Flashes of Lightning': Challenging the Foundations of Romantic Acting Theory," *ELH* 62, no. 4 (Winter 1995): 933–54.

Davis, Tracy C., ed. *The Broadview Anthology of Nineteenth-Century British Performance*. Peterborough, ON: Broadview Press, 2011.

Davis, Tracy C., and Peter Holland, eds. *The Performing Century: Nineteenth-Century Theatre's History*. Basingstoke: Palgrave Macmillan, 2007.

Davis-Fisch, Heather. *Loss and Cultural Remains in Performance: The Ghosts of the Franklin Expedition*. Basingstoke: Palgrave Macmillan, 2012.

Dawson, Melanie. "The Miniaturization of Girlhood: Nineteenth-Century Playtime and Gendered Theories of Development." In *The American Child: A Cultural Studies Reader*, edited by Caroline F. Levander and Carol J. Singley, 63–84. New Brunswick, NJ: Rutgers University Press, 2003.

Denisoff, Dennis. "Introduction." In *The Nineteenth-Century Child and Consumer Culture*, edited by Dennis Denisoff, 1–25. Burlington, VT: Ashgate, 2008.

Dickens, Charles. *The Life and Adventures of Nicholas Nickleby, vol. 1*. London: Chapman and Hall, 1858.

"The Drama." *Literary Chronicle and Weekly Review*, Nov. 3, 1821, p. 701. Google Books.

"The Drama." *London Magazine* 8 (July–Dec. 1823): 549. British Periodicals.

"The Drama." *New Monthly*, Nov. 1, 1823, 490. British Periodicals.

"The Drama." *Universal Magazine* 4 (Sept. [?] 1805): 248–50. Google Books.

"The Drama: English Opera House." *New Monthly Magazine and Historical Register* 6 (1822): 395.

"The Drama, and Public Amusements [English Opera House]." *Literary Chronicle and Weekly Review* 164 (July 6, 1822): 430. British Periodicals.

Drew, Mrs. John (Louisa Lane). *Autobiography of Mrs. John Drew*. New York: Charles Scribner's Sons, 1899.

Driscoll, Catherine. *Girls: Feminine Adolescence in Popular Culture and Cultural Theory*. New York: Columbia University Press, 2002.

"Drury Lane." *Mirror of the Stage; or, New Dramatic Censor*, Dec. 16, 1822, 152–53.

"Drury-Lane, Clara Fisher." Clipping, HTC.

Dubourg, George. *The Violin: Being an Account of that Leading Instrument and Its Most Eminent Professors*. London: Robert Cocks and Co., 1878.

Eagleton, Terry. *Literary Theory: An Introduction*. Hoboken: Blackwell, 1983.

Edinburgh Dramatic Review 1, no. 23 (13 Dec. 1824): 87–88.

Editorial. *Newfoundland Patriot*, Aug. 18, 1841. Clipping, Jean Davenport scrapbook, Box 11, F. W. Lander and J. M. Lander Papers, LC.

Elliston, Robert William. *Memoirs of Robert William Elliston, Comedian*. London: John Mortimer, 1845.

Engel, Laura. *Fashioning Celebrity: Eighteenth-Century British Actresses and Strategies for Image Making*. Columbus: Ohio State University Press, 2011.

———. "Stage Beauties: Actresses and Celebrity Culture in the Long Eighteenth Century." *Literature Compass* 13, no. 12 (2016): 749–61.

Engel, Laura, and Elaine McGirr, eds. *Stage Mothers: Women, Work, and the Theater, 1660–1830*. Lewisburg, PA: Bucknell University Press, 2014.

"English Opera House." *Literary Gazette; and Journal*, Aug. 3, 1822, 492. Google Books.

"English Opera House." *Literary Chronicle and Weekly Review*, 164 (May 22, 1819–Dec. 28, 1822): 429–30.

"English Opera House." *Theatrical Examiner*, Aug. 4, 1822, 761. British Periodicals.

"English Theatricals." *Belle Assemblee: Or, Court and Fashionable Magazine*, Jan. 1823, 232. Google Books.

"Eventful Careers: A Record of Over Seventy Years Upon the Stage, Mrs.
   Clara Fisher-Maeder's Remarkable Experience. A Chat with Mr. Actor,
   Mr. George C. Boniface." Clara Fisher clippings, HTC.
Falocco, Joe. "'So Much for Shakespeare': Cibber, Barrymore, Barton and
   the History of *Richard III* in Performance." *Upstart: A Journal of English
   Renaissance Studies* (August 2013), https://upstart.sites.clemson.edu
   /Essays/so-much/so-much.xhtml.
Fara, Patricia. *Pandora's Breeches: Women, Science and Power in the
   Enlightenment.* London: Pimlico, 2004.
Fawcett, Julia H. *Spectacular Disappearances: Celebrity and Privacy, 1696–
   1801.* Ann Arbor: University of Michigan Press, 2016.
Field, Corinne. "'Made Women of When They Are Mere Children': Mary
   Wollstonecraft's Critique of Eighteenth-Century Girlhood." *Journal of the
   History of Childhood and Youth* 4, no. 2 (Spring 2011): 197–222.
Field, Hannah. "'A Story, Exemplified in a Series of Figures': Paper Doll
   versus Moral Tale in the Nineteenth Century." *Girlhood Studies* 5, no. 1
   (Summer 2012): 37–56.
Filewod, Alan. *Performing Canada: The Nation Enacted in the Imagined
   Theatre.* Kamloops: Textual Studies in Canada, 2002.
Finlay, John. "Clara Fisher 1823." In *Miscellanies. The Foreign Relations of the
   British Empire: The Internal Resources of Ireland: Sketches of Character:
   Dramatic Criticism: Etc. Etc. Etc.* Dublin: John Cumming, lower Ormond-
   Quar, 1835, 272.
Fisher, Frederick George. *A Catalogue of the Various Articles Contained in
   Clara Fisher's Shaksperian [sic] Cabinet.* 1830.
———. *Fisher's New Brighton Guide.* London: Printed, for the Editor, 1804.
Fitzsimmons Frey, Heather. "Victorian Girls and At-home Theatricals:
   Performing and Playing with Possible Futures." Ph.D. dissertation,
   University of Toronto, 2015.
Formanek-Brunell, Miriam. *Made to Play House: Dolls and the
   Commercialization of American Girlhood, 1830–1930.* New Haven: Yale
   University Press, 1993.
Foulkes, Richard. *Performing Shakespeare in the Age of Empire.* Cambridge:
   Cambridge University Press, 2002.
Freeman, Lisa A. *Antitheatricality and the Body Public.* Philadelphia:
   University of Pennsylvania Press, 2017.
———. *Character's Theater: Genre and Identity on the Eighteenth-Century
   Stage.* Philadelphia: University of Pennsylvania Press, 2002.
Garber, Marjorie. *Vested Interests: Cross-Dressing and Cultural Anxiety.* New
   York: Routledge, 1992.

Garvey, Ellen Gruber. *Writing with Scissors: American Scrapbooks from the Civil War to the Harlem Renaissance*. New York: Oxford University Press, 2012 [online 2013].

Gaunt, Kyra D. *The Games Black Girls Play: Learning the Ropes from Double-Dutch to Hip-Hop*. New York: New York University Press, 2006.

Gollapudi, Aparna. "Recovering Miss Rose: Acting as a Girl on the Eighteenth-Century Stage." *Theatre Survey* 60, no. 1 (January 2019): 6–34.

Gonda, Caroline. *Reading Daughters' Fictions, 1709–1834: Novels and Society from Manley to Edgeworth*. Cambridge: Cambridge University Press, 1996.

Gonzalez, Eugenia. "'I Sometimes Think She Is a Spy on All My Actions': Dolls, Girls, and Disciplinary Surveillance in the Nineteenth-Century Doll Tale." *Nineteenth Century Literature* 39 (2011): 33–57.

Goodall, Jane. *Performance and Evolution in the Age of Darwin: Out of the Natural Order*. London: Routledge, 2002.

"Grand Juvenile Concert." 1840. George C. Howard, and Family. Series II, Acting Companies, 1833–1928, Subseries A. Fox Company, 1833–1846, HRC.

"Great Novelty." *Novascotian*, May 9, 1833, 139. Toronto Metro Reference Library Collections.

Green, London. "Edmund Kean's Richard III." *Theatre Journal* 36, no. 4 (Dec. 1984): 505–34.

Grobe, Christopher. *The Art of Confession: The Performance of Self from Robert Lowell to Reality TV*. New York: New York University Press, 2017.

Gubar, Marah. *Artful Dodgers: Reconceiving the Golden Age of Children's Literature*. Oxford: Oxford University Press, 2009.

———. "The Drama of Precocity: Child Performers on the Victorian Stage." In *The Nineteenth-Century Child and Consumer Culture*, edited by Dennis Denisoff, 64–78. Burlington, VT: Ashgate, 2008.

———. "Entertaining Children of All Ages: Nineteenth-Century Popular Theater as Children's Theater." *American Quarterly* 66, no. 1 (March 2014): 1–34.

———. "Who Watched *The Children's Pinafore*? Age Transvestism on the Nineteenth-Century Stage." *Victorian Studies* 54, no. 3 (Spring 2012): 410–26.

Gullette, Margaret Morganroth. *Aged by Culture*. Chicago: University of Chicago Press, 2004.

Halberstam, Jack. *Female Masculinity*. Durham, NC: Duke University Press, 1998.

Hall, D. G. "The Apprenticeship Period in Jamaica, 1834–1838." *Caribbean Quarterly* 3, no. 3 (1953): 142–66.

Hamlin, David. "The Structures of Toy Consumption: Bourgeois Domesticity and Demand for Toys in Nineteenth-Century Germany." *Journal of Social History* (Summer 2003): 857–69.

Hansen, Caitlin R. "The Infant Phenomenon: Shakespeare, the Mimetic Child, and Nineteenth-Century British Literature." Ph.D. dissertation, University of Washington, 2013.

Hanson, Willis T. *The Early Life of John Howard Payne*. Boston: Printed for members of the Bibliophile Society, 1913. British Library.

Harley, George Davies. *An Authentic Biographical Sketch of the Life, Education, and Personal Character of William Henry West Betty, the Celebrated Young Roscius*. London: Richard Phillips, 1804.

Harris, Daniel. *Cute, Quaint, Hungry and Romantic: The Aesthetics of Consumerism*. Cambridge, MA: Da Capo Press, 2001.

Harris, Jocelyn Margaret. "Jane Austen and Celebrity Culture: Shakespeare, Dorothy Jordan and Elizabeth Bennet." *Shakespeare* 6, no. 4 (Dec. 2010): 410–30.

Hartman, Saidya V. *Scenes of Subjection: Terror, Slavery, and Self-Making in Nineteenth-Century America*. New York: Oxford University Press, 1997.

———. *Wayward Lives, Beautiful Experiments: Intimate Histories of Social Upheaval*. New York: W. W. Norton, 2019.

Hatch, Kristen. *Shirley Temple: The Performance of Girlhood*. New Brunswick, NJ: Rutgers University Press, 2015.

Helgren, Jennifer, and Colleen A. Vasconcellos. *Girlhood: A Global History*. New Brunswick, NJ: Rutgers University Press, 2010.

Herrera, Brian Eugenio. *Latin Numbers: Playing Latino in Twentieth-Century U.S. Popular Performance*. Ann Arbor: University of Michigan Press, 2015.

Heuman, Gad. "A Tale of Two Jamaica Rebellions." *Jamaican Historical Review* 19 (Jan. 1996): 1–8.

Higonnet, Anne. *Pictures of Innocence: The History and Crisis of Ideal Childhood*. London: Thames and Hudson, 1998.

———. "Picturing Childhood in the Modern West." In *The Routledge History of Childhood in the Western World*, edited by Paula S. Fass, 296–312. Abingdon: Routledge, 2013.

Hill, Errol. *The Jamaican Stage, 1655–1900: Profile of a Colonial Theatre*. Ann Arbor: University of Michigan Press, 1992.

Hogan, Charles Beecher. *Shakespeare in the Theatre, 1701–1800. A Record of Performances in London 1751–1800*. Oxford: Oxford at the Clarendon Press, 1957. Houghton Library.

Hogan, Robert. *Dion Boucicault*. New York: Twayne, 1969.

Holdsworth, Sara, and Joan Crossley. *Innocence and Experience: Images of*

Children in British Art from 1600 to the Present. Manchester: Manchester City Art Galleries, 1992.

Honeyman, Susan. "Trans(cending) Gender through Childhood." In *The Children's Table: Childhood Studies and the Humanities*, edited by Anna Marie Duane, 167–82. Athens: University of Georgia Press, 2013.

Horwitz, Steve. "How Capitalism and the Bourgeois Virtues Transformed and Humanized the Family." *Journal of Socio-Economics* 41 (2012): 792.

Hughes, Alan. "Charles Kean in Victoria: Touring Actors and Local Politics in 1864." *BC Studies* (1987): 21–32.

Hunt, Leigh. *Critical Essays &c &c*. London: John Hunt, 1807. Google Books.

Hunter, Jane H. *How Young Ladies Became Girls: The Victorian Origins of American Girlhood*. New Haven: Yale University Press, 2002.

Hutton, Laurence. "Infant Phenomena." *Frank Leslie's Popular Monthly* 21, no. 4 (April 1886): 439 ff. American Periodicals.

———. *Talks in a Library with Laurence Hutton*, recorded by Isabel Moore. New York: G. P. Putnam's Sons, 1905.

"Impromptu on Miss Fisher." *Mirror of Literature, Amusement, and Instruction*, 2, no. 54 (Nov. 1, 1823): 383.

"Infant Phenomenon Is Now Mrs. Lander, in Philadelphia." *Lincoln Nebraska State Journal Newspaper*, Jan. 19, 1877.

Ireland, Joseph N. Scrapbook. HTC.

Isbell, Mary. "P(l)aying off Old Ironsides and the Old Wagon: Melville's Depiction of Shipboard Theatricals in *White-Jacket*." *Leviathan: A Journal of Melville Studies* 15, no. 1 (2013): 6–39.

James, Felicity. "Wild 'Tales' from Shakespeare: Readings of Charles and Mary Lamb." *Shakespeare* 2, no. 2 (Dec. 2006): 152–67.

"Jean Margaret Davenport Lander." Find a Grave.com, https://www.findagrave.com/memorial/37272951/jean-margaret-lander, accessed 21 August 2019.

Johnson, Odai. *Ruins: Classical Theater and Broken Memory*. Ann Arbor: University of Michigan Press, 2018.

Johnston, D. C. *The Aurora Borealis or Flashes of Wit Calculated to Drown Dull Care and Eradicate the Blue Devils*. Boston: Editor of the Galaxy of Wit, 1831.

Jones, Eugene H. "Fisher, Clara." In *Notable Women in the American Theatre: A Biographical Dictionary*, ed. Alice M. Robinson, Vera Mowry Roberts, and Milly S. Barranger, 278–79. New York: Greenwood Press, 1989.

Jones, Silas. *Practical Phrenology*. Boston: Russell, Shattuck, & Williams, 1836.

Joosen, Vanessa. "Second Childhood and Intergenerational Dialogues: How Children's Literature and Age Studies Can Supplement Each Other."

Children's Literature Association Quarterly 40, no. 2 (Summer 2015): 126–40.

—, ed. *Connecting Childhood and Old Age in Popular Media*. Jackson: University Press of Mississippi, 2018.

Kahan, Jeffrey. *Bettymania and the Birth of Celebrity Culture*. Bethlehem: Lehigh University Press, 2010.

Kaleidoscope: or Literary and Scientific Mirror; Liverpool 3, no. 115 (Sept. 10, 1822): 80.

Keeton, Guy Herbert. "The Theatre in Mississippi from 1840 to 1870." Ph.D. dissertation, Louisiana State University, 1979.

Kelly, Rivka. "The Duchess: An Analysis of the Life and Legacy of Louisa Lane Drew." Senior dissertation, Paper 23, University of Vermont, 2014.

Kemble, Frances Ann. *Records of a Girlhood*. 2nd ed. New York: Henry Holt and Company, 1883. Accessed Dec. 30, 2018, https://archive.org/details /recordsofgirlhooookembuoft/page/n7.

Kincaid, James R. *Child-Loving: The Erotic Child and Victorian Culture*. New York: Routledge, 1994.

"Kingston Theatre." *Morning Journal*, n.d. Jean Davenport scrapbook, Box 11, F. W. and J. M. Lander Papers, LC.

Klein, Jeanne. "An Epoch of Child Spectators in Early U.S. Theatre." *Journal of the History of Childhood and Youth* 10, no. 1 (Winter 2017): 21–39.

—. "Reclaiming Four Child Actors through Seven Plays in U.S. Theatre, 1794–1800." *Journal of American Drama and Theatre* 30, no. 1 (Fall 2017): 1–23.

—. "Without Distinction of Age: The Pivotal Roles of Child Actors and Their Spectators in Nineteenth-Century Theatre." *The Lion and the Unicorn* 36, no. 2 (April 2012): 117–35.

Klett, Elizabeth. *Cross-Gender Shakespeare and English National Identity: Wearing the Codpiece*. London: Palgrave Macmillan, 2009.

Knowles, Katie. *Shakespeare's Boys: A Cultural History*. Basingstoke: Palgrave Macmillan, 2014.

Kornmeier, Ute. "Almost Alive: The Spectacle of Verisimilitude in Madame Tussaud's Waxworks." In *Ephemeral Bodies: Wax Sculpture and the Human Figure*, edited by Roberta Panzanelli and Julius Ritter von Schlosser, 67–82. Los Angeles: Getty Research Institute, 2008.

Kotsilibas-Davis, James. *Great Times, Good Times: The Odyssey of Maurice Barrymore*. New York: Doubleday, 1977.

Kutzer, M. Daphne. *Empire's Children: Empire and Imperialism in Classic British Children's Books*. New York: Garland, 2000.

Lal, Ruby. *Coming of Age in Nineteenth-Century India: The Girl-Child and the Art of Playfulness*. Cambridge: Cambridge University Press, 2013.

Lancaster, E. R. *The Manager's Daughter*. Lord Chamberlain's Plays, fols. 893–903, BL.

Lander, Jean Margaret (Davenport). Letter to *Shakespeareana*. Y.c.736 (1 a–c), FSL.

Langmuir, Erika. *Imagining Childhood*. New Haven: Yale University Press, 2006.

"Last Night Miss Davenport ..." *Montreal Royal Gazette*, Aug. 6, 1849. Jean Davenport scrapbook, Box 11, F. W. and J. M. Lander Papers, LC.

Lavoie, Chantel. "*Tristram Shandy* and Breeching." *Eighteenth-Century Fiction* 28, no. 1 (Fall 2015): 85–107.

Ledoux, Ellen Malenas. "Working Mothers on the Romantic Stage: Sarah Siddons and Mary Robinson," in Engel and McGirr, eds., *Stage Mothers*, 79–104.

Leman, Walter M. *Reminiscences of an Old Actor*. San Francisco: A. Roman Co., 1886.

"Letter from a Contributor in Love." *Blackwood's Edinburgh Magazine*, 14 (Oct. 1823): 472. Google Books.

Levine, Lawrence. *Highbrow/Lowbrow: The Emergence of Cultural Hierarchy in America*. Cambridge: Harvard University Press, 1999.

Lipscomb, Valerie Barnes, and Leni Marshall, ed. *Staging Age: The Performance of Age in Theatre, Dance, and Film*. Basingstoke: Palgrave Macmillan, 2010.

Literary Gazette and Journal of Belles Lettres, Arts, Sciences, Part 2. No. 307, Dec. 7, 1822. Google Books.

"Little Cordelia Howard." *American Phrenological Journal* 23, no. 5 (May 1865): 107.

The London Stage, 1660–1800; A Calendar of Plays, Entertainments & Afterpieces, Together with Casts, Box-Office Receipts, and Contemporary Comment. [1st ed.] Carbondale: Southern Illinois University Press, 1960. Hathi Trust Digital Library.

Longman, W. *Tokens of the Eighteenth Century Connected with Booksellers & Bookmakers*. London: Longmans, Green and Co., 1916.

"Lowell Museum/Splendid Attraction!! The Foxes!" George C. Howard and Family. Series II, Acting Companies, 1833–1928, Subseries A. Fox Company, 1833–1846, HRC.

Luckhurst, Mary, and Jane Moody. "Introduction: The Singularity of Theatrical Celebrity." In *Theatre and Celebrity in Britain, 1660–2000*, edited by Mary Luckhurst and Jane Moody, 1–11. Basingstoke: Palgrave Macmillan, 2005.

Ludlow, Noah. *Dramatic Life as I Found It*. St. Louis: G. I. Jones and Company, 1880.

Lutz, Deborah. *Relics of Death in Victorian Literature and Culture.* Cambridge: Cambridge University Press, 2015.

MacArthur, Benjamin. *Actors and American Culture, 1880–1920.* Iowa City: University of Iowa Press, 2000.

MacKay, Ellen. "*RE*: Sources / The Wrong Stuff: Staffordshire Figures at the Folger Shakespeare Library." *Theatre Survey* 56, no. 3 (Sept. 2015): 389–401.

Maddock Dillon, Elizabeth. *New World Drama: The Performative Commons in the Atlantic World, 1649–1849.* Durham, NC: Duke University Press, 2014.

Maeder, Clara Fisher. *Autobiography of Clara Fisher Maeder*, ed. Douglas Taylor. New York: Burt Franklin, 1897 [1979].

Malabou, Catherine. *What Should We Do with Our Brain?* Translated by Sebastian Rand. New York: Fordham University Press, 2008.

Marcus, Sharon. *Between Women: Friendship, Desire, and Marriage in Victorian England.* Princeton, NJ: Princeton University Press, 2007.

———. *The Drama of Celebrity.* Princeton, NJ: Princeton University Press, 2019.

———. "The Theatrical Scrapbook." *Theatre Survey* 54, no. 2 (May 2013): 283–307.

Marra, Kim. *Strange Duets: Impresarios and Actresses in the American Theatre.* Iowa City: University of Iowa Press, 2006.

Marsden, Jean I. "Modesty Unshackled: Dorothy Jordan and the Dangers of Cross-Dressing." *Studies in Eighteenth-Century Culture* 22 (1993): 21–35.

———. "Shakespeare for Girls: Mary Lamb and *Tales from Shakespeare*." *Children's Literature* 17, no. 1 (1989): 47–63.

Martin, Carol. *Theatre of the Real.* Basingstoke: Palgrave Macmillan, 2013.

Mathews, Mrs. (Anne Jackson). *Memoirs of Charles Mathews, Comedian* vol. 4. London: Richard Bentley, New Burlington Street, 1838.

Matthews, Brander, and Laurence Hutton, eds. *Kean and Booth and Their Contemporaries: Actors and Actresses of Great Britain and the United States.* Boston: L. C. Page, 1900.

McGillis, Roderick. *A Little Princess: Gender and Empire.* New York: Twayne, 1996.

McLean [Maclean], Robert Simpson. "The Case of the Silent Figure: A Phenomenal Art Mystery Revealed." *Dickensian* 91, no. 436 (Summer 1995): 94–98.

———. "He Played with Crummles: The Life and Career of William Pleater Davidge, Anglo-American Actor, Author and Dickens Enthusiast." *Dickensian* 89, no. 430 (Summer 1993): 103–17.

———. "How 'the Infant Phenomenon' Began the World: The Managing of Jean Margaret Davenport (182?–1903)." *Dickensian* 88, no. 428 (1992): 133–52.

McWilliam, Rohan. "The Theatricality of the Staffordshire Figurine." *Journal of Victorian Culture* 10, no. 1 (2005): 107–14.

"Memoir of Master Burke." *Dramatic Magazine*, June 1, 1830, 130.

Merish, Lori. "Cuteness and Commodity Aesthetics: Tom Thumb and Shirley Temple." In *Freakery: Cultural Spectacles of the Extraordinary Body*, edited by Rosemarie Garland-Thomson, 185–203. New York: NYU Press, 1996.

Merrill, Lisa. *When Romeo Was a Woman: Charlotte Cushman and Her Circle of Female Spectators*. Ann Arbor: University of Michigan Press, 1999.

Michals, Teresa. "Experiments before Breakfast: Toys, Education, and Middle-Class Childhood." In *The Nineteenth-Century Child and Consumer Culture*, edited by Dennis Denisoff, 29–42. Aldershot: Ashgate, 2008.

Miller, Alice. *For Your Own Good: Hidden Cruelty in Child-Rearing and the Roots of Violence*. New York: Farrar, Straus and Giroux, 1983.

Miller, Derek. "Average Broadway." *Theatre Journal* 68, no. 4 (Dec. 2016): 529–33.

Miller, Gemma. "Cross-Gender Casting as Feminist Activism in the Staging of Early Modern Plays." *Journal of International Women's Studies*, 16, no. 1 (2014): 4–17.

———. "'Many a Time and Oft Had I Broken My Neck for Amusement': The Corpse, the Child, and the Aestheticization of Death in Shakespeare's *Richard III* and *King John*." *Comparative Drama* 50, nos. 2–3 (Summer and Fall 2016): 209–32.

Mintz, Steven. *Huck's Raft: A History of American Childhood*. Cambridge: Harvard University Press, 2004.

"Miss Clara Fisher." *Drama; Or, Theatrical Pocket Magazine* 4, no. 3 (Sept. 1822): 157–65.

"Miss Clara Fisher: To the Editor." *Kaleidoscope: or, Literary and Scientific Mirror*. June 11, 1822, 392. Google Books.

"Miss Davenport." Dec. 28, 1839. Clipping, Jean Davenport scrapbook, Box 11, F. W. and J. M. Lander Papers, LC.

"Miss Davenport." *Newfoundland Times*, Aug. 4, 1841. Clipping, Jean Davenport scrapbook, Box 11, F. W. and J. M. Lander Papers, LC.

"Miss Davenport's Juliet." *Kingston Dispatch*, Sept. 24, 1840. Clipping, Jean Davenport scrapbook, F. W. and J. M. Lander Papers, LC.

"Miss Lane." Playbills, female stars, HTC.

Monks, Aoife. "Human Remains: Acting, Objects, and Belief in Performance." *Theatre Journal* 64, no. 3 (October 2012): 355–71.

"Monthly List of Bankruptcies from the London Gazette." *Monthly Visitor, and New Family Magazine* 5, no. 20 (Dec. 1805): 424–27. British Periodicals.

Montreal Royal Gazette. Aug. 8, 1839. Jean Davenport scrapbook, Box 11, F. W. and J. M. Lander Papers, LC.

Morgan, Simon. "Material Culture and the Politics of Personality in Early Victorian England." *Journal of Victorian Culture* 17, no. 2 (2012): 127–46.

Morley, Malcolm. "Dickens Goes to the Theatre." *Dickensian* 59 (1963): 165–71.

———. "More about Crummles." *Dickensian* 59 (1963): 51–56.

———. "Where Crummles Played." *Dickensian* 58 (1962): 23–29.

"Mr. Cull on a Case of Musical Talent [Monday, 21st September]." *Phrenological Journal and Magazine of Moral Science* 14, no. 66 (1841): 25–31.

Mulleneaux, Nan. "Our Genius, Goodness, and Gumption: Child Actresses and National Identity in Mid-Nineteenth Century America." *Journal of the History of Childhood and Youth* 5, no. 2 (2012): 283–308.

Mullenix, Elizabeth Reitz. *Wearing the Breeches: Gender on the Antebellum Stage.* New York: St. Martin's Press, 2000.

Myers, Mitzi. "'A Taste for Truth and Realities': Early Advice to Mothers on Books for Girls." *Children's Literature Association Quarterly* 12, no. 3 (Fall 1987): 118–24.

Nathans, Heather S. *Hideous Characters and Beautiful Pagans: Performing Jewish Identity on the Antebellum American Stage.* Ann Arbor: University of Michigan Press, 2017.

Newfoundland clippings. *Gazette,* Aug. 18, 1841. Toronto Metro Reference Library.

Newfoundland Times. Aug. 11 and 18, 1841. Toronto Metro Reference Library.

New-York Mirror, and Ladies' Literary Gazette. Clara Fisher, clipping. HTC.

Ngai, Sianne. *Our Aesthetic Categories: Zany, Cute, Interesting.* Cambridge, MA: Harvard University Press, 2012.

Norcia, Megan A. "Playing Empire: Children's Parlor Games, Home Theatricals, and Improvisational Play." *Children's Literature Association Quarterly* 29, no. 4 (Winter 2004): 294–314.

"Notice to Correspondents." *Edinburgh Dramatic Review* 1, no. 29 (Dec. 20, 1824): 113.

"Notices Relating to the Fine Arts in Edinburgh." *Scots Magazine and Edinburgh Literary Miscellany,* 78, part 1. Edinburgh: Archibald Constable and Company, 1816, 207.

Nussbaum, Felicity. *Rival Queens: Actresses, Performance, and the Eighteenth-Century British Theater.* Philadelphia: University of Pennsylvania Press, 2010.

Nyong'o, Tavia. "Racial Kitsch and Black Performance." *Yale Journal of Criticism* 15, no. 2 (Fall 2002): 371–91.

O'Flaherty, Patrick. *Lost Country: The Rise and Fall of Newfoundland, 1843–1933*. St. John's: Long Beach Press, 2005.

"The Olympic Theatre." *Literary Gazette: A Weekly Journal of Literature, Science, and the Fine Arts* 102 (Jan. 2, 1819): 142.

O'Neil, Paul. *The Oldest City: The Story of St. John's*. St. John's, Newfoundland: Press Porcepic, 1975.

O'Neill, Patrick. "Blake, William Rufus" and "Nova Scotia, The Theatre of." In *The Oxford Companion to Canadian Theatre*, edited by Eugene Benson and L. W. Conolly. Toronto: Oxford University Press, 1989–.

———. "Theatre in the North: Staging Practices of the British Navy in the Canadian Arctic." *Dalhousie Review* 74, no. 3 (1994): 356–84.

Owens, Tammy C., et al. "Towards an Interdisciplinary Field of Black Girlhood Studies." *Departures in Critical Qualitative Research* 6, no. 3 (2017): 116–32.

Oxberry's Dramatic Biography and Histrionic Anecdotes. Volume 4; The Literary Gazette and Journal of Belles Lettres, Arts, Sciences, Part 2, no. 307, Dec. 7, 1822, 105–6. Google Books.

Pande, Raksha. "Strategic Essentialism." Wiley Online Library, 2017, https://doi.org/10.1002/9781118786352.wbieg1170, accessed August 22, 2019.

Pangloss, Peter. *The Young Rosciad, An Admonitory Poem. Well-Seasoned with Attic Salt*. London: J. Roach, Russell Court, 1805. HTC.

Papageorgiou, Ionna. "Enchanting Evil: English Romantic Criticism on Edmund Kean's Interpretation of *Richard III* and Schiller's Theory on the Immortal Characters in Art." *Restoration and Eighteenth-Century Theatre Research* 23, no. 1 (2008): 19–33.

Pascoe, Judith. *The Sarah Siddons Audio Files: Romanticism and the Lost Voice*. Ann Arbor: University of Michigan Press, 2013.

———. "Tales for Young Housekeepers: T. S. Arthur and the American Girl." In *The Girl's Own: Cultural Histories of the Anglo-American Girl, 1830–1915*, 34–51. Athens: University of Georgia Press, 2010.

"The Passing of Mrs. Lander." *Dramatic Mirror*, Aug. 15, 1903. Clippings. HTC.

"Performing Girlhoods." Special issue. *Theatre Survey* 60, no. 1 (January 2019).

Perry, Claire. *Young America: Childhood in Nineteenth-Century Art and Culture*. New Haven: Yale University Press, 2006.

Perry, Gill. "Ambiguity and Desire: Metaphors of Sexuality in Late Eighteenth-Century Representations of the Actress." In *Notorious Muse: The Actress in British Art and Culture 1776–1812*, edited by Robyn Asleson, 111–26. New Haven: Yale University Press, 2003.

————. *Spectacular Flirtations: Viewing the British Actress in Art and Theatre*. New Haven: Yale University Press, 2007.

————. "Staging Gender and 'Hairy Signs': Representing Dorothy Jordan." *Eighteenth-Century Studies* 38, no. 1 (2004): 145–63.

Perry, Ruth. *Novel Relations: The Transformation of Kinship in English Literature and Culture, 1748–1818*. Cambridge: Cambridge University Press, 2006.

Phelps, Henry Pitt. *Players of a Century: A Record of the Albany Stage*. Albany: Joseph McDonough, 1880.

Phillips, Chelsea. "Bodies in Play: Maternity, Repertory, and the Rival *Romeo and Juliet*s, 1748–51." *Theatre Survey* 60, no. 2 (May 2019): 207–36.

Phillipson, J. D. "The Inconvenience of the Female Condition, Anne Oldfield's Pregnancies," in Engel and McGirr, eds., *Stage Mothers*, 43–62.

Phrenological Society [Edinburgh]. *Transactions of the Phrenological Society*, vol. 1. Edinburgh: John Anderson Jr., 1824.

Plotz, Judith. *Romanticism and the Vocation of Childhood*. New York: Palgrave, 2000.

Poole, S. *Old and Young*. Manuscript, John Larpent papers, 1737–1824, Huntington Library.

————. *The Popular Farce Called Old and Young* (From the French of Eugène Scribe and Germond Delivne). London: J. Tabby, Mr. Miller, 1822.

Porter, Roy, and G. S. Rousseau. *Gout: The Patrician Malady*. New Haven: Yale University Press, 2000.

Purinton, Marjean D. "Cross-Dressing and the Performance of Gender in Romantic-Period Comic Plays by Women." In *Spheres of Action: Speech and Performance in Romantic Culture*, edited by Alexander Dick and Angela Esterhammer, 178–93. Toronto: University of Toronto Press, 2009.

Quarterly Oriental Magazine Review and Register [Dinapore, India]. Vol. 6 (Nov. 25, 1826): cxxxxv. Google Books.

Quinn, Arthur Hobson. "Chapter 1: The Heritage." In *Edgar Allan Poe: A Critical Biography*, edited by Arthur Hobson Quinn, 1–50 (1941), https://www.eapoe.org/PAPERS/misc1921/quinnc01.htm#fn01011.

Raven, James. "Libraries for Sociability: The Advance of the Subscription Library." In *The Cambridge History of Libraries in Britain and Ireland*, edited by Peter Hoare, 241–63. Cambridge: Cambridge University Press, 2008.

Redcap. "Letter to the Editor." *Kingston Morning Journal*, Sept. 21, 1840. Jean Davenport scrapbook, Box 11, F. W. and J. M. Lander Papers, LC.

Reed, Joseph P., and William S. Walsh. "Beauties of the American Stage." *The Cosmopolitan* 14 (1893): 294–304.

"Remarks." *Newfoundland Patriot*, Aug. 25, 1841. Clipping, Jean Davenport scrapbook, Box 11, F. W. and J. M. Lander Papers, LC.

Richard III. Playbills collection, Thr. A3, box 2, folder 2, (King) Richard III, March 15, 1819–September 6, 1824, LC.

Richards, Sandra L. "Horned Ancestral Masks, Shakespearean Actor Boys, and Scotch-Inspired Set Girls: Social Relations in Nineteenth-Century Jamaican Jonkonnu." In *The African Diaspora: African Origins and New World Identities*, edited by Carole Boyce Davies, Ali Mazrui, and Isidore Okpewho, 254–71. Bloomington: Indiana University Press, 1999.

Roach, Joseph. *Cities of the Dead: Circum-Atlantic Performance*. Ann Arbor: University of Michigan Press, 1996.

———. *It*. Ann Arbor: University of Michigan Press, 2007.

———. "Public Intimacy: The Prior History of It." In *Theatre and Celebrity in Britain, 1660–2000*, edited by Mary Luckhurst and Jane Moody, 15–30. Basingstoke: Palgrave Macmillan, 2005.

Robson, Heather. *Men in Wonderland: The Lost Girlhood of the Victorian Gentleman*. Princeton, NJ: Princeton University Press, 2001.

Russell, Anne. "Tragedy, Gender, Performance: Women as Tragic Heroes on the Nineteenth-century Stage." *Comparative Drama* 30, no. 2 (Summer 1996): 135–57.

Salter, Denis. "William Rufus Blake and the Gentlemanly Art of Comic Acting." In *The Proceedings of the Theatre in Atlantic Canada Symposium*, edited by Ric Knowles, 68–99. Anchorage Series 4. Sackville, NB: Centre for Canadian Studies, 1988.

Sam's-Son, Sam. "Provincial Drama." *British Stage and Literary Cabinet* 5, no. 57 (Sept. 1821): 298–303.

Sánchez-Eppler, Karen. *Dependent States: The Child's Part in Nineteenth-Century American Culture*. Chicago: University of Chicago Press, 2005.

Sansonetti, Anthony. "Master Joseph Burke." *Ambassadors of Empire: Child Performers and Anglo-American Audiences, 1800s–1880*, http://childperformers.ca/master-joseph-burke/.

Savran, David. *Highbrow/Lowdown: Theater, Jazz, and the Making of the New Middle Class*. Ann Arbor: University of Michigan Press, 2009.

Schanke, Robert A., and Kim Marra, eds. *Passing Performances: Queer Readings of Leading Players in American Theater History*. Ann Arbor: University of Michigan Press, 1998.

Schechner, Richard. *Between Theater and Anthropology*. Philadelphia: University of Pennsylvania Press, 1985.

Schneider, Rebecca. *Performing Remains: Art and War in Times of Theatrical Reenactment*. New York: Routledge, 2011.

Schweitzer, Marlis. "Consuming Celebrity: Commodities and Cuteness in the Circulation of Master William Henry West Betty." In *The Retro-Futurism of Cuteness*, edited by Jen E. Boyle and Wan-Chuan Kao, 111–35. Santa Barbara: Punctum Books, 2017.

———. "Three Sentences: A Child Actress in Halifax." In *Canadian Performance Histories and Historiographies*, edited by Heather Davis-Fisch, 280–98. Toronto: Playwrights Canada Press, 2017.

———. "'Too Much Tragedy in Real Life': Theatre in Post-Emancipation Jamaica." *Nineteenth Century Theatre and Film* 44, no. 1 (May 2017): 8–27.

———. "An 'Unmanly and Insidious Attack': Child Actress Jean Davenport and the Performance of Masculinity in 1840s Jamaica and Newfoundland." *Theatre Research in Canada*, 35, no. 1 (Winter 2014): 49–68.

Scott, Charlotte. "Incapable and Shallow Innocents." In *Childhood, Education and the Stage in Early Modern England*, edited by Richard Preiss and Deanne Williams, 58–78. Cambridge: Cambridge University Press, 2017.

Segel, Elizabeth. "The Gypsy Breynton Series: Setting the Pattern for American Tomboy Heroines." *Children's Literature Association Quarterly* 14, no. 2 (Summer 1989): 67–71.

Senelick, Laurence. *The Age and Stage of George L. Fox, 1825–1877.* Iowa City: University of Iowa Press, 1999.

———. *Sex, Drag, and Theatre.* New York: Taylor & Francis, 2003.

Sentilles, Renée M. *American Tomboys 1850–1915.* Amherst: University of Massachusetts Press, 2018.

Sharpe, Christina. *In the Wake: On Blackness and Being.* Durham, NC: Duke University Press, 2016.

Sheridan, Richard Brinsley. *Pizarro; A Tragedy*, edited by Alexander Dick and Selena Couture. Peterborough, ON: Broadview Press, 2017.

Siddons, Henry. *Practical Illustrations of Rhetorical Gesture and Action: Adapted to the English Drama from a Work on the Subject by M. Engel.* 2nd ed. London: Sherwood, Neely, and Jones, 1822 [1807].

"Since Then I'm Doom'd: A New Song as Sung by Mrs. Jordan." Dublin: published by F. Rhames, No. 16, Exchange St. [1800?]. British Library.

Slout, William L. ed. *Old Gotham Theatricals: Selections from a Series "Reminiscences About Town,"* by Col. Tom Picton. San Bernadino, CA: The Borgo Press, 1995.

Slout, William L., and Sue Rudisill. "The Enigma of the Master Betty Mania." *Journal of Popular Culture* 8, no. 1 (Summer 1974): 81–90.

Smith, Geddeth. *The Brief Career of Eliza Poe.* Teaneck, NJ: Fairleigh Dickinson University Press, 1988.

Smith, Michelle J. *Empire in British Girls' Literature and Culture: Imperial Girls, 1880–1915.* London: Palgrave Macmillan, 2011.

Some Account of the English Stage from the Restoration in 1660 to 1830,
    vol. 8 - Bath. Bath: H. E. Carrington, 1832.

Stack, David. *Queen Victoria's Skull*. London: Hambledon Continuum, 2008.

Steedman, Carolyn. *Strange Dislocations: Childhood and the Idea of Human
    Interiority, 1780–1930*. Cambridge, MA: Harvard University Press, 1995.

Stephenson, Jenn. *Insecurity: Perils and Products of Theatres of the Real*.
    Toronto: University of Toronto Press, 2019.

Stewart, Susan. *On Longing: Narratives of the Miniature, the Gigantic, the
    Souvenir, the Collection*. Durham, NC: Duke University Press, 1992.

Straub, Katrina. "Performing Variety, Packaging Difference." In *The Oxford
    Handbook of the Georgian Theatre 1737–1832*, edited by Julia Swindells
    and David Francis Taylor, 229–46. Oxford: Oxford University Press, 2014.

———. *Sexual Suspects: Eighteenth-Century Players and Sexual Ideology*.
    Princeton, NJ: Princeton University Press, 1992.

Studlar, Gaylyn. *Precocious Charms: Stars Performing Girlhood in Classical
    Hollywood Cinema*. Berkeley: University of California Press, 2013.

Sunday Times. May 22, 1836, clipping. Jean Davenport scrapbook, Box 11,
    F.W. and J.M. Lander Papers, LC.

Tasch, Peter A. *The Dramatic Cobbler: The Life and Works of Isaac
    Bickerstaff*. Lewisburg, PA: Bucknell University Press, 1971.

Taylor, Diana. *The Archive and the Repertoire: Performing Cultural Memory
    in the Americas*. Durham, NC: Duke University Press, 2003.

Tedeschi, Anthony. "Vale Shakespeare: Highlights from the Turnbull
    Collection." National Library of New Zealand, https://natlib.govt.nz
    /blog/posts/vale-shakespeare-highlights-from-the-turnbull-collections,
    accessed Feb. 19, 2019.

"Theatre." *Acadian Recorder*, June 1, 1833, 3.

"Theatre." *Kingston Dispatch*, Sept. 8, 1840. Clipping, Jean Davenport
    scrapbook, Box 11, F. W. and J. M. Lander Papers, LC.

"Theatre." *Kingston Dispatch*, Sept. 11, 1840. Clipping, Jean Davenport
    scrapbook, Box 11, F. W. and J. M. Lander Papers, LC.

"Theatre." *Newfoundlander*, Aug. 19, 1841. Clipping, Jean Davenport
    scrapbook, Box 11, F. W. and J. M. Lander Papers, LC.

"The Theatre." *Newfoundland Ledger*, Aug. 10, 1840, n.p.

Theatre Glocester playbill, July 24, 1805. In *Collecteana*, p, 95.

Tomalin, Claire. *Mrs. Jordan's Profession: The Actress and the Prince*. New
    York: Alfred A. Knopf, 1995.

"Under the Patronage of His Honor and the Administrator of the
    Government." *Newfoundland Public Ledger*, July 31, 1841, n.p.

Van Wyhe, John. *Phrenology and the Origins of Victorian Scientific
    Naturalism*. Aldershot: Ashgate, 2004.

Varty, Anne. *Children and Theatre in Victorian Britain: "All Work, No Play."* Basingstoke: Palgrave Macmillan, 2008.

Vey, Shauna. *Childhood and Nineteenth-Century American Theatre: The Work of the Marsh Troupe of Juvenile Actors.* Carbondale: Southern Illinois University Press, 2015.

Wahrman, Dror. *"Percy's* Prologue: From Gender Play to Gender Panic in Eighteenth-Century England." *Past and Present* 159, no. 1 (May 1998): 113–60.

Walen, Denise A. "Such a Romeo as We Had Never Ventured to Hope For." In *Passing Performances: Queer Readings of Leading Players in American Theater History,* edited by Robert A. Schanke and Kim Marra, 41–62. Ann Arbor: University of Michigan Press, 1998.

Wallace, Heather E. "Women's Education According to Rousseau and Wollstonecraft," *Feminism and Women's Studies, Feminism- eserver.org.* Jan. 1, 2005, accessed Aug. 8, 2016, http://feminism.eserver.org/theory /papers/womens-education.txt.

Warner, Kristen J. "In the Time of Plastic Representation." *Film Quarterly* 71.2 (Winter 2017), https://filmquarterly.org/2017/12/04/in-the-time-of -plastic-representation/, accessed 17 January 2020.

Warren-Crow, Heather. *Girlhood and the Plastic Image.* Hanover, NH: Dartmouth College Press, 2014.

"Wars of Independence: Robert (1) the Bruce." *future museum.co.uk,* http:// www.futuremuseum.co.uk/collections/people/lives-in-key-periods/the -medieval-period-(1100ad-1499ad)/wars-of-independence/robert-(i)-the -bruce/robert-the-bruce,-cast-of-his-skull.aspx, accessed Dec. 28, 2015.

Waters, Hazel. "'That Astonishing Clever Child': Performers and Prodigies in the Early and Mid-Victorian Theatre." *Theatre Notebook* 50, no. 2 (1996): 78–94.

"We Feel Pleasure." *Kingston Dispatch,* Aug. 31, 1840. Untitled clipping, Jean Davenport scrapbook, Box 11, F. W. and J. M. Lander Papers, LC.

"We Hope the People." *Kingston Dispatch,* June 8, 1840. Untitled clipping, Jean Davenport scrapbook, Box 11, F. W. and J. M. Lander Papers, LC.

Wesley, John. *The Works of the Rev. John Wesley.* Vol. 6. New York: J. & J. Harper, 1826. Google Books.

Whittaker, Robin C. "Un/Disciplined Performance: Nonprofessionalized Theatre in Canada's Professional Era." Ph.D. dissertation, University of Toronto, 2010.

Williams, Deanne. "Introduction: *'Look on't Again.'*" In *Childhood, Education and the Stage in Early Modern England,* edited by Richard Preiss and Deanne Williams, 1–13. Cambridge: Cambridge University Press, 2017.

———. *Shakespeare and the Performance of Girlhood*. Basingstoke: Palgrave Macmillan, 2014.

Wilson, Kathleen. "Introduction: Three Theses on Performance and History." Special issue "Performance," *Eighteenth-Century Studies* 48, no. 4 (Summer 2015): 375–90.

———. *The Island Race: Englishness, Empire and Gender in the Eighteenth Century*. London: Routledge, 2003.

Winter, William. *Brief Chronicles*. New York: Dunlap Society, 1889.

Winton, Henry. "Editorial." *Newfoundland Public Ledger*, Aug. 20, 1841. Clipping, Box 11, F. W. and J. M. Lander Papers, LC.

Woo, Celestine. *Romantic Actors and Bardolatry: Performing Shakespeare from Garrick to Kean*. New York: Peter Lang, 2008.

———. "Sarah Siddons's Performances as Hamlet: Breaching the Breeches Part." *European Romantic Review* 18, no. 2 (Dec. 2007): 573–95.

Wordsworth, William. "Ode 536: Intimations of Immortality from Recollections of Early Childhood." Bartleby.com, 1999. Accessed July 30, 2016, http://www.bartleby.com/101/536.html.

Wright, Nazera Sadiq. *Black Girlhood in the Nineteenth Century*. Champaign: University of Illinois Press, 2016.

Wright, Richardson. *Revels in Jamaica, 1682–1838: Plays and Players of a Century, Tumblers and Conjurers*. New York: Dodd, Mead, 1937.

Wycherley, William. *The Double-Dealer*. In *The Dramatic Works of Wycherley, Congreve, Vanbrugh, and Farquhar*, edited by Leigh Hunt, 173–210. London: George Routledge and Sons, 1875.

Zelizer, Viviana. *Pricing the Priceless Child: The Changing Social Value of Children*. Princeton, NJ: Princeton University Press, 1994.

Ziegler, Georgianna. "Introducing Shakespeare: The Earliest Versions for Children." *Shakespeare* 2, no. 2 (2006): 132–51.

Zimmerman, Calin Rashaud. "The Penalty of Being a Young Black Girl: Kindergarten Teachers' Perceptions of Children's Problem Behaviors and Student-Teacher Conflict by the Intersection of Race and Gender." *Journal of Negro Education* 87, no. 2 (Spring 2018): 154–68.

Ziter, Edward. *The Orient on the Victorian Stage*. Cambridge: Cambridge University Press, 2003.

INDEX

travel and transportation, 5, 104, 161, 170–71

travesty roles, 68–69, 71–72, 108–13; and disguise roles, 81. *See also* breeches roles

Wesley, John, 69, 73–74, 76

white privilege, 12, 59, 64, 102, 155, 173–74, 192

white supremacy, 8–9, 12, 48, 54–57, 58–59, 62–65, 102, 156, 169, 173–74, 176, 187–88, 192–93

whiteness, 1, 8–9, 12, 54–56, 58–59, 62–64, 147, 168, 178–79, 192–93

willfulness, 74, 76, 85; willful child/children, 62, 69, 74, 76, 80, 85. *See also* Ahmed, Sara

Wilson, Kathleen, 168, 177

Winning a Husband; Or Seven's the Main, 118–19, 191

Winton, Henry, 182–83

Wollstonecraft, Mary, 80, 110–11

Wordsworth, William, 10, 75–76, 80, 110

Young Norval (*Douglas*), 1, 19, 20, 26, 36, 47, 89, 116, 143, 172, 191; Clara Fisher as, 47, 116; Master Betty as, 19, 20; Jean Fisher as, 26, 36, 89; Jean Margaret Davenport as, 143, 172

Zelizer, Viviana, 10, 153–54

STUDIES IN THEATRE HISTORY AND CULTURE